PERPLEXITY IN THE
MORAL LIFE
Philosophical and Theological
Considerations

EDMUND N. SANTURRI

PERPLEXITY IN
THE MORAL LIFE

Philosophical and Theological

Considerations

University Press of Virginia

Charlottesville

THE UNIVERSITY PRESS OF VIRGINIA
Copyright © 1987 by the Rector and Visitors
of the University of Virginia

First published 1987

Library of Congress Cataloging-in-Publication Data
Santurri, Edmund N., 1950–
  Perplexity in the moral life.

  (Studies in religion and culture)
  Bibliography: p.
  Includes index.
  1. Ethics.   I. Title.   II. Series: Studies in
religion and culture (Charlottesville, Va.)
BJ1012.S24   1987   170   87-16211
ISBN 0-8139-1155-9

CONTENTS

PREFACE

This book has profited immensely from numerous exchanges I have had with teachers and colleagues over several years. Conversations with Robert Fogelin, Ruth Marcus, and Michael Williams helped me to explore the philosophical dimensions of moral perplexity. On such philosophical matters, I am particularly indebted to Timothy Jackson, Michael Levine, and Robert McKim, all of whom took considerable time to think through along with me some difficult conceptual issues. From Margaret Farley I learned a good deal about the foundations of Thomistic natural law, which forms the centerpiece of the third chapter. Stanley Hauerwas read and commented on portions of the study. His own work stimulated many of my thoughts on the theological interpretation of moral conflict and moral tragedy.

I am especially grateful to seven persons, without whose assistance this project could not have been completed. James Childress and Nathan Scott were kind enough to suggest that I submit the manuscript to the University Press of Virginia. John Reeder responded exhaustively to the first two chapters and thus aided me in my efforts to make clear a set of rather technical arguments. David Little's influence has been general in nature but enormously significant nonetheless. From him more than from anyone else I learned what it means to think as a moral philosopher. The contributions of Gene Outka have been countless. Apart from the fact that he scrupulously read and critically analyzed every bit of the essay, his teaching and scholarship have served as a model of serious and sophisticated philosophical reflection on fundamental issues in theological ethics. To my friend and intellectual cohort, William Werpehowski, I am deeply indebted in so many ways. His constant words of encouragement and advice sustained me immeasurably through the entire process of writing. Finally, but foremost, I thank Rachel D. Santurri for her painstaking editorial work in the last stages of manuscript preparation and for her consistently generous, loving support during the time of composition.

INTRODUCTION

IT IS an indisputable fact of our practical lives that we are sometimes perplexed about what morality requires of us. This is to say that it sometimes appears as though a moral transgression is unavoidable, as though whatever course of action we take will involve the commission of a moral wrong. The source of the kind of perplexity I am referring to is a seemingly irresolvable conflict between moral requirements, which we ordinarily regard as unproblematically binding on our actions. We typically believe, for instance, that we ought to keep our promises and that we ought to aid those in distress. Yet sometimes these requirements conflict in a given case, and we are forced to choose between them. Consider the following example. A person has promised a friend that she would be present at a meeting that is crucial to the friend's livelihood. We may assume that the meeting is a once-in-a-lifetime affair; that is, for certain reasons it cannot be rescheduled. On the way to the meeting she finds a young child who is obviously lost and is wandering about in a very dangerous section of the city. She realizes that if she takes the time to aid the child she will be unable to honor the commitment to her friend. She is, therefore, perplexed as to what morality dictates in the situation. Regarding a similar example, it is hardly controversial to say that a doctor ought to promote the health of her patients and that she ought to be truthful with them. The problems arise when these requirements conflict. Should a placebo be administered when it is judged that such an action would benefit the patient's health? Should the doctor lie to a patient when it is determined that the latter is not psychologically equipped to face the fact of terminal illness? The answers to these questions are not overwhelmingly obvious. And we can think of a host of instances that generate questions of this type.

The following discussion concerns how such situations of *moral perplexity* are to be construed and, more particularly, how the interpretation of these situations might be constrained by the presuppositions of Christian ethics. On the one hand, while conceding that moral perplexity is a daily affair, one might attribute its occurrence to a deficiency in our moral knowledge. It might be the case that we just do not *know* the morally correct answer in these sorts of situations. To make this claim is not to deny that there *is* a morally correct answer to be discovered (e.g., that one particular course of action is required or that any course is permissible). Given this way of looking at the matter, the task with which we are faced in such situations is one of determining what that answer is, unless there are reasons for believing that our moral ignorance is incorrigible. Moral perplexity, according to this view, is purely and simply an epistemic problem. On the other hand, instances of such perplexity might be read as signs of the existence of genuine *moral dilemmas*. As I shall use the expression, a moral dilemma is a situation in which it actually *is* the case (rather than merely *seems* to be the case) that a moral transgression is unavoidable. Thus, to acknowledge the existence of a genuine moral dilemma would be to rule out *in principle* the possibility of finding an unequivocal moral solution to the problem. Moral perplexity, according to this rendering, is not to be interpreted as a deficiency in our moral knowledge but rather as a function of the way the moral universe is structured. In genuinely dilemmatic circumstances we know all there is to know, namely, that whatever course of action we take will embroil us in some moral transgression.

Consider another situation that might be construed as a genuine moral dilemma.[1] The mayor of a populous city learns from reliable sources that a terrorist organization has planted bombs in a large number of family dwellings, though she does not learn which of the dwellings are affected. The size of the city and a projected short period of time before the explosions preclude the possibility of large-scale evacuations. The well-known leader of the terrorist organization is captured almost immediately, however. Unfortu-

nately, even under torture he refuses to divulge the bombs' loca-
tions. Moreover, psychiatric evaluation based on the leader's personality history yields the prediction that he will provide the
relevant information only if his young child is tortured before his
very eyes. Thus, the mayor must decide whether or not to order
the torture of the child. Now this situation, excruciatingly per-
plexing as it might be for the mayor, qualifies as a genuine moral
dilemma only if something like the following analysis holds:
Whatever the mayor does she commits a moral wrong since she
ought to order the child's torture (reason: one ought to minimize
the generation of evil in the world) *and* she *ought not* to order the
child's torture (reason: one ought not to torture innocent human
beings). Overall, moral dilemmas exist if situations exhibiting
this general structure exist.

The central question raised by this essay is whether or not
moral perplexity is ever to be interpreted as a sign of genuine
moral dilemma as just defined. In a variety of forms this question
has been addressed by a number of recent philosophical discussions. A good many of the discussions have suggested that genuine
moral dilemmas do exist and that any denial of this fact ignores,
among other things, important features of our moral experience.[2]
Philosophers taking this line do not always agree on the precise
normative considerations that are supposed to justify such dilemmatic assessments. The immediately preceding example exploits
the oft-mentioned confrontation between utilitarian and nonutilitarian values. While some proponents of the view that moral
dilemmas exist trade on this confrontation, not all do.[3] Alleged
instances of moral dilemma are often portrayed as emerging from
wholly nonutilitarian considerations.[4] The following example is
representative: Jane promises John that she will not reveal his sordid past. Later, however, she is asked by Jill whether John did in
fact commit the shameful deed. She reasons that only an outright
lie would convince Jill. Since the principles of morality include
one enjoining the keeping of promises and another forbidding the
telling of lies, Jane, according to the standard account, is faced
with a moral dilemma; that is, morality demands that she ought
to tell Jill the truth and that she ought not to tell Jill the truth. A
moral transgression is involved no matter what she does. This example, as opposed to the preceding one, lacks any appeal to utility. And in general the thesis stating that genuine moral dilemmas
do exist (hereafter designated *the moral dilemmas thesis*) has not

been associated exclusively with any particular normative ethical
theory.[5]

Proponents of the moral dilemmas thesis collide with an established philosophical tradition holding that no adequate ethical
theory can countenance the existence of genuine dilemmas.[6] The
philosophical concerns that prompt this tradition's rejection of dilemmas are not always clear and, most likely, are quite diverse.
There has been a tendency, however, to suggest that admitting the
existence of moral dilemmas is tantamount to acknowledging the
presence of a debilitating incoherence in one's system of moral
reasoning.[7] At least implicitly, the incoherence is linked in various ways to fundamental constructs of ethical theory such as prescriptivity, universalizability, and certain principles of deontic
logic. But whatever the precise nature of the links involved, the
claim is made that coherence considerations *simpliciter* rule out
the possibility of moral dilemmas in principle. In this view, moral
perplexity, where it is acknowledged at all, presumably must be
taken as a function of moral ignorance. And it is precisely this interpretation that has been called into question by recent advocates of the moral dilemmas thesis.

I contend in this essay that the issue of whether genuine moral
dilemmas exist cannot be resolved on the basis of philosophical
arguments typically advanced either by the traditional or by the
revisionist views. On the one hand, appeals to coherence as justifications for the theoretical rejection of dilemmas are finally inconclusive and derive whatever plausibility they might have from
concealed substantive premises about the nature or function of
morality. On the other hand, standard philosophical affirmations
of dilemmas, whether they rely on pragmatic, phenomenological,
or normative considerations, are likewise inconclusive. More generally, I maintain that moral perplexity is a phenomenon that cannot be interpreted apart from answering certain fundamental
questions of moral ontology: Are moral codes simply systems of
convention or do these codes refer to a transcendent moral reality? If such codes do wholly or partially reflect an independent
moral reality, what is the character of that reality? Is the world of
moral value irreducibly pluralistic or monistic? If pluralistic, are
the constituent values orderable or are they incommensurable and
beyond the possibility of mutual ordering? Is moral requirement
to be regarded as a function of divine providential directive or of
divine command? If either, what is the nature of the God who

issues these providential directives or commands? My contention is that unless such questions are resolved it will be impossible to determine just how our experiences of moral perplexity are to be construed.

Having established the importance of these fundamental matters for the issue, I then consider what sorts of constraints a Christian view of morality imposes on the interpretation of moral conflict. Specifically, I evaluate two representative types of Christian ethical theory—Thomistic natural law and theological voluntarism. My overall conclusion will be that, on the terms of either theory, it would be extraordinarily difficult to countenance the existence of genuine moral dilemmas. In the case of Thomistic natural law, acknowledging the reality of such dilemmas would pose problems for the doctrine of providence and for the idea that God's power is sufficient to realize his creative purposes. In the case of theological voluntarism, accepting the existence of dilemmas would mean attributing incoherence to the divine will, thereby admitting God's practical irrationality. These conclusions, at the very least, establish a burden of proof for any Christian ethicist who advances the moral dilemmas thesis. Unless that burden can be borne theoretically, Christian ethics will have to assume that situations of moral perplexity are essentially problems of moral knowledge; in such situations, that is, we are unclear about what morality requires, but in principle resolutions of the conflicts are available.

Finally, I attend to a range of positions that have been or might be employed in Christian ethical arguments for the reality of irresolvable moral conflict. These positions most often arise out of reflection on specific moral issues such as the nature of Christian love, the Sermon on the Mount and the use of coercion, Christian political responsibility, and so forth. Occasionally, however, the positions are tied more or less systematically to basic theological notions such as the doctrine of justification *sola fide* and the idea of a sinful world in rebellion against the will of God. At any rate, my general conclusion will be that these positions, whatever plausibility they may appear to have, do not require the acknowledgment of genuine moral dilemmas. The proposed normative analyses frequently do bring out real tensions in the moral life, but nothing in these analyses excludes the possibility that such tensions are resolvable. Moreover, in spite of persistent claims to the contrary, there seems to be no necessary theoretical connection between the moral dilemmas thesis and fundamental theological constructs related to the doctrine of justification or to the notion of a sinful world. If my assessments are accurate, then, the afore-mentioned burden of proof cannot be borne by certain standard Christian affirmations of the moral dilemmas thesis. As a result, for Christian ethics moral perplexity will have to be interpreted as a function of deficiencies in our moral knowledge rather than as a sign of irresolvable conflict in the structure of the moral universe.

1

MORAL PERPLEXITY
AND CONSISTENCY

As I have already noted, an established philosophical tradition claims that no adequate moral theory can admit the existence of moral dilemmas since such dilemmas would signify the presence of an incoherence in moral reasoning. In the present chapter I examine this claim. Of course, discussions of coherence and incoherence in the history of philosophy are notorious for their imprecision. Yet we shall see that the controversy over the existence or possible existence of moral dilemmas clearly does raise certain issues regarding *consistency* in the moral life. These consistency issues relate to the various connections among the *general* principles and *singular* judgments of a moral system.[1] In showing how the moral dilemmas discussion generates such issues, I shall consider a question often aired by participants in the debate: What rationale, if any, do situations of moral perplexity offer for *revising* the principles of one's moral system? Of four arguments supporting the claim that moral perplexity provides some rationale for systemic revision, I shall examine the first (from prescriptivity) briefly and the other three (from universalizability, from deductive logic, and from deontic metaprinciples) at greater length. All four of these arguments appeal to the notion of consistency in one form or another, and all four conclude that consistency considerations provide the grounds for systemic revision, which is putatively a sign of the resolution of moral conflict. I shall try to show that none of the four arguments establish what they purport to establish. As we shall see, the conclusions drawn will have important implications for the moral dilemmas debate.

The advocates of systemic revision in the face of moral perplexity convey a distinctive picture of the moral life, a picture that can be captured in the following overly simple, but for our purposes adequate, scenario. We are to imagine a moral ingenue—that is, an individual possessing an elementary moral education—whom we will call Innocent. His education has equipped him with a battery of moral principles, each of which is characterized by a low degree of specificity. In other words, the principles by and large are devoid of *ceteris paribus* or exception clauses limiting their respective scopes of application. Moreover, the moral system as a whole contains no ordering device assessing the relative importance of each of the principles. Now imagine further that among the principles in the system are these two: (P_1) 'One ought to keep one's promises' and (P_2) 'One ought not to perform acts that foreseeably will lead to the harm of other human beings'. These are principles that, along with the others in the system, Innocent has learned at his mother's knee and that for the longest time have served him without difficulty. In accordance with the dictates of his moral register, that is, Innocent has always been able to keep his promises and has always been able to refrain from actions foreseen to be harmful to other persons. One day, however, this happy state of affairs is disrupted. On the scene appears Innocent's friend—call him X—who is enraged at his adulterous wife and accordingly announces his intention to kill her. He demands that Innocent keep his promise to return a gun borrowed sometime before for a hunting trip. Innocent foresees that returning the gun would result in the wife's harm, but he also remembers his promise to X. Thus, he is morally perplexed. From his moral register and from the facts of the situation he infers both that he ought to keep his promise to X and that he ought not to keep his promise to X. Ultimately our ingenue determines (the source of the determination is not for the moment my concern) that he ought not to return the gun as promised. From this determination he concludes that one of his moral principles requires revision. The dictum 'One ought to keep one's promises' now becomes 'One ought to keep one's promises except when . . . '

According to this account of the moral life, situations of moral perplexity such as the one just depicted represent recalcitrant experiences that eventually call for appropriate adjustments in one's moral system. Revision of this sort is putatively a sign of the dissolution of moral perplexity. Conflict is said to be dissolved partly in virtue of our discovery in these instances that the principles which are *genuinely* binding on us are not the principles which generated the conflict to begin with. This general line of reasoning might be supported with either of the following two claims: (1) We come to the realization that our original principles are not genuinely binding *through the practical judgments we inevitably make in such situations.* These judgments, coupled with certain consistency constraints, compel us to modify the contents of our moral code with the result that perplexity is dissolved. As we shall see, the arguments from prescriptivity and universalizability are elaborations on this theme. (2) We discover that our original principles are not genuinely binding *from the mere fact that they conflict in a given case.* This fact alone shows us that there is an incoherence in our moral reasoning, and given this state of affairs we are required to revise our moral codes. Again, as we shall see, the arguments from deductive logic and deontic metaprinciples trade on this claim in one form or another. In the view of either (1) or (2), then, situations of moral perplexity are never to be construed as genuine moral dilemmas. Since proponents of the moral dilemmas thesis would take issue with this conclusion, it is essential to be clear about its possible theoretical underpinnings.

The Argument from Prescriptivity

The least plausible argument in support of the claim that moral perplexity requires moral revision is tied to a strong theory of the prescriptivity of moral discourse. Given this theory, moral 'ought'-sentences, at least in their nondegenerate forms, are tied logically to imperatives, and this relation between 'ought'-sentences and imperatives imposes constraints on the moral principles one can accept as binding. In short, assent to a general moral principle *entails* assent to a singular 'ought'-judgment, and assent to a singular judgment, in its turn, *entails* assent to an imperative. To return to our example, if Innocent had truly assented to the simple general principle 'One ought to keep one's promises', then, according to the theory under consideration, he also would have assented to the singular judgment 'I, Innocent, ought to return the gun to X', and this latter assent, in its turn, would have committed him, as a matter of logic, to accepting the imperative 'Let me, Innocent, return the gun to X'. Now on the terms of the theory in question, since an agent's assent to a first-person singular imperative logically entails at least a resolution to obey its dictates and since Innocent resolved not to return the gun, he cannot have truly assented to the imperative; this fact, in its place, shows that he has assented neither to the judgment nor to the principle in question. Consequently, from the vantage point of this theory of prescriptivity, we should conclude that Innocent has rejected the simple principle 'One ought to keep one's promises' or that he *should* reject that principle as a matter of consistency given his resolution to disobey it. His earlier behavior showed, however, that he does not believe one always ought to break one's promises. The theory, then, provides a justification for Innocent's particular revision.[2]

The problem with this rationale resides in the implausibility of a theory of prescriptivity as strong as the one indicated. For the theory, so rigorously stated, rules out the possibility of moral weakness, the phenomenon of an agent's resolving to violate one of her own moral principles. Thus, the account drives one to the Socratic paradox of denying that an agent ever determines to do what she believes to be morally wrong. Of course, proponents of the theory, wishing to avoid the paradox, usually resort to ad hoc explanatory devices such as the one proposed in the work of R. M. Hare.[3] Yet these sorts of devices fail to achieve the degree of simplicity attained by weaker theories of prescriptivity, which admit some relation between moral principle and action but deny the existence of *entailment* relations between principles and resolutions to perform. And this last is the important point. For if such entailment relations are denied, then the argument we have been considering fails to provide the rationale for revision it purports to provide.

The Argument from Universalizability

A more plausible line of reasoning invokes the so-called universalizability condition.[4] The thesis of universalizability states that a singular 'ought'-judgment issued for a determinate reason (rather than arbitrarily) logically implies an 'ought'-principle having universal application. For the purposes of discussion let us assume that any singular positive 'ought'-judgment ascribes the property of *oughtness* to an act falling under some description (negative 'ought'-judgments ascribe the property of *oughtnotness* or *not-oughtness*). Given this characterization, issuing a singular 'ought'-judgment for a determinate reason amounts to ascribing the property of oughtness O to an act A on the basis of some condition C satisfied by A. The condition C *ceteris paribus* must be considered sufficient to warrant the ascription of O since otherwise the reason in question would fail to *justify* the ascription of O to A. Now, inasmuch as C is regarded as a condition sufficient to warrant the ascription of O to A, it must be regarded *ceteris paribus* as a condition sufficient to warrant the ascription of O to any act; this is to say, of course, that the singular judgment initially issued implies logically a principle of universal application. Any refusal to acknowledge the implication results in an inconsistency. For assume that with respect to some other act B, which satisfies C, the ascription of O is denied. This denial coupled with the ascription of O to A would issue in a contradiction since in the case of A it is suggested that C *is* a sufficient condition for ascribing O while in the case of B it would be implied that C *is not* a sufficient condition for ascribing O. This *reductio* leads us to conclude that a singular 'ought'-judgment stating that some act ought to be done for some reason logically implies a principle stating that any act *ceteris paribus* ought to be done for that reason.[5]

To return to the issue at hand, the universalizability constraint, as it is characterized here, would seem to afford a compelling reason for revising one's moral principles in the face of moral perplexity. For determining with reason that one ought or ought not to take a particular course of action in such a situation commits one to a principle that appears to be inconsistent with one of the original principles constituting the conflict. Consider the case of our moral ingenue once again. Innocent determined that he ought not to keep his promise to X *because* the kept promise foreseeably would result in harm to some human being. In accordance with the thesis of universalizability, we should say that this singular judgment commits him to the principle (P_3) 'One ought not to keep one's promises when doing so will result foreseeably in the harm of some human being'. Now this principle collides with one of Innocent's original principles, namely, (P_1) 'One ought to keep one's promises'. Given this incompatibility, both principles cannot be retained. Consequently, the latter is rejected for a more modest version, (P_4) 'One ought to keep one's promises except when the keeping of them will lead foreseeably to the harm of some human being'. With this revision in the system the inconsistency is removed. It is in this way that the universalizability thesis purportedly provides a theoretical foundation for adjusting one's moral system in response to the recalcitrant experience of moral perplexity. Given this adjustment, of course, the perplexity dissolves.

Assuming the truth of the universalizability thesis, one would think that a situation of moral perplexity could be construed as a genuine moral dilemma only if the possibility of issuing a reasoned determining 'ought'-judgment regarding the proper course of action were to be denied. Certain defenders of the moral dilemmas thesis have refused to accept this conclusion. They have maintained, rather, that even in a situation of genuine moral dilemma an individual may determine what she ought or ought not to do and support this determination with reasons. In other words, these philosophers have contended that a rationally supported judgment in favor of a certain course of action in situations of moral perplexity need not erase the dilemmatic nature of such situations. To put the point still another way, *moral* dilemmas, they would suggest, do not necessarily amount to *practical* dilemmas.[6]

In support of this position Roger Trigg has presented an argument that utilizes a distinction between cases in which a rule does not apply because it has been modified to account for an exception and cases in which a rule does apply but is broken for countervailing reasons. The distinction is illustrated in the following account of a country's traffic laws.[7] In country Z the rule of the road is that one ought to keep to the left. Call this principle *PL*. On a one-way street, however, moving to the right is legally permitted in Z. Such moving to the right, then, *does not* constitute a *violation* of *PL* since the rule is duly modified to make room for the practice. On the other hand, sometimes for contravening reasons *PL* ought to be violated, as in a case when turning to the right is the only way to avoid an accident. Clearly, all other things being equal, travelers on Z's roads ought to turn to the right in such instances despite the fact of *PL*'s directing otherwise, but this 'ought' affords no obstruction to our saying that *PL* *applies* in such cases. *PL* does apply though it ought to be broken. There is, then, as the example shows, a clear distinction between modifying a rule and resolving to break a rule, and given this distinction, the way is left open for suggesting that determinations about what one ought to do or ought not to do in moral conflict situations are instances of the latter phenomenon rather than of the former. By this account, Innocent's determination that he ought not to return the gun to X would amount to a determination for a specified reason to *violate* the moral principle (P_1) 'One ought to keep one's promises'. Trigg goes on to give independent arguments purporting to establish grounds sufficient for construing moral conflict situations in this manner, but I shall not attend to these arguments at the moment. The important point for now is that, given the distinction between modification and violation, it is at least arguable, according to Trigg, that rationally supported singular 'ought'-judgments issued in moral conflict situations involve rational determinations to violate binding moral principles. And if under these conditions determinations to *violate* binding moral principles are inescapable, then these situations can only be read as genuine moral dilemmas.

Yet, *pace* Trigg, a question can be raised as to whether judgments about the proper course of action in situations of moral perplexity are relevantly similar to our case of judging that *PL* ought to be broken. One would think there are grounds for disputing the analogy. Consider the traffic example once again. It was determined that, despite *PL*, an individual ought to move to the right on a two-way street in order to avoid an accident. This 'ought', given the constraint of universalizability, commits one to a principle something like the following: 'Despite the existence of traffic rules relevantly similar to *PL*, one ought to move to the right on two-way streets whenever such is necessary to avoid accidents'. Call this principle *PR*. What is *its* status? Two interpretations are equally plausible given the details of the example. Either (1) the principle is a dictate of *prudence* or (2) it is a directive of *morality;* exactly which is not now my concern. What is essential to note is that *PR* cannot itself be part of the law of Z. For if it were, then one could not say, as the example stipulates, that *PL applies* in cases where following its dictates would lead to an accident since a departure from the principle would be required *legally* in virtue of *PR*. In other words, were *PR* a law of Z, then moving to the right in order to avoid an accident would constitute a practice akin to that of moving to the right on a one-way street in Z, that is, a practice legally allowed through modification of *PL*. Now, inasmuch as it is ruled out that *PR* is a part of Z's law, a potential for absurdity is removed. For whatever we want to say about the situation, we should not want to say that we have uncovered an inconsistency internal to Z's legal system; that is, we should not want to say that Z's law states that on a two-way street one ought to keep to the left and one ought not to keep to the left (when accidents can be avoided by moving to the right). Rather, what we should want to say is that either *morality* or *prudence* directs us to disobey Z's law. And this claim in and of itself does nothing to impugn the consistency of Z's legal system. Neither does the claim uncover an inconsistency in the moral or prudential system in question. The upshot is that consistency considerations *simpliciter* afford no impediment to our saying in this instance that *PL* ought to be broken for determinate reasons.

Things would appear to be different, however, with situations of moral perplexity, for by arguing that in such situations rationally supported singular judgments about the proper course of action involve determinations to break moral rules, one seems ipso facto to be acknowledging the existence of an inconsistency internal to one's moral system. Suppose, for example, Innocent's judgment not to return the gun to X were to be interpreted as a determination to *violate* (P_1). This supposition suggests that his moral system contains two mutually incompatible principles—the principle that putatively *applies* to his situation and is thereby *violated* (P_1) and the principle arrived at via universalizability (P_3).[8] If this line of reasoning is correct, then an absurdity, which was absent in the legal example, manifests itself in the moral case, and, consequently, Trigg's analogy would appear to break down at this juncture.[9] In contrast to the traffic case, consistency considerations seem to pose obstructions to analyzing Innocent's determination as a reasoned resolution to break a rule, in this instance a moral rule.

The only way to save the analogy would be to deny that the new principle resulting from the resolution of the conflict was a *moral* principle at all. This is the strategy employed by Bernard Williams.[10] According to Williams, rational judgments in favor of prosecuting a particular course of action in situations of moral perplexity should not be interpreted as *moral* judgments. Such judgments are said to provide answers to the question, 'What ought I to do?'; their role is, as he puts it, "deliberative" rather than moral. The significance of Williams's contention for our purposes should be clear. If deliberative 'ought'-judgments in situations of moral perplexity turned out to be nonmoral, as he suggests, then the principles that such judgments generate via universalizability could not be *moral* principles, whatever else they might be. And if these principles are nonmoral, then the moral absurdity discussed above will fail to materialize. In Innocent's case the conflict between (P_1) and (P_3) would not amount to an inconsistency internal to his moral system since (P_3) would be nonmoral. According to Williams's account, then, Innocent's rationally supported determination not to return the gun to X should be read as analogous to a resolution to break a law for good, extralegal reasons. In other words, the determination in question should be interpreted as a resolution to violate a moral principle for good, nonmoral reasons. Consistency considerations of the type discussed would, in and of themselves, be insufficient to rule out such an analysis.

Is Williams's contention plausible? Is it reasonable to suggest that deliberative 'ought'-judgments issued in situations of moral perplexity necessarily amount to *nonmoral* judgments, which give rise to *nonmoral* principles via universalizability? Williams provides the following defense of his claim: Suppose I am faced with a situation in which morality unequivocally requires that I do *A* though I clearly prefer not to do *A* (e.g., I perceive that it is not in my interest to do *A*). In such a situation I can pose the deliberative question, 'What ought I to do?' and arrive at an answer to the question. If the question's 'ought' were a *moral* 'ought', then the question itself would be vacuous. *Ex hypothesi* I *know* what morality requires. Since the question is an open one and since, indeed, its ultimate answer may be repugnant to morality, its 'ought' cannot be a moral 'ought'. And if the question's 'ought' is nonmoral, then the answer's 'ought' must be nonmoral in a relevantly similar sense. Williams's conclusion, then, is that the role of the deliberative 'ought' qua deliberative "is not tied to morality." The only way to avoid this conclusion, presumably, is to assume, as he puts it, "the necessary supremacy of the moral," in other words, a theory of moral discourse that equates, as a matter of definition, the 'ought' acted on with the *moral* 'ought'. Because this theory leads (as does the strong theory of prescriptivity) to the Socratic paradox discussed earlier, it is, Williams implies, implausible and should be rejected. With this rejection the nonmoral status of the deliberative 'ought' is preserved. Moreover, this status, Williams contends, is retained even under conditions of moral conflict. In such contexts the deliberative 'ought'-judgment is putatively second-order, that is, a judgment advising action on one of the original 'ought'-judgments constituting the conflict. In this account, Innocent's resolution not to return the gun to X is presented most perspicuously in the following form: 'I, Innocent, ought to act on the judgment, *I, Innocent, ought not to return the gun to X*'; or, alternatively, 'I, Innocent, ought not to act on the judgment, *I, Innocent, ought to return the gun to X*'. In other words, the deliberative 'ought' is of a different order than the moral 'oughts'; the deliberative 'ought' is nonmoral.

Now Williams is certainly correct inasmuch as he limits himself to the claim that deliberative judgments issued in situations of moral perplexity *need not* be moral in character. Assume, for instance, that Innocent's resolution to act on the judgment dictated by (P_2) rather than that by (P_1) were based on prudential considerations. That is, he reasons in the following manner: "From the point of view of my moral system alone, no decisive determination for or against returning X's gun can be effected. I fear, however, that X wrongly suspects me as his wife's lover. So, given the moral stalemate, self-interest tips the deliberative balance. I ought to follow (P_2)." Under these conditions, clearly, it would be perfectly reasonable (assuming that prudence and morality are of a different order) to describe Innocent's deliberative verdict as non-moral. This description derives its plausibility from the prudential character of the justification Innocent gives for his decision. Suppose, however, he reasoned in this way: "My moral register leads me to an impasse. Yet, I must make the best of the situation so I shall embark on the course of action that generates the least evil in the world. Since the evil of frustrated expectation that I would bring to X by breaking my promise to him would be quite minimal in comparison with the evil that would result from my returning the gun, I ought to act on (P_2)." What are we to make of this final judgment? Its underlying rationale would seem to be moral. Let us assume that it is. Doesn't this assumption require that we interpret the judgment itself as moral in character? Williams denies that it does. Though a deliberative judgment may be grounded in moral considerations, he states, its status remains nonmoral. Yet he provides no argument in support of this conclusion, and the omission is a serious matter since it is eminently plausible to suggest that the status of a deliberative judgment remains *indeterminate* prior to any assessment of the character of its grounds. Given this analysis, the status of the simple deliberative question, 'What ought I to do?'—unless the question is to be interpreted as a request for an ungrounded order rather than for reasoned advice—remains ambiguous until it is made clear just what sort of counsel (legal? moral? prudential?) is being sought.

The general point is that while deliberative 'oughts' *need not* be moral in character, it seems hasty to conclude, as does Williams, that they *cannot* be moral *even when moral reasons are given in their support.* And if a deliberative judgment issued in a moral conflict situation did turn out to be moral, then, as demonstrated earlier, an absurdity would result from interpreting that judgment as one *violating*, rather than *modifying*, a moral rule. The inconsistency would show itself at the level of principle. To illustrate once again, suppose that Innocent's determination not to return

the gun to X were read as a judgment that he ought to violate
(P_1)—presumed to *apply* to his case—for the reason that such a
violation would minimize the generation of evil in the world.
Given the presumption for the moment that the reason is a *moral*
one and given the condition of universalizability, this singular
judgment would lead to the following *moral* principle: (P_5) 'One
ought not to keep one's promise whenever (*a*) the keeping of that
promise involves the violation of some other generally applicable
moral principle (relevantly similar to $[P_2]$) and (*b*) the breaking of
the promise would result in less evil than the keeping of it would'.
Now it would appear that (P_5) is inconsistent with (P_1); consequently, if both principles were presumed to be part of a unitary
moral system, the system would have to be judged incoherent.
This potential for absurdity, in turn, would provide a rationale for
revising the moral code. The desired revision would be achieved,
and thus the absurdity would be avoided by an appropriate modification of (P_1) to something like (P_6) 'One ought to keep one's
promises except under conditions specified by (P_5)'. The consequence of this revision, of course, is that the original conflict
would be dissolved.

The problem with this general reply to Williams's argument is
that it rests on the possibility of citing unequivocally *moral* reasons for deliberative judgments. In view of the seemingly endless
debate about what sorts of reasons or considerations count as distinctively *moral*, such reliance is dubious dialectical strategy.[11]
For example, while some defenders of the moral dilemmas thesis
agree that deliberative judgments delivered in contexts of moral
conflict should be governed by some type of utilitarian standard
(either a principle enjoining promotion of the greater good or one
enjoining promotion of the lesser evil), certain of them suggest
that the appeal to such a standard is not a *moral* appeal at all.
Thus, E. J. Lemmon writes:

> The situation is such that no moral, or at least purely moral, con-
> siderations are relevant, in the sense that no appeal to our own
> given morality can decide the issue. . . . We may approach our deci-
> sion by a consideration of ends—which course of action will lead to
> the best result. (I do not think of it as an accident, by the way, that
> the word "good," or rather its superlative "best," makes its first ap-
> pearance at this point in our discussion; for it is typically when we
> are torn between courses of conduct that the question of comparing
> different actions arises, and hence the word "good," a comparative

adjective unlike "right," is at home here; the consequence, admittedly paradoxical, of this view of "good" is that it is not properly a word of moral appraisal at all, despite the vast attention it receives from ethical philosophers; and I think I accept this conclusion.)[12]

Implicit in Lemmon's remarks and seemingly shared by other proponents of the moral dilemmas thesis is the following more general position. No genuinely *moral* reason can be given in support of a deliberative judgment issued in the face of moral conflict. It is, according to this view, simply an institutional fact about our system of morality that it contains a finite number of determinate principles fixed in content and exhibiting a low degree of specificity. Given their general nature and given the conditions of the world, these principles inevitably lead to moral conflict, and indeed, having generated the conflict, morality has exhausted its role, so to speak, in such situations. In other words, moral perplexity by this account always turns out to be morally dilemmatic. As soon as one begins the business of determining what ought to be done in situations of moral perplexity, one has left the realm of the moral. As D. Z. Phillips and H. O. Mounce express the point:

> Moral principles . . . are not the means by which moral problems are removed. Moral principles are the source of moral problems, they create them rather than solve them. For example, the reason why a man who has to choose between telling the truth or helping a friend is in a dilemma is that he considers it important to tell the truth and to help a friend. If he could look on either of these as not having moral importance he would no longer be in a dilemma. His dilemma is a direct consequence of holding certain moral principles. One's principles in a technique are the means by which problems are solved, whereas in morality they are the very things which give rise to one's problems.[13]

On the terms of this position, then, the nature of morality is such that deliberative judgments delivered in situations of moral perplexity can be supported *only* by nonmoral reasons. If this view is correct, then the theoretical foundation for systemic revision putatively afforded by the universalizability constraint is lost. A *nonmoral* principle (arrived at from a *nonmoral* reason via universalizability) directing violation of a *moral* principle constitutes, in itself, no *moral* absurdity, and, it will be remembered, it was the appearance of such an absurdity that provided in the first place a rationale for adjustments in the system when faced with moral conflict.

Now the claim that deliberative judgments of the relevant sort admit of only nonmoral justification is not a claim beyond debate. On its face the issue appears to be a semantic one (What does the term 'morality' mean?), but, more than likely, how one assesses the status of a deliberative judgment will turn on substantive matters related to the general theory of morality. For instance, if one viewed morality as a corporate creation generated by a particular historical community in its establishing the conditions necessary for social life, then one might be inclined to regard the institution as one consisting of a body of principles identifiable in terms of content alone. Given this rendering, the particular resolution of a conflict produced by those principles might be interpreted as one whose source is outside the moral institution itself. On the other hand, if the institution of morality, as we know it, were seen to incorporate a body of principles approximating, but not fully capturing, an independent moral reality, one might be inclined to regard the resolution of a moral conflict as itself fully moral in the sense that its source was the moral reality insufficiently captured by the body of principles. The important point is that these sorts of considerations would have to be attended to prior to any decision on the status of a deliberative judgment in cases of conflict. In any event, we can conclude that the simple appeal to the constraint of universalizability as a way of providing theoretical backing for the type of moral revision we have considered is an appeal insufficient to establish what it sets out to establish.

The Argument from Deductive Logic

We have seen that invoking the constraint of universalizability as a maneuver designed to justify the type of moral revision under consideration fails in virtue of the ambiguous status of a deliberative judgment. We come now to a pro-revision argument that avoids explicit discussion of deliberative judgments altogether. The position presented by David Lyons may be considered representative of this sort of argument.[14] According to Lyons, *weak* moral principles may be distinguished from *strong* moral principles; the former are constrained by *ceteris paribus* conditions limiting their respective scopes of application while the latter lack such conditions and thus are to be obeyed in every relevant circumstance. This distinction, Lyons claims, has substantive implications. In cases of conflict moral judgments deduced from weak principles will give way to judgments deduced from strong principles. Situations of conflict between weak moral judgments and strong moral judgments, therefore, turn out not to be genuine moral dilemmas since the putative bindingness of the former dissolves in the face of the actual bindingness of the latter. Cases of conflict between two weak moral judgments, on the other hand, are to be adjudicated by assigning relative weights to the relevant principles. But what about a conflict between two strong moral judgments, a conflict that, given the sense of the terms, would have to be construed as a genuine moral dilemma? Lyons notes that if two conflicting judgments are both strong judgments, then "we have moral incompatibility." And such a situation would, according to him, attest to an *incoherence* in moral reasoning itself. Given this state of affairs, then, one of the original principles constituting the putative dilemma must be assessed as incorrect. The point is that the appearance of moral conflict between putatively strong judgments provides *simpliciter* a rationale for revising one's moral system, and the revision is in order on grounds of consistency.

The difficulty with this general line of reasoning is that the critical notion of *incoherence* remains uninterpreted. In what sense can it be said that a moral dilemma in and of itself attests to an incoherence in moral reasoning? In response to this question Ruth Marcus has argued that, whatever *incoherence* might mean in such instances, it need not signify an *inconsistency* in the set of principles generating the dilemma.[15] Marcus distinguishes consistency as defined for a set of sentences or propositions from consistency as defined for a set of rules (including moral principles). With respect to sets of propositions or sentences, consistency is said to be a property possessed by a set if it is possible for all members of that set to be true. This possibility is guaranteed if a contradiction would not be the logical consequence of supposing that each member of the set is true. Thus, the sentences 'Snow is green' and 'Grass is white', though false, form together a consistent set since there is an unactualized possible world in which both sentences are true. Similarly, consistency for a set of rules is defined as a property possessed by that set if in some possible world all the rules of that set could be obeyed in every circum-

stance of that world. According to this account, the moral principles 'One ought to keep one's promises' and 'One ought not to
lie' form a consistent set inasmuch as there is a possible world in
which both principles can be obeyed under all conditions of that
world. On the other hand, the set containing the principles 'One
ought to keep one's promises' and 'One ought not to keep one's
promises' is inconsistent since there is no possible world in which
both principles of that set can be obeyed under any condition of
that world.

Given this definition of consistency for moral principles, one
would have to conclude that the appearance of a genuine moral
dilemma need not signify an inconsistency in the relevant system
of moral principles. Assume, for instance, that the principles enjoining the keeping of promises and forbidding the telling of lies
are *strong* moral principles in Lyons's sense of the terms. Assume,
furthermore, the conditions of our earlier example of Jane's promising John that she would not reveal his sordid past.[16] We may infer
from the foregoing that there is some particular act—her denial—
whose commission or omission will involve Jane in a moral wrong.
On the terms of the example, in other words, Jane is faced with a
genuine moral dilemma. Nonetheless, assuming the correctness
of Marcus's definition, this state of affairs does not impugn the
consistency of the set incorporating the principles. For indeed
there *is* some possible world in which under any condition of that
world both principles can be obeyed, namely, the possible world in
which, among other things, no one makes the sort of promises
that Jane made.

Thus, if Marcus is correct, a *consistent* moral code could generate genuine moral dilemmas given the proper combination of facts
about the world. Construing moral conflict situations as moral dilemmas, therefore, would not necessarily jeopardize the coherence
of one's system of moral principles. The upshot is that consistency
considerations of this sort provide no indefeasible warrant for revising one's moral code in the face of conflict. Moreover, we have,
according to Marcus, compelling reasons (having nothing to do
with consistency per se) for *not* revising our system in such situations: (*a*) Adjusting our system with the result that the conflict is
dissolved without residue impoverishes moral theory by rendering it incapable of capturing features of our moral experience that
point to the *reality* of moral dilemmas. (*b*) Regarding situations of
moral perplexity as genuine moral dilemmas preserves the conviction that inevitably something wrong is done in these situa

tions, and this conviction in its turn generates the motivation necessary to change the world so that these situations will not arise. I shall have occasion to discuss questions raised by (a) and (b) in the following chapter. For the moment I want to dwell on the matter of consistency. Have all consistency issues been resolved by Marcus's argument?

I think not. Marcus's discussion addresses the claim that a moral dilemma betrays an inconsistency *internal to one's code of general moral principles* or, to put the matter another way, *internal to the set of one's general moral beliefs*. Yet, more likely than not, philosophers such as Lyons have not been primarily concerned with advancing this particular claim. Rather, what seems to be behind such a position is the contention that one can acknowledge the existence of genuine moral dilemmas only at the expense of admitting an inconsistency *internal to a broader set of beliefs, in particular, the set consisting both of one's general moral beliefs and of one's nonmoral beliefs about the world*. In this view the incoherence attested to by the acknowledged existence of a genuine moral dilemma is discovered only on examination of the practical (moral) syllogisms that structure such situations. For instance, with reference to Jane's predicament, where '*a*' is a singular expression denoting some particular act performable by Jane (namely, at time/place, Jane's denying that John committed the shameful deed):

> One ought to keep one's promises.
> *a* is an act of keeping a promise.
> _____
> *a* ought to be performed.

At the same time:

> One ought not to lie.
> *a* is an act of lying.
> _____
> *a* ought not to be performed.

Now, given the presumption that the respective conclusions of the two arguments are inconsistent with one another (a presumption that, as we shall see, raises important questions) and given that the patterns of inference here conform to the canons of ordinary deductive logic, we must conclude, it would seem, that at least one of the four premises in either of the two arguments is unacceptable; that is, we must conclude that *the set of beliefs (moral and factual) captured by the premises of both arguments is an inconsistent set*. If we can assume further, as we can uncontroversially in nearly all cases of this kind, that the *factual* premises are acceptable (in this instance, that the act denoted by *a* is in fact an act of keeping a promise *and* an act of telling a lie), then, it would appear, we must conclude that at least one of the distinctively *moral* premises (one of the moral principles) is unacceptable. The judgment that one of the principles is unacceptable provides, at the very least, a rationale for reducing that principle's status from strong to weak in Lyons's sense of the terms. Thus, consistency considerations would appear to provide a reason for adjusting one's moral system in the face of moral conflict, though the specific consistency considerations determinative here differ from those Marcus presumably has put to rest.

There are at least three possible responses to this argument from deductive logic, each focusing on different stages in the argument. One might reason (1) that, while the syllogistic conclusions are inconsistent in the form presented, the premises of such syllogisms when properly understood do not generate conclusions of this form; or (2) that, while syllogisms of this type do generate conclusions of this form, such conclusions are not authentically inconsistent; or (3) that, while syllogisms of this type do generate conclusions of this form and while these conclusions are incompatible in a certain sense, the nature of moral pronouncements is such that neither member of such a pair must be rejected without remainder as one *must* reject either of two inconsistent propositions. I shall consider each of these responses in order.

(1) The first response to the argument from deductive logic concedes the inconsistency between two moral judgments having the ought/ought not form but denies that the premises of syllogisms structuring putatively dilemmatic situations generate pairs of conclusions having these forms. In this rendering, consistency constraints pose no obstacle to the acknowledgment of a moral dilemma since the syllogisms producing the dilemma do not yield inconsistent moral judgments. The result is that canons of consistency need not dictate a revision of one's moral system in the face of moral conflict.

In order to illustrate this line of reasoning let us return to our earlier syllogistic representation of Jane's predicament. In that case we inferred morality's requirement that a particular act of Jane's called *a* (at time/place, her denying that John committed the shameful deed) both ought to be performed and ought not to be performed. According to the present account this inference was unjustified. We were entitled to infer from the facts of the situation and the relevant moral principles only that Jane's act of keeping her promise to John at time/place$_i$ (call it b) ought to be performed and that her act of lying to Jill at time/place$_i$ (call it c) ought not to be performed. Our mistake occurred when we substituted a neutral act-description, 'at time/place$_i$ Jane's denying that John committed the shameful deed', for the appropriate act-descriptions demanded by the principles binding on the situation, 'at time/place$_i$ Jane's keeping her promise to John' and 'at time/place$_i$ Jane's lying to Jill'. Had we stayed aright on this matter, so this line of reasoning goes, the inconsistent judgments would have been avoided. While 'a ought to be performed' and 'a ought not to be performed' may represent an inconsistent pair, there is no inconsistency exhibited in the pair 'b ought to be performed' and 'c ought not to be performed'.

The thesis presupposed in the foregoing argument states that moral concepts such as obligated (ought) and prohibited (ought not) attach only to certain descriptions of acts and thus that even when different descriptions appear to denote the same act we are not entitled to transfer moral predicates from one description to another. In defense of this thesis either of two appeals might be made, one to a putative referential opacity of deontic contexts, the other to the claim that different descriptions sometimes denote different acts, appearances to the contrary notwithstanding. It should be emphasized that the thesis we are examining requires *some* defense inasmuch as it would seem to generate counterintuitive conclusions. To take as an example the case we have been discussing, if we admit that the description 'at time/place$_i$ Jane's keeping her promise to John' denotes the same act as the description 'at time/place$_i$ Jane's denying that John committed the shameful deed' and if we admit that Jane ought to keep her promise, the presumption would appear to be that she *ought* to issue the denial specified in the second description. Moreover, analogous considerations related to the stricture against lying would seem to establish that she *ought not* to issue said denial. Yet these conclusions are precisely those the thesis would force us to resist.

(a) *Referential Opacity.* It is generally accepted that the application of certain notions such as *necessity* and *belief* generates conditions under which substitution of terms having identical references cannot be made while preserving truth. For example, the truth of 'Twelve is necessarily greater than ten' does not ensure the truth of 'The number of the apostles is necessarily greater than ten', even though twelve is the number of the apostles. Similarly, the truth of 'Joe believes that Eisenhower was the thirty-fourth president' does not ensure the truth of 'Joe believes that the leader of the Normandy invasion was the thirty-fourth president', even though 'Eisenhower' and 'the leader of the Normandy invasion' pick out the same individual. The question we are interested in is whether moral notions similarly establish referentially opaque contexts. In other words, we want to know whether phrases like ' . . . ought to be performed' and ' . . . ought not to be performed' create contexts in which substitutions of act-descriptions having identical references cannot be made *salve veritate*. If the referential opacity of deontic contexts can be established, then the thesis limiting the transfer of moral predicates from one act-description to another will be justified. And if this thesis is justified, then, as indicated above, a case would have been made for the claim that the acknowledgment of a moral dilemma poses no threat to the consistency of one's moral reasoning.

The problem is that it is difficult to see how the referential opacity of deontic contexts might be established without begging the question. In the cases of necessity and belief, certain *independent* arguments are available to show that the relevant substitutions do not ensure truth. We know that 'The number of the apostles is necessarily greater than ten' is false because we know that, logically speaking, the world *might* have been different, that there is some possible world in which, for instance, the number of the apostles is nine. Similarly, we know that the truth of 'Joe believes that the leader of the Normandy invasion was the thirty-fourth president' is not guaranteed by the truth of 'Joe believes that Eisenhower was the thirty-fourth president' because we realize that Joe might be unaware that Eisenhower was the leader of the Normandy invasion. In the case of deontic notions, however, these sorts of explanations would appear to be unavailable. As intimated above, the fact that the relevant descriptions have identical references serves as a *prima facie* reason for holding that the truth of 'At time/place$_i$ Jane's keeping her promise to John ought to be performed' guarantees the truth of 'At time/place$_i$ Jane's denying that John committed the shameful deed ought to be performed' (Imagine what we would say to Jane if she assented to the first claim and denied the second). Moreover, there appears to be no independent reason—independent, that is, of the concern to establish the opacity thesis—for denying the truth of the second sentence given the truth of the first. Similar conclusions apply to the sentences 'At time/place$_i$ Jane's lying to Jill ought not to be performed' and 'At time/place₁ Jane's denying that John committed the shameful deed ought not to be performed'. Therefore, there appears to be no reason for assuming that referential opacity obtains in the deontic case. The appeal to referential opacity thus fails to sustain this objection to the argument from deductive logic.

(b) *Different Descriptions Denoting Different Acts.* In the previous discussion it was suggested that the fact of two or more act-descriptions' denoting the same act serves as a reason for allowing the transfer of moral predicates from one description to another. Thus, one way of supporting the thesis denying entitlement to such transfers is to hold that in the relevant cases, appearances to the contrary notwithstanding, the different act-descriptions denote different acts. In this rendering, the act-descriptions involved in our syllogistic representation of Jane's predicament, while putatively covering the same act, in fact pick out discrete acts. In discussing this nonidentity theory of act-individuation I shall limit myself to considering what I regard as the strongest argument for the position, an argument presented by Alvin Goldman.[17]

This argument appeals to what Goldman calls the principle of the indiscernibility of identicals. If "X and Y are identical, then X must have all and only the properties that Y has." Yet on close inspection we find that certain supposedly identical acts do not possess all the same properties:

> Let us look, for example, at John's pulling the trigger and John's killing Smith, which were mentioned in one of the examples above. According to the identity thesis, these acts are supposed to be one and the same act. But are they really identical? Surely not. It would be extremely odd to say that John's killing Smith caused the gun to go off. But now consider John's act of pulling the trigger. It is certainly true of *this* act that it caused the event in question, i.e., that it caused the gun to fire. Thus, John's pulling the trigger has the property of causing the gun to fire. However, since one of these acts has a property which the other lacks, they cannot be one and the same act.[18]

Goldman goes on to give a series of similar examples, all of which purport to show that act-descriptions ostensibly denoting identical acts in fact exemplify divergent properties and thus denote different acts. What consequences do Goldman's analyses have for the matter at hand?

First, it should be clear that Goldman's argument yields no immediately obvious conclusions regarding our presentation of Jane's predicament. His strategy is to proceed ad hoc, putatively showing in each specific instance that a seeming case of identity is only apparent. We still need to determine whether the act-descriptions involved in our syllogistic representation of Jane's situation manifest divergent properties. Perhaps such divergence can be established, but it does not follow immediately from Goldman's analyses.

More important, a direct criticism can be lodged against Goldman's general argument. In particular, his analyses appear to ignore the fact that different act-descriptions normally taken to pick out the same act are more often than not shorthand descriptions identifying a limited (i.e., less than exhaustive) range of properties possessed by that act. Yet if act-descriptions are often shorthand in this sense, it is hardly surprising that the properties identified by different act-descriptions covering the same act will themselves possess divergent subproperties. Indeed, a similar phenomenon manifests itself in descriptions of physical objects. I might pick out, for example, the *same* object with either of two distinct phrases, 'the red book' or 'the largest object on the table', each of which identifies discrete properties possessed by that object. In this case a property identified by one phrase itself possesses a subproperty lacked by the property picked out by the other phrase. More specifically, the property of *redness*, picked out by the phrase 'the red book', has the subproperty of reflecting light to a certain degree. The fact that the property *largeness*, picked out by the phrase 'the largest object on the table', does not possess the subproperty of reflecting light to a certain degree is not grounds for ruling out the possibility that the phrases pick out the *same* object. Similarly, the fact that the phrase 'John's pulling the trigger' designates an act-property possessing a subproperty (*causing the gun to fire*) lacked by the act-property denoted by the phrase 'John's killing Smith' does not ipso facto show that the phrases in question fail to denote the same act. Analogous arguments apply to Goldman's treatment of other cases as well. Consequently, his analyses do not establish the nonidentity theory even in cases he examines, much less in the ones we are assessing. And, therefore, given the considerations here, the theory cannot be appealed to in the way of blocking exchanges of moral predicates between different act-descriptions that may plausibly be construed as denoting the same act. All in all, then, it is reasonable to conclude that the first response to the argument from deductive logic fails.

(2) The second response to the argument from deductive logic concedes that the premises of arguments structuring conflict situations can generate pairs of conclusions having the ought/ought not form but denies that conclusions such as these are genuinely inconsistent. It is difficult to see how Marcus herself could make use of this response without limiting her theory in a way that bears a special burden of proof. Indeed, extending her consistency definition to apply to singular judgments as well as to general principles yields the result that pairs of conclusions having the ought/ought not form *are* inconsistent pairs; for there is no possible world in which two dictates having the relevant structures ('ought *x*' and 'ought not *x*') can be jointly obeyed in every circumstance of that world. Thus, if Marcus's consistency definition were to be given general application, she would be obliged to hold that conclusions such as the ones we have considered *are* inconsistent. Of course, it is open to her to refrain from extending her consistency definition to apply to singular judgments; that is, she might argue that a different consistency criterion applies to judgments. Yet multiplying consistency definitions in this way bears a special burden of explanation, especially in view of the fact that in the analogous case of propositions or sentences the consistency definition remains the same whether one is dealing with statements of general or of singular form.

The issue we have before us, then, is whether there are any theoretical considerations that would command such a qualification of Marcus's consistency definition. More generally, are there compelling reasons for suggesting that judgments having the forms 'ought *x*' and 'ought not *x*' are *not* inconsistent? It is clear enough that such judgments are not contradictories in the technical sense of the expression. Pairs of contradictories are characterized by the fact that if one of any such pair is true, the other is false, and vice versa. Yet, the existence of a realm of the morally indifferent ensures the *possibility* that two judgments having the relevant forms (e.g., 'I ought to scratch my head' and 'I ought not to scratch my head') are both false (given for the moment that moral judgments are the sorts of things that can be true or false). If judgments having these forms are not contradictories, are they inconsistent in another sense? Are they contraries, for instance?

Lemmon has provided an argument purporting to show that pairs of judgments having these forms are not contraries.[19] The argument, which might be labeled the argument from disanalogy, goes as follows: Although alethic modal logic and deontic logic are analogous in many ways, they are dissimilar in at least one important respect. Consider the modal auxiliary denoting necessity. Clearly, if necessarily p (where p represents some state of affairs), then p. But if this conditional is true, the following statement must be false, 'necessarily p and necessarily not p', since from it we can infer 'p and not p', which is a contradiction. Thus 'necessarily p' and 'necessarily not p' cannot both be true. Yet both might be false; for example, p might be true but only *contingently* so. A relation of contrariety, therefore, can be shown to obtain between 'necessarily p' and 'necessarily not p'. The case is otherwise with the deontic operators 'ought' and 'ought not'. While, as we have seen, 'ought p' and 'ought not p' can both be false (if p is merely permissible), we cannot show that they cannot both be true. That is, from 'ought p and ought not p' we cannot deduce the contradiction 'p and not p' as we were able to do in the case of 'necessarily p and necessarily not p'. For, indeed, in order to deduce the contradiction, we would need to assume that 'ought p' entailed p. Yet, clearly no such entailment relation obtains. If it did, then of necessity what ought to be the case would be the case. Lemmon thus concludes that, since a contradiction cannot be deduced from 'ought p and ought not p', there is no good reason to suppose that 'ought' and 'ought not' are contraries.

The problem with Lemmon's disanalogy argument resides in its assumption that a relation of contrariety between two statements can be revealed only in the manner exhibited in the treatment of the alethic modal operator, that is, only by deducing a contradiction from the pair. That this is not the case can be gathered from an inspection of certain contrary pairs in nonmodal contexts. Take, for instance, the statements 'Jimmy Carter is now in Sarasota, Florida' and 'Jimmy Carter is now in Sacramento, California'. These statements are not contradictories, of course, since both of them might be false. Yet they are contraries because they cannot both be true. What is noteworthy for our purposes is the way we come to this latter conclusion. We do not do so by deducing a contradiction from the contrary pair. Rather, we ground our judgment in a certain bit of knowledge about the nature of the world: A person cannot be in two places that far apart at once.

The question we have before us is whether there are considerations—apart from those concerning the deducibility of contradiction—prompting us to judge that a relation of contrariety obtains in the deontic case. Consider the following line of argument.[20] A concern of any moral theory is to capture and preserve, to an extent that is consistent with other theoretical constraints, the formal relations governing our deontic concepts. And it would appear to be uncontroversial to say that the following relations hold:

(a) If ought p, then permissible p.

(b) If permissible p, then it is not true that ought not p.

Yet, if (a) and (b) hold, then so does the following via the inference rule of the hypothetical syllogism:

(c) If ought p, then it is not true that not ought p.

And from (c) via *modus tollens:*

(d) If ought not p, then it is not true that ought p.

Of course, (c) and (d) jointly express the claim that 'ought' and 'ought not' are contraries. The point is that if one were to reject this claim, then one would be forced to reject either (a) or (b). In other words, denying that 'ought' and 'ought not' are contraries commits one to denying what appear to be some obvious conceptual connections among moral obligation (ought), permission (may), and prohibition (ought not).

Perhaps we may say that the preceding argument establishes a presumption in favor of the view that 'ought' and 'ought not' are contraries in some sense. But the crucial thing to note is that one could hardly appeal to the argument as a way of showing that dilemmas are to be dismissed *on the grounds of consistency alone.* For here the claim that dilemmatic judgments are inconsistent (that they are contraries) rests on considerations that clearly go beyond the realm of formal logic *simpliciter.* That is, the conceptual connections among obligation, permission, and prohibition employed by the argument cannot be established apart from substantive presuppositions related to the nature and function of morality. If, for instance, an obligation to lie in order to keep a promise implies the permission to lie to keep the promise, the implication is not one that follows solely from the principles of logic; on the contrary, if there is a connection here, it will depend on a certain understanding of the character of the moral universe, an understanding that excludes the possibility morality will ever require what it does not permit. And, interestingly enough, it is precisely such an interpretation of the moral universe that is rejected by the proponent of the moral dilemmas thesis since, on the terms of that thesis, there may be cases where we are obliged to do precisely what we are not permitted to do. This last judgment may be in error, but if so, the mistake is not in logic but in interpreting the nature of the moral world. The general point is that whether one regards dilemmatic judgments as inconsistent or incompatible will depend on one's constructions of fundamental deontic concepts, and the nature of these constructions will rely, in turn, on the various background beliefs one holds about the structure of the moral universe. In this respect, then, the argument from deductive logic simply begs the question against the moral dilemmas thesis and drives us toward consideration of more substantive matters.

(3) The third response to the argument from deductive logic admits that the premises of syllogisms structuring putatively dilemmatic situations generate pairs of conclusions having the ought/ought not form, concedes that such conclusions are inconsistent in a sense, but denies that either member of such a pair must be rejected without remainder as one must reject either of two inconsistent propositions. This response is grounded in a dismissal of the theory of *moral realism*.

Moral realism is the doctrine holding that morality deals with truth, that there is a sphere of reality which moral language seeks to capture. According to this account, moral judgments are genuine assertions that admit of assessment as either true or false, and a system of moral principles is seen to be logically similar to a body of lawlike generalizations, which likewise can be evaluated in terms of truth. Realistic moral theories may be contrasted with antirealistic theories, which deny that moral pronouncements are genuine assertions. For the antirealist, moral judgments are not things that can be either true or false. On the contrary, they are analogous to imperatives, which are fundamentally prescriptive rather than assertive. Similarly, antirealistic theories can be distinguished from realistic theories in that the former treat systems of moral principles as something akin to systems of legal rules, which might be assessed on general pragmatic grounds but not in terms of truth and falsity.

The response under consideration rejects the realist's account of moral discourse and suggests, furthermore, that this rejection has crucial implications for the way we understand the role consistency considerations play in reflection on moral matters. From the realist's perspective the appearance of two inconsistent judgments, such as the conclusions of arguments structuring putatively dilemmatic situations, provides one with a compelling reason for revising one's moral system since one of two such conclusions must be rejected unequivocally. The rejection is called for in view of the supposed fact that the point of a moral judgment is to depict moral truth, and *per definitionem* one of two inconsistent truth claims must be false. By implication it would seem that, in the realist view, situations of moral perplexity never could be construed as genuinely dilemmatic, for to assume that they could be would be to assume that the moral reality captured by dilemmatic judgments was itself *incoherent*. And, after all, reality cannot be incoherent.

The antirealist sees the matter differently. According to this account, the role that consistency plays in morals is analogous to the role it plays in a conventional system of rules such as a legal system. If two laws of a particular system conflict in a given case, the issue of whether or not to change the laws turns on pragmatic considerations. Is the conflict likely to occur again? Will the modification of the laws generating the conflict engender confusion about what is legally required? Is the bringing about of legal change so involved that it is not worth undertaking to avoid this sort of situation? The point to stress here is that in legal conflict cases, questions of truth or falsity just do not arise. The situation is analogous in the moral case given the antirealist's position. If the antirealist is correct, questions of truth or falsity are not generated by moral conflict since the point of a moral pronouncement is not to express truth at all. Consequently, the role that consistency plays in moral discourse will be judged differently by the realist and the antirealist. For the latter, inconsistency is a problem in conflict cases because it disrupts the action-guiding function of a moral code. Yet this concern is a pragmatic one that needs to be weighed against other pragmatic concerns similar to those mentioned in the legal case (e.g., What sort of purpose might be thwarted by modifying the moral code in order to avoid conflict situations?)[21] And it would appear to be the case that in the antirealist account there is no problem, from the point of view of consistency at any rate, with interpreting situations of moral perplexity as genuinely dilemmatic. Again, in this respect moral codes are seen to be similar to legal codes. Whether or not they generate dilemmas will depend on the extent of their completeness in anticipating possible instances of application. Indeed, just as it would be foolish to expect a legal system to evince perfect completeness in the relevant sense, it is likewise unreasonable to think that a moral code will do so. Thus, genuine moral dilemmas, according to the antirealist theory, would appear to be not only conceivable but likely.[22]

Granting the presumption that moral realism is false, then, consistency considerations of the sort traded on by the argument from deductive logic would seem to pose no necessary obstacle to claiming that genuine moral dilemmas exist. Yet suppose this presumption were not granted. Could the defender of the argument from deductive logic find ultimate refuge in the doctrine of moral realism? There are, of course, two ways of addressing this question. First, one might ask whether moral realism is a plausible doctrine. This is a complex query, discussion of which must be deferred until the next chapter. Second, one might ask whether the realist's and the antirealist's respective evaluations of consistency ought to differ in the way the foregoing discussion suggests. Might one argue that the realist's account of consistency ought to be closer to the antirealist's account than first thought?

An affirmative answer to this last question has been buttressed with the following line of argument.[23] Just as consistency is only one of a set of ideals to be striven for by practical systems (e.g., legal codes), so consistency is merely one of a number of methodological ideals (including simplicity, explanatory power, comprehensiveness, etc.) governing the construction or modification of theoretical systems whose overriding aim is the discovery of truth. Circumstances, therefore, might be such that an inconsistency in a theoretical system would need to be tolerated because tinkering with the system to do away with the inconsistency would require the sacrifice of some systemic feature satisfying another methodological ideal judged to be of paramount concern in the given case. Take, for example, a system of lawlike generalizations that yielded accurate predictions in almost every case but that now and then issued inconsistent predictions. Imagine further that the inconsistencies can be eliminated only at the expense of attenuating seriously the system's predictive power by reducing the level of generality of its laws. Such a modification would sacrifice a good measure of comprehensiveness for the sake of a small saving in coherence. And it would be reasonable to say that the proposed adjustment in the system would on balance reduce the degree of truth captured by the system as a whole. Similar conclusions could be drawn with respect to a moral system realistically construed. Perhaps it is the case that such a system generates inconsistent judgments on occasion. Does this sort of occurrence provide a knockdown argument for revising the system's principles? Not necessarily. It could be that other methodological ideals would be sacrificed as a result of such a modification. Suppose the only way to avoid the inconsistencies was to reduce the scope of the principles to an extent that seriously limited the comprehensiveness of the moral system (the extreme case being the allowance of only singular judgments). Such a reduction, it could be argued, would lessen significantly the degree of moral truth captured by the system, that is, would lessen it to an extent not offset by the gain in coherence. In such a case methodological constraints would require tolerating the inconsistency.

This is a compelling argument, but it is important to be clear about what it demonstrates. It does not show that moral realism can admit the possibility of genuine moral dilemmas. What it does show is that the theory must allow for the possibility that the best moral code available, given certain canons of system building, is one generating inconsistencies. In other words, the argument shows that even if moral realism turned out to be true, situations of moral conflict would not necessarily call for systemic revision. Yet the best available moral system is not of necessity the best system *in principle*. And, indeed, it would still have to be the case that in the realist view a moral code generating genuine inconsistency would always be ultimately unsatisfactory, though it might be provisionally acceptable. Such a system would be unsatisfactory from the realist's perspective because it would be partially false (even granting that it might be *minimally* false given the best available system). And, of course, it would show its falsity precisely at the point of conflict, that is, precisely where the inconsistent judgments manifested themselves. Thus, were we to assume that dilemmatic judgments were genuinely inconsistent, we would have to conclude that the moral realist could never interpret a particular instance of moral perplexity as a genuine dilemma.

We are driven once again to the issue of the compatibility between dilemmatic judgments. It has been suggested already that the resolution of this issue will depend on one's interpretation of basic deontic concepts and that these interpretations in turn will depend on certain background beliefs about the nature and foundation of morality. Indeed, I shall try to show eventually that given certain readings of the moral 'ought' a realist could countenance dilemmas without difficulty. Suffice it to say at this juncture that the argument from deductive logic is inconclusive inasmuch as it trades implicitly on two problematic assumptions, that moral realism is true and that, because dilemmatic judgments are incompatible, realism cannot countenance the moral dilemmas thesis. I shall consider these and related matters in the next chapter.

The Argument from Deontic Metaprinciples

Before turning to these matters, I want to consider one final pro-revision argument. The position under consideration holds that moral perplexity can never be assessed as dilemmatic since the judgment that a moral dilemma exists is inconsistent with two metaprinciples said to be binding on all moral systems: a deontic factoring principle and the familiar "'ought' implies 'can'" principle. The deontic factoring principle states, seemingly trivially, that if I ought to do x and I ought to do y, then I ought to do x and y. The 'ought'/'can' principle states, of course, that if I ought to do x, then I can do x. Given the bindingness of these principles, it can be shown that the acknowledgment of a genuine moral dilemma leads to an inconsistency. The inconsistency is represented in the following:[24]

(1) I ought to do a
(2) I ought to do b
(3) I cannot do both a and b
(4) I ought to do both a and b (from the deontic factoring principle plus [1] and [2] via *modus ponens*)
(5) It is not the case that I ought to do both a and b (from the 'ought'/'can' principle and [3] via *modus tollens*)

It should be clear that (1), (2), and (3) represent the admission that a moral dilemma exists; (4) and (5) illustrate the inconsistency generated by the coupling of this admission with the aforementioned metaprinciples. Given the argument's validity, one may conclude that moral perplexity always calls for the revision of one's moral system in order to remove the inconsistency. In other words, the judgment reflected in either (1) or (2) must be rejected; this rejection in turn forces one to modify the moral principle from which the judgment was deduced.[25]

In objection to this line of reasoning it might be argued that the possibility of moral dilemmas can be preserved and thus that the necessity to revise can be eliminated by justifiably calling into question either of the two metaprinciples. Of course, without the two metaprinciples the argument loses its validity. Are there good reasons for rejecting at least one of the principles?

Apart from certain question-begging maneuvers, it has been suggested that factoring principles do not apply in other areas of evaluative discourse and that this circumstance should cause us to wonder about applicability in the moral case.[26] For example, it has been said that one may speak of *a*'s being advisable and *b*'s being advisable without speaking of the advisability of *both a* and *b* or that one may claim the desirability of *a* and the desirability of *b* while denying the desirability of *both a* and *b*. Two points should be registered here. First, what has been established about a factoring principle's applicability in these other evaluative areas is not at all clear. More than likely, rejecting the principle will depend on appealing to examples in which equivocations occur. Take the matter of desirability. True enough, it might be desirable for Bill to marry Jean and desirable for him to marry Barbara but not desirable for him to marry both Jean and Barbara. Yet this instance hardly serves as a counterexample to the factoring principle's applicability in this evaluative area generally since it is surely the case that 'desirable' is used here in different senses at crucial points, and the principle's application presumes univocity of meaning. Thus, marriage to Jean might be desirable in virtue of her beauty and marriage to Barbara desirable in virtue of her wealth but marriage to both undesirable in virtue of the legal consequences. One could still hold that where the meaning of 'desirable' is univocal the principle applies. Although one would have to examine each case on its own merits, my suspicion is that most putative counterexamples to a factoring principle's applicability in evaluative areas could be analyzed in similar terms.

Second, even if it were the case that a factoring principle did not apply in other areas, this circumstance in and of itself would not prove decisive in determining the principle's status in the moral context. Nonetheless, we have learned something from examining the nonmoral case. If it could be shown that similar equivocations always occurred in the use of moral 'oughts' to describe conflict situations, then one would have reason to reject the metaprinciple's relevance to those situations. For example, one might argue that saying a particular act both ought to be done and ought not to be done is *at bottom* to say that the act possesses both the property of fidelity (the keeping of a promise) and the property of insincerity (the telling of a lie). If such an analysis is appropriate in a given case, then an equivocal use of 'ought'-language will have been identified. Of course, whether this sort of semantic rendering most accurately displays what is involved in conflict cases will depend on certain fundamental constructions of morality's nature (e.g., Are properties such as fidelity and insincerity wholly discrete and independent or are they features of some more basic moral property—the right—captured by our 'ought'-language?). The point is that substantive questions are begged by any argument appealing to the metaprinciple.

The 'ought'/'can' principle has come under fire in recent philosophical discussions.[27] Among other things, it has sometimes been suggested that the nature of the ability required by the 'can' of the principle is less than clear. At a minimum the term would appear to denote *logical* and some form of *physical* possibility. But is this physical possibility to be construed stringently or loosely? For instance, does the fact that one's legs have been broken an hour before dissolve, on the terms of the principle, one's obligation to attend an important business meeting, even though strictly speaking one is *able* to make the meeting? And what about *psychological* possibility? Does the psychological inability of, say, moral weakness serve as a counterexample to the doctrine that 'ought' implies 'can' (e.g., "John really ought to tell Richard the truth, but he just *can't* bring himself to do so.")? Such questions are difficult to answer. We need not address them here, however, since the 'ought'/'can' principle requiring logical and physical possibility *strictly* construed is sufficient for the argument under consideration.

Why accept the 'ought'/'can' principle? Hare seems to give the following defense, which focuses on the notion of implication expressed in the doctrine.[28] According to Hare, the 'implies' of the principle denotes not a relation of entailment but rather one of presupposition, a relation analogous to that claimed by Strawson to exist between the statements 'The King of France is wise' and 'There is a King of France'.[29] The first sentence presupposes the truth of the second in the sense that were the latter false the question of the King's wisdom could not arise. Similarly, the sentence 'x ought to be performed' is said to presuppose the truth of 'x can be performed' in the sense that, were the latter false, the *prescriptive* question ('Ought x to be performed?'), to which the former serves as answer, likewise could not arise because its intelligibility rests on the possibility of raising a related *practical* question ('Shall x be performed?'), and the practical question is senseless without presuming that x *can* be performed. In Hare's own words, "it is because they are prescriptive that moral words possess that property which is summed up, perhaps over-crudely, in the slogan '"Ought" implies "can"'."[30]

This argument trades on the controversial assumption that all moral judgments are prescriptive in the way specified, that they all are generated by practical questions and thus are action-guiding in intent.[31] In defense of this assumption it might be argued that moral judgments issued without prescriptive intent have no point. Yet apart from its vagueness, this defense in its turn makes two further assumptions that are similarly problematic. The first is that determining whether such moral judgments have a *point* is relevant to the matter at hand. To presume relevance here is to risk confusing considerations of intelligibility or truth with considerations of pragmatics. Perhaps it is the case that a moral judgment is meaningful or true even though its issuance serves no particular function.[32] Perhaps not. But to deny the possibility requires further argument, and such an argument would almost certainly include general theoretical claims about the nature and purpose of morality as a whole. The second assumption is that the point of issuing a moral judgment can only be to guide action. That this assumption begs certain questions about the function of morality should be obvious. Indeed, we can at least imagine other purposes that moral judgments might serve.[33] For instance, saying that an agent ought to have kept his promise even though he could not have done so (through circumstances beyond his control) might be a way of underlining the unsatisfactory nature of the situation (a promise having gone unfulfilled) or of affording the unsuccessful agent a reason for doing all in his power to avoid such situations in the future. Whether these sorts of considerations provide sufficient grounds for jettisoning the 'ought'/ 'can' principle is another matter. Much will depend, of course, on the availability of further arguments supporting the principle's retention. What the foregoing discussion does highlight is the incompleteness of Hare's defense.

Along with others, I suspect that behind the concern to retain the 'ought'/'can' principle is a deep motivation to capture theoretically certain intuitions we have about the inappropriateness of blaming an agent for failing to perform a task she *could not* perform. The question is whether retention of the principle is necessary to do justice to the intuitions.[34] It has been suggested, for example, that moral theory would be advanced if the subtheory of obligation (the subtheory that determines what an agent *ought to do*) were independent of the subtheory of blame (the subtheory that determines when an agent might be held blameworthy).[35] Assuming the existence of a blameworthy agent would not, in this account, be a necessary condition for assuming the existence of a failed obligation. Given the independence of the subtheories, the way would be paved for rejecting the 'ought'/'can' principle without sacrificing the connection between blame and ability since it would now be possible to speak of an agent's being *blameless* for having failed to perform some act that *ought* to have been performed but *could not* have been performed. The virtues of such a theory would include the aforementioned capacities to portray the unsatisfactoriness of a situation in which an obligation went unfulfilled through nonculpable inability and to provide the unsuccessful agent with a reason for doing everything to avoid such situations in the future (by stating in both cases that something which ought to have been done was not done). This sort of theory, moreover, preserves the distinction between excuse and justification. To say that an agent has been excused for having failed to perform an act because of inability is not to say that the omission was justified, is not to deny that the act was one that ought to have been done. Adhering to the 'ought'/'can' principle prevents us from making this distinction, however, since inability on the principle's terms dissolves obligation.[36]

For our purposes it is enough to note at this point that if the motivation behind the 'ought'/'can' principle is to capture these intuitions about blame and ability, then the concern the principle generates about moral dilemmas is ill-founded, even given the truth of the deontic factoring principle. A moral theory that, while rejecting the 'ought'/'can' principle, salvaged these intuitions by maintaining the independence of the subtheories of blame and obligation would have no problem admitting the existence of genuine moral dilemmas, for the theory would allow one to speak of situations in which a blameless agent inevitably committed some moral wrong. Thus, unless the 'ought'/'can' principle admits of further justification, this antidilemmas argument from deontic metaprinciples fails. It is difficult to imagine that such justification could be provided apart from substantive discussion of the nature and purpose of morality as a whole.

Conclusion

In the foregoing discussion I have assessed variations of the claim that consistency considerations compel the revision of moral systems in response to moral conflict, a revision that presumably signifies the dissolution of such conflict. I have tried to demonstrate that none of the four arguments succeeds since each of them either relies on counterintuitive assumptions or begs any of a number of substantive questions about the nature of morality. (1) The argument from prescriptivity fails because it rests on an implausible theory of the relation between moral commitments and resolutions to perform what is morally required, a theory that denies the possibility of moral weakness. (2) The argument from universalizability is inconclusive because it resorts to a controversial interpretation of deliberative judgments in conflict cases. The interpretation assumes that our *practical* resolutions of moral perplexity have their source in *morality* itself, and this assumption presupposes, in turn, the substantive assessment that morality's content is rich enough to adjudicate apparent dilemmas. (3) The argument from deductive logic is unsuccessful inasmuch as it presumes (*a*) that moral realism is true and (*b*) that dilemmatic judgments are incompatible (that they are contraries). Both presumptions call for further discussion, and both beg certain questions about the structure of the moral universe. (4) Finally, the argument from deontic metaprinciples fails because the axioms it employs are problematic. The factoring principle presumes that the use of 'ought'-language in describing conflict situations is unequivocal, and the 'ought'/'can' principle embraces a number of controversial assumptions about morality's function. In both cases the presuppositions require further defense of a sort that draws on arguments relating to substantive moral theory.

If my assessments are correct, then the issue of moral perplexity's solubility cannot be assessed on the basis of consistency considerations alone. On the contrary, in attempting to determine whether moral conflict is adjudicable, we are forced to confront substantive matters regarding the content, nature, and function of morality. As we shall see, such matters raise questions about the practical effects of moral constructions, the implications of our moral experience, and the fundamental character of moral reality. In what follows, I attend to these questions and related issues.

2

PERPLEXITY AS

DILEMMA

IF consistency considerations in and of themselves do not suffice to rule out the possibility of genuine moral dilemmas, are there any reasons for believing that such dilemmas do exist? In this chapter I shall attend to this question by assessing recent philosophical arguments designed to show that moral perplexity, at least in a good number of cases, ought to be construed dilemmatically. I shall conclude in general that these arguments are unsuccessful. More particularly, I shall suggest that the pragmatic and phenomenological considerations often cited by these arguments do not lead inevitably to the moral dilemmas thesis, that, contrary to what one might expect, antirealism or what I shall refer to as moral positivism provides no firm foundation for that thesis, and that a full-fledged salvaging of the moral dilemmas thesis requires, therefore, a particular version of moral realism, a realism whose distinctive ontology allows for the existence of moral dilemmas. I shall end by considering two philosophical accounts of such an ontology in an attempt to demonstrate their inadequacy. Finally, I shall suggest that no ultimate assessment of the moral dilemmas controversy is possible apart from an airing of certain kinds of foundational questions about the nature of the world and about morality's place within it.

A Pragmatic View

I want to examine first an argument advanced by Ruth Marcus.[1] The argument maintains that the issue of interpreting moral conflict experience is to be assessed at least partially against the background of general pragmatic considerations. In particular, the argument assumes that whether or not the existence of genuine moral dilemmas is to be admitted depends on whether such admission contributes to the goals of morality itself. According to this view, the problem of moral perplexity is regarded as a problem of practice as much as one of theory.

In the previous chapter we concluded that consistency considerations *simpliciter* provided no indefeasible warrant for revising one's moral code on occasions of moral perplexity. In response to this conclusion it might be suggested that while consistency canons are indeed insufficient in this respect, practical considerations certainly do dictate such revision. After all, if a moral code is to do anything at all, it is to guide action, and in cases of conflict it is precisely this action-guiding function of morality that has stalled. Consequently, in the systematization of one's moral code one should account as much as possible for the contingencies of the world by providing guidelines for action in even the most extraordinary of circumstances. Of course, because of our limited knowledge and because of the complexity of the world's affairs, it is hardly likely that one could construct a code whose principles never conflicted. Nonetheless, the general concern to preserve morality's prescriptive function should stimulate revision of the code when conflict does occur.

It is this line of reasoning that serves as the point of departure for Marcus's pragmatic counterargument. Essentially her response is that while action guidance is one concern of morality, it is not the only concern. We adopt moral principles not simply because they prescribe actions but also because they prescribe actions of a particular type. In other words, we accept moral principles because we have reason to believe that they identify which actions are right and which are wrong, which actions are to be performed in virtue of their rightness and which are to be avoided in virtue of their wrongness. Thus, morality's purpose is not only to bring forth actions but to bring forth actions that will make the world what it ought to be. Given morality's concern to provide this *special* sort of action guidance, revision of one's moral code is inappropriate unless the revision is justified on grounds independent of the mere concern to resolve moral conflict, that is, unless we have separate reason to believe that the principles do not in fact identify which actions are right and which wrong (and Marcus implies that for a wide range of our principles we hardly ever have such reason). On this matter comparison between the principles of morality and the rules of a game is instructive. Imagine a game in which play is brought to a standstill because of a conflict in the rules. Obviously such a game is deficient in that it violates the canon of game formation requiring that a game be playable to its conclusion. When such intragame conflict occurs, the players have two alternatives, the relative feasibility of both depending, among other things, on the nature and extent of the conflict. They may abandon the game, or they may save the game by altering its rules so that the conflict will not reoccur.

Neither alternative, according to Marcus, is available to the players of the moral game. The moral player cannot abandon the game because its rules impinge on the everyday activities of human life. Nor ought the player to revise the principles of the code, and this for the following reason: Given that the principles were adopted in the first place because they were believed to identify rightness and wrongness, revising the code obscures the fact that the world has fallen away from what morality requires (e.g., a promise must be broken; a lie must be told). The obfuscation of this fact through revision of the moral code can serve only to weaken the motivation to avoid such situations in the future, therefore depriving us of an incentive to bring the world closer to what morality demands. Since we ought to avoid wrong actions, we ought to avoid situations of conflict in which wrong actions inevitably occur. It is thus mistaken to be concerned about tailoring our principles to fit the world in the way the advocates of revision suggest. Rather, we ought to shape the world so as to maximize conformity with our principles. But if by revising our codes in the face of moral conflict we disguise the fact that the world has in an important sense fallen short of our principles, we thereby weaken the impulse to change the world, to alter our lives and institutions so that the likelihood of moral conflict's recurrence will be minimized. Thus, in Marcus's view, refusal to acknowledge the existence of moral dilemmas is bound to impede progress in the moral transformation of the world.

In assessing Marcus's argument, let us take the case of a political executive who reasons that the passing of a particular piece of legislation will advance the cause of equality in her society. She calculates, moreover, that the necessary votes will be secured only if recalcitrant legislators are subjected to political blackmail. Of course, she reasons further, in ordinary circumstances such blackmail is wrong inasmuch as it violates the autonomy and personal integrity of those involved. She concludes, nevertheless, that reservations of this type are overridden by the substantial social good that will be achieved by the legislation. She thus decides on the blackmail.

How ought the politician to regard her decision and subsequent action? Consider these two options: (1) She views her behavior as fully and unequivocally justified from the moral point of view. While political blackmail is wrong in ordinary cases, she reasons, this is an extraordinary case. Thus she suffers from no residual moral compunction. True enough, she does *regret* the pain and suffering that she must generate in committing the blackmail. Yet she feels no moral *guilt* or *remorse* in doing so. Indeed, there is no reason to feel guilty or remorseful, she thinks, since her action is not morally wrong. (2) She regards her behavior as justified on balance but not without some moral ambiguity. This is to say she believes that her decision is the correct one considering all the factors, but she also feels that her action in some sense constitutes a moral transgression, that she commits a moral wrong in doing what she ought to do *all things considered.* She thus feels not merely regret in taking the measures she does but also moral guilt. Now for Marcus, even if we assume that the chosen course of action is the rational one, we must conclude that it is this second sort of attitude that should be exhibited by the politician, and this judgment is grounded partially in pragmatic considerations. The politician who experiences guilt in such situations, who feels that something has gone morally awry, most likely will be the politician who is motivated to change the world so that repetition of the incident is avoided. In the present case the guilty experience may, for instance, stimulate endeavor on the part of the executive to bring about the election of legislators who do not need to be blackmailed into a concern for equality. This kind of effect is likely, Marcus would argue, because guilt by its very nature tends to generate resolutions not to repeat moral transgressions: "Most important, an agent in a predicament of conflict will also 'wish to act properly in the future and strive to modify his actions accordingly.' He will strive to arrange his own life and encourage social arrangements that would prevent, to the extent that it is possible, future conflicts from arising. To deny the appropriateness or correctness of ascriptions of guilt is to weaken the impulse to make such arrangements."[2] In short, the guilt inevitably generated by an agent who has acted in circumstances perceived to be dilemmatic serves as a stimulus to change the world so that similar situations will not arise. "The point to be made is that, although dilemmas are not settled without residue, the recognition of their reality has a dynamic force. It motivates us to arrange our lives and institutions with a view to avoiding such conflicts."[3]

Marcus's argument makes use of two claims that require further examination. One asserts that guilt characteristically involves the resolution and the endeavor to avoid relevantly similar moral transgressions. The other asserts that failure to experience moral guilt or remorse in situations of moral perplexity will diminish the incentive to change the world so that such situations will not recur.

The status of the first claim is less than clear. Just what is the precise nature of the relation between guilt feelings and the sort of dispositional characteristics described? In the abstract there are at least three possibilities. (1) The relation in question could signify a *normative requirement* stipulating that persons who experience moral guilt *ought* to be disposed not to repeat the offense. Put in this way the requirement expresses a virtual truism; for moral guilt, at least when experienced nonpathologically, denotes the violation of a binding moral principle, and, of course, such a principle ought not to be violated. Yet if this were Marcus's meaning, her pragmatic argument, which suggests that the guilt experience *does in fact* have the stated dispositional effects, would lose its force since there is no guarantee that persons will form the sort of dispositions that they *ought* to form. (2) The relation intended by Marcus could be a *logical connection* between the concepts of guilt and the relevant dispositional attitudes. According to this account, the guilt experience *per definitionem* generates resolutions and endeavors not to repeat moral offenses. Given this understanding, a feeling that did not lead to the formation of the dispositional attitudes in question by definition could not count as an instance of guilt. If this is Marcus's meaning, then her claim is much too strong. Indeed, it is at least logically possible for an agent to experience genuine moral guilt—the uneasy feeling one has in response to one's own violation of a moral principle—without acquiring the dispositions described in Marcus's argument. Such an occurrence may be judged normatively deficient or even unlikely, but it is not a contradiction in terms. (3) Marcus's claim is rendered most plausible if the relation in question is interpreted as a *causal connection*. Intuitively, it seems reasonable to characterize the experience of moral guilt as a causal factor generating dispositions not to repeat moral transgressions. The problem here is that it is difficult to determine guilt's effectivenss in this regard with any great degree of precision. Eventually, such a characterization, if it is to reflect anything more than a hunch, will have to be grounded in empirical (e.g., sociological or psychological) evidence—a sort not provided by Marcus.

Nonetheless, let us grant on the basis of our intuitions that a strong causal connection exists. What, then, are we to make of the second claim that failure to experience moral guilt in conflict situations weakens the incentive to alter the world so that such situations do not recur? Consider the case of our political executive once again and imagine that she embarks on her chosen course with the greatest regret and reluctance but without feeling moral guilt, that is, without the sense that she commits a moral wrong. Must we then assume that as merely regretful she will be any less motivated to work for conditions that would make such actions unnecessary in the future? I think not. For agent regret is a painful emotion prompted by a person's belief that she has brought about some evil (though not necessarily *morally* evil) state of affairs. As a painful emotion, it is one "that agents are motivated to avoid."[4] And if agents are motivated to avoid regret, they will also be motivated to avoid the conditions perceived to give rise to it. Imagine the situation of an army medic who, under battlefield conditions, is forced to amputate the gangrenous leg of a soldier with insufficient anesthetic. In this case there can be no question of moral guilt, but the medic is agonizingly regretful of the pain she must inflict. Such an experience seems as likely as any to provide the motivation for changing the world. Similarly, it is just as reasonable to think that our political executive, deeply affected by her predicament, will feel impelled to transform the world so that she will not have to face similar situations in the future. It is reasonable to think this, it should be emphasized, without assuming that she sees herself as morally guilty.

The general point is that we need not construe conflict situations as genuinely dilemmatic in order to ensure the practical effects Marcus describes. Regret, as much as guilt, can serve as a causal factor generating dispositions to avoid conflict situations. Now in response to this position Marcus suggests that the ascription of regret rather than guilt to an agent embroiled in moral conflict is "inappropriate" and "false to the facts," the implication being that the nature of conflict experience demands the description of the agent's attitude as one governed by the perception of dilemmatic circumstances.[5] Unfortunately, she does not explain why conflict situations demand such descriptions. Arguments impinging on this matter will be considered below. In any event, it is important to note here that Marcus's phenomenological claim is independent of her practical argument. It may be true that regret and guilt have the same practical effects and yet still be the case that there are phenomenological grounds for ascribing guilt to an agent rather than regret and thus for reading situations of perplexity as genuinely dilemmatic.

Phenomenological Considerations

In evaluating the possible phenomenological grounds for admitting the existence of moral dilemmas, it is useful to begin by considering W. D. Ross's theory of *prima facie* duties.[6] Ross provides an interesting point of departure since certain features of his theory have been drawn upon in the way of supporting the moral dilemmas thesis. More particularly, it has been suggested that Ross's own phenomenological account of conflict situations cannot be sustained unless the existence of genuine moral dilemmas is acknowledged. The suggestion is especially interesting because the theory's distinction between *prima facie* and *actual* or *absolute* duties is designed to do justice to our moral experience of conflict situations without denying that apparent moral dilemmas are fully adjudicable in principle.

The distinction may be characterized roughly as follows.[7] Our actual duty in a given situation is what we ought to do (morally speaking), all things considered. A *prima facie* duty, on the other hand, is a duty *ceteris paribus;* that is, it is our actual duty in a particular case as long as it is not overridden by other morally relevant considerations. Hence, *prima facie* duties are defeasible. For instance, although keeping one's promise is, as Ross sees it, a *prima facie* duty, and although it is often the case that one's actual duty is to keep one's promise, in a particular situation one's actual duty may require the breaking of a promise (e.g., if this is the only way to save someone's life).[8] It is this distinction between *prima facie* and actual duty that allows Ross to rule out the existence of dilemmas while doing justice to their *apparent* existence. By Ross's account, ostensible moral dilemmas can be regarded as adjudicable in principle because such predicaments are constituted by conflicts between *prima facie* duties, some of which may be overridden with moral justification. The possibility of such resolutions, according to Ross, is not dependent on an ordering of the *prima facie* duties in accordance with some standard of relative importance. Indeed, Ross claims, for the most part such an ordering is impossible. Judgments as to what constitutes actual duty in a given situation putatively rest on "perception."[9] Nonetheless, fallible as that perception may be, actual duty is fully determinate, appearances to the contrary notwithstanding.

Ross never explains why we are to believe that actual duties are fully determinate in every case, apart from hinting vaguely that the nature of ethical judgment demands such. To this extent his theory is deficient.[10] What is particularly important for our purposes, however, is his suggestion that the belief in the adjudicability of moral conflict coupled with an appreciation of the phenomenological structure of conflict situations *requires* the theoretical distinction between *prima facie* and actual duty:

> If, as almost all moralists except Kant are agreed, and as most plain men think, it is sometimes right to tell a lie or to break a promise, it must be maintained that there is a difference between *prima facie* duty and actual or absolute duty. When we think ourselves justified in breaking, and indeed morally obliged to break, a promise in order to relieve some one's distress, we do not for a moment cease to recognize a *prima facie* duty to keep our promise, and this leads us to feel, not indeed shame or repentance, but certainly compunction, for behaving as we do; we recognize, further, that it is our duty to make up somehow to the promisee for the breaking of the promise. We have to distinguish from the characteristic of being our duty that of tending to be our duty. Any act that we do contains various elements in virtue of which it falls under various categories. In virtue of being the breaking of a promise, for instance, it tends to be wrong; in virtue of being an instance of relieving distress it tends to be right.[11]

Ross's point can be put as follows: We are often faced with situations in which every available course of action involves the violation of some moral principle. In such cases, after a measure of deliberation, we determine which course is morally required, all things considered, and by implication which principle must be overridden. Yet this is not the end of the matter; for in acting on the determination we feel a certain "compunction" about our behavior as well as an obligation to make reparations for having set aside the moral principle. How can these latter features of our experience be explained, given that in such instances we regard ourselves as fully justified in taking (and, indeed, in being obliged to take) the chosen course? Such features, Ross answers, can be accounted for only by recognizing that the overridden principle specifies a *prima facie* duty, which "tends" to bind our actions morally under any circumstances. When a principle specifying a *prima facie* duty is overridden, this "tendency" manifests itself through the residual effects noted, namely, through a feeling of compunction and a recognition of reparative obligation.

Ross's account has been criticized as an attempt to hold together two incompatible claims: (1) that conflict situations admit of unambiguous resolutions (that one course of action is unequivocally justified from the moral point of view) and (2) that overridden moral principles have certain residual phenomenal effects. The first claim, it is suggested, implies that the moral principle set aside is not in any way binding on the agent; that is, it does not create any genuine obligation in the given case. This implication is consistent with Ross's claim that justifiably overridden *prima facie* duties do not constitute actual obligations. But if overridden *prima facie* duties are without the force of genuine obligation, then it is difficult to understand how they can generate the residual phenomenal effects mentioned in the second claim. Why should we feel compunction or come to recognize a reparative obligation if no genuine obligation has been violated in the first place? Of course, Ross's reply would be that the residual effects are the result of the tendency of *prima facie* duties to be binding. Yet, his appeal to the concept of tendency has itself come under severe criticism. To say that things of type x have a tendency to exhibit property z is to say that most x's exhibit z (while some do not) and not that each individual x has the property of tending to exhibit z. Ross's argument, however, depends on the second reading. Thus, John Searle writes:

> To say, as he [Ross] does, that promise keeping has a "tendency" to be our duty is like saying glass windows have a tendency to break when struck. If I strike this window and it does not break, it is just as unbroken as if I had never struck it at all. Similarly if all that promises do is generate tendencies to be duties, then the fact that in this case I have no duty at all to keep the promise renders the conflict situation exactly as if I had never made a promise in the first place, for in this case the "tendency" is inoperative. But this view is unacceptable because it makes it mysterious and inexplicable that I should have any "compunction" about breaking the prom-

ise and that I should have "a duty to make up to the promisee for the breaking of the promise". If the promise does not create any actual obligations but only seems to (*"prima facie"*) then I should be able to ignore it altogether once all the facts are known.[12]

If Searle is correct, then Ross would need to adjust his moral theory in at least one of two ways. Either he would have to abandon his first claim that conflict situations are unequivocally adjudicable and admit that the duties overridden in such situations are actual rather than *prima facie* (i.e., he would need to abandon the doctrine of *prima facie* duties, at least as he expounded it), or he would have to modify his second claim about the residual phenomenal effects of overridden moral principles. Both Searle and Bernard Williams suggest the former course, in part because they believe that Ross's phenomenological account is close to being correct.[13] Whether the account is correct is especially important to determine. For it is Ross's phenomenological explanation or some version of it that has been adopted by Williams and others in arguing that conflict situations inevitably issue in the violation of genuinely binding moral principles.[14] In other words, this sort of explanation has been appealed to as a warrant for construing moral conflict situations as authentically dilemmatic.

What are we to make of Ross's phenomenological account? Let us take the matter of compunction first. As defined by the *Oxford English Dictionary*, 'compunction' denotes "a pricking or stinging of the conscience or heart, regret or uneasiness of mind consequent on sin or wrongdoing; remorse, contrition." Compunction is, in other words, a state of consciousness whose intentional object is a moral transgression. We can thus see how the case for the moral dilemmas thesis might be strengthened by the adoption of Ross's phenomenological analysis. For to say that an agent feels a certain compunction in conflict situations presupposes the agent's belief that she has committed or is about to commit a moral offense. Yet is Ross correct in citing this emotion as an inevitable datum of the conflict experience? And even if he is correct, need this datum be explained by appealing to the fact of a failed obligation?

It is clear that, unless the agent is an insensitive sort, conflict situations are prone to engender distressing emotive states, and any adequate moral theory is going to have to do justice to this fact. But Ross's particular account is not the only one that yields a plausible explanation of this feature of conflict experience. In fact, there are at least four plausible phenomenological accounts of moral conflict, each providing a reasonable explanation of the distressing nature of such conflict. Conflict situations may be said to generate (a) distress as a result of the uncertainty characterizing moral perplexity; (b) regret whose object is the loss of some good; (c) regret whose object is a moral transgression, that is, the feeling of remorse or the feeling of guilt; or (d) pathological remorse or guilt. I shall consider each of these descriptions in turn.

(a) It could be said that the unpleasant emotions associated with conflict experience are a function of uncertainty about the morally appropriate course of action. Agents faced with moral conflict can never be absolutely sure about what they ought to do, and this uncertainty engenders anxiety. Interestingly enough, Ross's own theory provides a foundation for this account. While, in his view, we know *prima facie* duties as self-evident truths, our judgments about actual duties in particular cases are not self-evidently true. Indeed, Ross claims, in conflict situations "we are taking a moral risk" in deciding on a specific course of action.[15] Though he does not say so, the recognition of this risk on the part of a morally sensitive agent is bound to produce distress. It would appear, moreover, that a defender of the moral dilemmas thesis is going to have difficulty accounting for this distress in any straightforward way.[16] For recognizing such a risk involves recognizing the possibility of taking the wrong course of action rather than the right one. Yet talk of *the* wrong course over against the right cannot be countenanced by the moral dilemmas thesis since on its terms *both* courses of action in conflict situations are wrong and *both* are right in some sense. Now it is open to defenders of the thesis to charge in response that any distress generated by *uncertainty* regarding the morally correct action, though understandable perhaps, is nonetheless irrational or pathological since there is no action that admits of unequivocal moral justification in these contexts. Yet this claim, while accounting for the occurrence of the emotion under consideration, *presupposes* the truth of the moral dilemmas thesis.

(b) Even if one grants the fact of epistemic distress under conflict conditions, noting this fact does not suffice as a full-blown description of conflict experience. For it is reasonable to expect that agents embroiled in moral conflict will feel not only epistemic anxiety but also a certain regret. So stated, this claim is ambiguous partly because regret can be given either a moral or a nonmoral interpretation. As we have seen, Ross and those who adopt his phenomenological analysis construe this regret in moral terms. Yet as we have seen also in our discussion of the political executive's plight, there is a way of talking about conflict regret that does not make reference to perceived moral transgressions. This last point forms the basis of Maurice Mandelbaum's criticism of Ross:

> In the case of sacrificing a chance to discharge my debt of gratitude to X for the sake of giving a truthful [negative] opinion of his capacities, I find no element of moral regret. What I do regret is having been placed in this situation in which I had to choose between a concern for his welfare and telling the truth; I regret the effect which the loss of his position will have on his welfare; I regret that I was in part the instrument of this loss; I regret what he may think of me, possibly viewing me as ungrateful; and I regret that a huge opportunity to show him my gratitude has slipped by. But none of these regrets constitutes the peculiar moral regret which is usually termed remorse. For remorse is that regret which we feel when we contemplate an act which we have done, and each of *these* regrets refers to some specific aspect or consequence of that action, not to the fact that the action was done. In other words, regret is distinguishable from remorse in having as its object a contemplated disvalue, not a contemplated wrongness.[17]

In this view, the regret experienced by an agent in conflict situations is a nonmoral regret whose object is the loss of some nonmoral good. To say that the good in question is nonmoral is not to say that it is irrelevant to the determination of moral goodness or rightness but only that it is not in itself sufficient to establish such goodness or rightness. Thus, to act in such a way as to damage or irretrievably lose such a good is not necessarily to commit a moral wrong. Still, the feeling of nonmoral regret is appropriate in such cases, and it is this sort of regret, Mandelbaum claims, that is experienced by agents confronted with conflict. If Mandelbaum is correct, then the appropriate phenomenological description of moral conflict cannot provide support for the moral dilemmas thesis.

It has been suggested that whatever plausibility an account such as Mandelbaum's might have, it cannot be extended to cover all cases of conflict because citing the loss of a *nonmoral* good is often inappropriate as an explanation of agent regret. "A man may, for instance, feel regret because he has broken a promise in the course of acting (as he sincerely supposes) for the best; and his regret at having broken the promise must surely arise *via* a moral thought."[18] The point is that explaining the occurrence of regret in such cases requires appealing to the agent's belief that she has violated a *moral* rule ('One ought to keep one's promises.'). And such regret is inexplicable unless it is presumed that the agent perceives the rule to be binding, that the agent regards keeping the promise as an actual obligation. But if this is true, then phenomenological ground is established for asserting the existence of a genuine moral dilemma.

That an appropriate phenomenological description of cases such as the broken promise requires the ascription of moral regret is, I think, indisputable. Thus, Mandelbaum's analysis is deficient to the extent that it denies the necessity of this description. Yet attributing moral regret to an agent does not demand postulating further that agent's recognition of a violated moral *requirement*. True enough, to break a promise is to sacrifice a *moral* value. One can hardly deny that a world in which promises were kept would be better, *morally* speaking, than our actual world in which promises are not kept. And, therefore, a broken promise affords a suitable occasion for *moral* regret. But the loss of a moral value or a moral good does not entail the violation of a moral obligation or a moral requirement. To assume that it does is to confuse the categories of the moral good and the moral right. We may thus take issue with Mandelbaum when he suggests that moral regret is not an ingredient in the experience of moral conflict, without disputing his claim that the intentional object of that experience is "a contemplated disvalue, not a contemplated wrongness." Yet if it is open to us to speak of the agent's perception as one of the loss of a moral good rather than the commission of a moral wrong, we need not posit the existence of a genuine moral dilemma in order to explain the agent's moral regret.

(c) If the moral dilemmas thesis is to be established along these lines, then it must be shown, at the very least, that agents under conflict conditions experience not *merely* moral regret but also the peculiar sort of moral regret we ordinarily associate with the recognition of a moral transgression, that is, the feeling of remorse or guilt. The problem here is that it is difficult to see how the occurrence of conflict remorse could possibly be established without begging the question in favor of the dilemmas thesis. The proponent of that thesis might argue that guilt or remorse can be identified by its distinctive nonlinguistic behavioral markings.

For example, it might be said that guilt is a moral feeling that manifests itself in the disposition to avoid relevantly similar circumstances in the future. Yet, as I have mentioned already, it is questionable that this disposition is a necessary attribute of the guilt feeling. Furthermore, as we have seen also, this behavioral characteristic is not sufficient to distinguish guilt from nonmoral regret. Alternatively, it might be argued that guilt or remorse is identifiable in virtue of the distinctive internal sensations or kinesthetic feelings necessarily attached to it. Thus, it might be maintained that guilt is characteristically accompanied by "a tightening of the muscles, a retraction of the limbs, as if the person were trying to make himself smaller." Yet it is as natural to associate such sensations with shame as it is with guilt, and some have even claimed that these "attitudes are on the dark and heavy side of regret."[19] In short, attempts to identify guilt or remorse by appealing to such behavioral or sensational criteria would appear to be futile.[20] The appropriate principle of identification almost assuredly would have to be grounded in our initial insight that remorse is an experience whose intentional object is a moral transgression. More particularly, the identification of remorse in any given case would seem to require the *prior* identification of the agent's recognition that she had violated a binding moral requirement. But if such a prior identification is necessary, then the proponent of the moral dilemmas thesis could hardly appeal to the fact of remorse in order to establish the fact of an agent's perception of a moral transgression since the determination of the latter would be necessary to establish the former.

(d) As a last resort the defender of the dilemmas thesis might suggest that the relevant guilt experience can be verified by agent report, that agents immersed in situations of conflict do in fact or would characterize their experience as remorseful. The obvious response to this claim is that it is possible for emotions such as remorse to be felt pathologically or irrationally. That any emotion admits of this possibility is, of course, a function of its intentional nature. Put simply, an emotion is irrational or pathological when its intentional object has no referent. Now agents who experience remorse believe that they have violated some binding moral principle, and it is conceivable that they are mistaken in this belief, that the intentional object of their experience fails to refer to any actual state of affairs. It is, moreover, easy to understand how, if these beliefs are mistaken in conflict situations, the agent has come to have them, nonetheless. For after all, conflict situations are those in which an agent has no choice but to set aside principles that are binding under ordinary circumstances. Even if the course taken in these situations admits of full and unequivocal moral justification, it is understandable that the agent might fail to realize this and consequently feel remorseful. There is, then, a certain slack between our emotional lives and the real world, and this slack renders problematic any pro-dilemmas argument grounded in the emotive response of the perplexed agent.

For various reasons, then, the first part of Ross's phenomenological account fails to provide any conclusive support for the existence of dilemmas. We are thus left with the second part of that account, which asserts that an unmistakable feature of conflict experience is the agent's recognition of a reparative obligation, that is, a duty to "make up somehow" for the violated moral principle. Presumably, this reparative obligation can take various forms. For example, an instance of a broken promise might require explaining the reasons for failure to the promisee or apologizing for that failure. It might call for fuller reparation in the sense of meeting the conditions of the promise at some later date or compensating any loss sustained by the promisee as a result of the failure. In any event, as mentioned already, philosophers have come to focus on such reparative obligations in constructing arguments for the dilemmas thesis.[21] These obligations are putatively *residual* in nature; that is, they are the by-product of a failure to meet the requirements stipulated by moral principles, and as such they can be explained only as the outcome of an overridden obligation that is genuine rather than apparent. Reparative obligations of this sort, then, would appear to demand construing moral conflict dilemmatically.

The issue before us is whether residual obligations generated by conflict situations must be accounted for as the result of unfulfilled duties that actually bind the agent. As a way of assessing this matter, consider once again the example of the army medic who is forced to operate with insufficient anesthetic. It is certainly reasonable to suppose that the medic is morally obliged at some point to explain to the soldier why the course of action was taken, to provide an explicit justification for the action, and to express her deep sorrow and regret over the fact that the action had to be performed. True enough, these are obligations the medic would not have except for the fact that she did what she did. Yet barring some further explanation, it would be mistaken to suggest that they resulted from some unfulfilled actual duty. The general point is that obligations incurred as consequences of an agent's bringing evil (e.g., pain) into the world need not be seen as by-products of a moral transgression. And this principle provides the foundation of an alternative analysis of conflict situations. For example, in the case of a broken promise the agent's conviction that he has incurred residual obligations may be explained as the consequence of his recognition that he has brought evil into the world through his failure. The evil in this instance might be the evil of frustrated expectation undergone by the promisee or any other harm suffered in virtue of the broken promise. Indeed, drawing on earlier remarks, we may speak of these residual obligations as the outcome of agent contribution to the loss of moral value signified by the broken promise without implying thereby that a moral wrong has been committed. Again, the possibility of speaking this way rests on the categorical distinction between the moral good and the moral right.[22] And given this possibility, we may do justice to this feature of Ross's account without embracing the view that dilemmas exist.

The foregoing has not been presented as a general assessment of Ross's doctrine of *prima facie* duties or obligations, though my suspicion is that its reliance on the mysterious language of tendency renders it untenable. My only concern has been to show that Ross's phenomenological insights may be either interpreted or reconstructed so as to avoid the conclusion that actual duties or obligations genuinely conflict. Thus, certain elements of our moral experience can be accounted for without acknowledging the existence of moral dilemmas. There do remain, however, other features of the experience that are not noted by Ross but have been cited as grounds for adopting the moral dilemmas thesis. I shall conclude this discussion by considering two standard arguments, one focusing on the generally unsatisfactory nature of conflict situations and the other on the normative structure of conflict experience.

As I noted in the previous chapter, one reason given for the abandonment of the 'ought'/'can' principle is that its retention poses an obstacle to explaining why certain moral situations are unsatisfactory. Consider, for example, an agent who is unable to keep a promise because of circumstances beyond his control (an appointment is missed because of a broken leg). Jettisoning the 'ought'/'can' principle allows us to account for the unsatisfactory nature of such a case by permitting us to say that what ought to have been done was not done. Similar considerations have been advanced as justification for characterizing conflict situations as clashes between obligations that are genuinely binding. Unless we can speak of such clashes, it is claimed, there is no way of explaining what is clearly attested to in our experience, namely, that cases of conflict are unsatisfactory from the moral point of view. The argument is sometimes presented as follows: Situations of moral conflict are situations that we have moral reason to avoid. We have moral reason to avoid them because they are unsatisfactory from the moral point of view. Yet it is difficult to understand why they are unsatisfactory in this sense unless it is assumed that they inevitably issue in the violation of obligations that actually do bind the agent.[23] The possibility of theoretically capturing this element in our moral experience, therefore, would appear to require assent to the existence of dilemmas.

Now it should be said that accounting for the *generally* unsatisfactory nature of moral conflict need not require the positing of dilemmas in every case. After all, conflict situations typically involve unpleasant consequences (e.g., frustrated expectations, missed opportunities, broken friendships, physical and psychological harms) that admit of description without the use of distinctively moral categories. Yet it is also clear that noting such features will not suffice to meet the challenge posed by the argument just considered since what is stressed in that argument is an unsatisfactoriness from the *moral* point of view. For instance, it is not merely the consequence of a broken promise (e.g., frustrated expectation) that renders a particular situation less than satisfactory; it is also the fact of the broken promise itself. This conclusion is confirmed by our intuitions about cases in which neither the promisee nor anyone else is vulnerable to harm resulting from the broken promise (e.g., the promisee has died, has no living relatives, etc.). Even when such promises are justifiably left unfulfilled there is a residual loss from the *moral* point of view, and this loss must be captured by any adequate ethical theory.

The issue, of course, is whether explaining this moral loss requires reference to a moral wrong. From our previous discussion it should be clear that no such reference is necessary. We may speak of a loss of *moral* value—a loss that is unsatisfactory from the moral point of view—without speaking of a violated moral requirement. A broken promise, to take this example once again, is always to be lamented because it represents the loss of a moral good (fidelity), and in general we have moral reason to avoid such losses. But this is not to say that a broken promise is always in some sense morally *wrong*. To repeat, the assumption that the one statement entails the other rests on an unwarranted conflation of disparate notions, the moral good and the moral right. Keeping these notions separate allows the construction of an explanatory account that will do justice to the morally unsatisfactory nature of conflict experience without acknowledging the existence of genuine moral dilemmas.

The final phenomenological argument to be considered may be dealt with in a similar fashion. As mentioned above, this argument focuses on the normative structure of certain conflict experiences. In particular, it notes that moral conflict often has victims, that these victims have a *just complaint* about the manner of their treatment, and that our intuitions about the *justice* of this complaint serve as evidence of a moral transgression. The argument has been advanced by Bernard Williams in his discussion of the political problem of dirty hands, and it is this discussion that will occupy my attention.[24]

Williams's point of departure is what he regards as a standard feature of political life, namely, the situation in which a politician is required to do something morally disagreeable. Thus, in order to achieve some political goal a politician may be forced to deceive, break promises, advance special interests, forge alliances with moral undesirables, or compromise just causes. As Williams sees it, such activities are often justified on moral as well as on purely political grounds. The reason is that the institutions of politics have moral foundations that make "moral claims" on the life of the politician, claims requiring engagement in the activities described. "But it is a predictable and probable hazard of political life that there will be these situations in which something morally disagreeable is clearly required. To refuse on moral grounds ever to do anything of that sort is more than likely to mean that one cannot seriously pursue even the moral ends of politics." Still, the justification of such acts notwithstanding, there is a moral remainder that resists complete extirpation, and this remainder is attested to in our normative intuition "that the victims can justly complain that they have been wronged."[25] It is, according to Williams, not merely a matter of a politician's being obliged to explain to these victims the rationale informing such actions; it is also a matter of the victims having a right to complain on hearing the explanation. In light of these considerations, Williams maintains that the sort of politician we should want is one who, while recognizing the necessity of these activities, will be reluctant to engage in them. We should want this sort of politician for two reasons explicitly. First, it is, more than likely, this kind of person who will refrain from engaging in the morally disagreeable when it is not necessary from the moral point of view. Second, reluctance is the "correct reaction" to cases of this type because such an attitude reflects a "sensibility to moral costs."[26] For Williams it is important to emphasize that the costs involved are *moral* costs, that is, costs amounting to the violation of moral right. This notion of a moral cost that is the by-product of a morally justified action cannot be accounted for by utilitarian theory, Williams claims, since on its terms the moral right is exhaustively interpreted as the most favored course of action judged from the perspective of utility maximization. Such a notion of the moral right leaves no room for a fundamental datum of our "moral consciousness," namely, that the most favored course of action from the moral point of view can generate a residual moral wrong.

Williams's criticism of utilitarianism would appear to be unassailable. An ethical theory unable to do justice to the experience of moral cost is unquestionably impoverished. Yet, conceding this point, we are still left with the issue of whether Williams's particular analysis of the phenomenon of moral cost is the most adequate. According to that analysis, to speak of the moral cost of an action can only be to speak of a moral wrong as its by-product. By now, however, we should be able to see that an alternative account is available. In a given case a moral cost may be understood as involving the loss of a moral value or moral good without presupposing the commission of a moral wrong. It is hardly questionable that a world lacking unsavory political activities of the sort considered would be—morally speaking—a better world than the one we know, and thus it is meaningful to speak of the real world as one that is less than ideal from the moral point of view, as one whose constitutive activities often bear a moral price. But all of this can be captured theoretically without introducing the concept of a moral wrong (i.e., the violation of moral right). In this alternative account, the victim's plight is seen as the signification of the world's having fallen away from the moral ideal, not as evidence of moral transgression. That plight, according to this reading, is akin to the situation of victims of natural disasters, victims whose plaints attest to the injustices and inequities of the cosmic lottery. Such is the stuff that makes for theodicies, of course; in characterizing such situations, however, we need not speak of moral dilemmas.

I have not meant to suggest that this latter account of political life must, on phenomenological grounds, be judged superior to the analysis provided by Williams. My only point is that this account is available as an alternative that does justice to those features of moral experience that Williams has brought to light. In the final analysis, how one interprets the details of the experience will depend on other theoretical assumptions that need to be made explicit. And in general we may conclude that phenomenal data *simpliciter* are not going to be sufficient to suggest the proper reading of situations of moral perplexity. These data may be interpreted plausibly from the perspectives of theories that either do or do not admit the existence of genuine moral dilemmas.

The Rejection of Moral Realism

In the previous chapter I noted that an antirealist account of moral discourse would appear to have no special problem in admitting the existence of genuine moral dilemmas. In this account, in fact, dilemmas seem not only possible but likely. The judgment of likelihood is a consequence of the antirealist's assessment that moral codes are akin to legal codes in genesis and structure. More particularly, this assessment has it that, like legal codes, moral codes are systems embodying rules or principles *created* by human beings over time for the purpose of meeting the problems endemic to community life. Because of the finitude of human imagination manifested in its inability to conceive of every practical circumstance likely to call for arbitration, it is virtually inevitable that the rules of a legal code will be incomplete, not only in the sense that the criteria of application will be ambiguous for certain circumstances but also in the sense that there will be occasions on which the rules conflict without the availability of some explicitly created metarule designed to adjudicate the conflict. Of course, despite such conflict, life goes on in the law by virtue of the existence of an adjudicative administrative body (be it legislative, judicial, or some other type) invested with authority to *create* solutions. But the important point is that prior to such explicitly created adjudication there is embedded in the law itself no solution to this sort of conflict.[27] This last point is crucial in analyzing the analogous moral case. While we may speak of ad hoc creative adjustments by individuals or groups in response to a conflict between moral rules, it is, according to the antirealist, mistaken to assume that solutions to such conflicts are embedded in morality itself. To make this assumption requires postulating the existence of some objective moral reality, some moral fact of the matter, insufficiently captured by the explicitly created rules that generated the conflicts to begin with. But there is, in the antirealist's view, no such reality, no such fact of the matter. In the final analysis, then, moral perplexity is seen by the antirealist as the product of sheer indeterminacy, an indeterminacy that itself is the virtually inevitable outcome of a practical system created by finite, albeit rational, beings. Henceforth, I shall refer to this view of morality as *moral positivism.*

If moral positivism turned out to be correct, instances of perplexity would seem to require dilemmatic construal since, independent of the rules that generated the conflict, there would be available no moral facts to provide resolutions. A good deal would appear to turn, therefore, on this positivistic rejection of an independent realm of objective moral reality. For this reason it is important to be clear about the grounds of the rejection. What sort of considerations warrant the dismissal of a realm of moral fact that could, in principle at least, serve as a source of conflict resolution? I shall attend to three claims, which appear on their face to provide backing for such a dismissal: (1) Belief in an independent realm of objective moral reality is vitiated by the general fact of moral indeterminacy, whether it be the indeterminacy of moral perplexity, intracultural disagreement, or cross-cultural variation. (2) Such belief requires including in one's ontology entities that are so bizarre as to render implausible any theory that relies on them. (3) Such belief, along with the belief in any implied ontology, is superfluous in any reasonable explanatory account of moral convictions and moral practices. An exhaustive assessment of these claims would require fuller treatment than I can possibly give them here. I propose merely to generate a measure of doubt about their truth, a measure that is sufficient to render inconclusive any rejection of moral realism founded on them.

(1) The first claim focuses on the general fact of moral indeterminacy as a means of justifying this rejection. As noted, such indeterminacy is prevalent not only in the form of moral perplexity but also in the forms of moral disagreement between persons of a given culture and variations in moral codes across cultures. It should be pointed out that the mere presence of indeterminacy does not in itself constitute disproof of an independent and objective state of affairs; this is shown by the fact that there are other sorts of inquiry that we readily admit as objective in the relevant

sense but that are also marked by indeterminacy at various points. Literary historians, for example, often disagree about text authenticity, yet this indeterminacy does not preclude our assuming that there is a solution to such questions, that there is a fact of the matter. What is decisive, rather, is the way this sort of indeterminacy is explained. In the case of scientific or historical inquiry, disagreement is attributed to inadequate evidence or to misreadings of the evidence that is available. Nonetheless, it is simply unreasonable, according to the positivist, to explain moral indeterminacy in the same way. The root of such indeterminacy is not an inadequate perception of some independent moral reality on the part of an individual or group. Rather, moral indeterminacy is to be seen as a reflection of diverse life-styles. In the case of intercultural variation this appears to be obvious. "Disagreement about moral codes seems to reflect people's adherence to and participation in different ways of life. The causal connection seems to be mainly that way round; it is that people approve of monogamy because they participate in a monogamous way of life rather than that they participate in a monogamous way of life because they approve of monogamy."[28] Other sorts of moral indeterminacy admit of explanation in similar terms. Thus, disagreement between a pacifist and nonpacifist is best explained as a function of competing sets of mores anchored respectively in the peculiar lifestyles of each (the pacifist is a Mennonite; the nonpacifist is a Catholic) and not as a result of confused perceptions by either of some moral state of affairs. Analogously, the indeterminacy of moral perplexity can be seen as a collision between disparate ways of life that form part of the background of a single individual, the inevitable result of living in a pluralist society. The general point is that moral indeterminacy, according to the positivist, is most adequately explained along these lines and not by talk about distorted perceptions of objective moral fact.[29]

Much hangs on the notion of *most adequate explanation* in the positivist argument since the phenomenon in question can be given *some explanation* even by a realist who believes that indeterminacy is resolvable in principle. As implied already, moral indeterminacy for a realist of this type will always be the result of some confused perception or mistaken belief, and often, though not in every case, the error will be accounted for in terms that are consistent with realist premises.[30] Given this possibility, the positivist will need to identify some relative defect in the realist's explanatory scheme, and almost assuredly this defect will have something to do with the peculiarity of the realist's ontological commitments. The upshot is that the force of the first claim advanced as a reason for rejecting moral realism will most likely depend on the strength of the second claim regarding the bizarre character of realist ontology.

(2) The positivist argument resting on ontological considerations begins with the following question: What precisely would we need to assume about the world in order to posit the existence of some moral state of affairs that was not fully captured by any humanly created moral system and that made itself available, at least in principle, as a source of conflict resolution? The positivist answer to this question is, in short, that we would have to assume the existence of objective values, entities having the most peculiar characteristics. Such entities could not be the objects of our ordinary sensory awareness or introspection. They would have to be known, as some philosophers have claimed, by *intuition* or another similarly mysterious mode of apprehension. Knowledge of them, moreover, would have to have a strange motivational force. Finally, these entities would have to be capable of forging the most fantastic relations with natural properties:

> Another way of bringing out this queerness is to ask, about anything that is supposed to have some objective moral quality, how is this linked with its natural features. What is the connection between the natural fact that an action is a piece of deliberate cruelty—say, causing pain just for fun—and the moral fact that it is wrong? It cannot be an entailment, a logical or semantic necessity. Yet it is not merely that the two features occur together. The wrongness must somehow be "consequential" or "supervenient"; it is wrong because it is a piece of deliberate cruelty. But just what *in the world* is signified by this "because"? And how do we know the relation that it signifies, if this is something more than such actions being socially condemned, and condemned by us too, perhaps through our having absorbed attitudes from our social environment? It is not sufficient to postulate a faculty which 'sees' the wrongness: something must be postulated which can see at once the natural features that constitute the cruelty, and the wrongness, and the mysterious consequential link between the two. Alternatively, the intuition required might be the perception that wrongness is a higher order property belonging to certain natural properties; but what is this belonging of properties to other properties, and how can we discern them?[31]

If moral realism is correct, the positivist claims, then moral ontology will include the problematic entities just described. But
the theoretical costs of accepting such an ontology are too great to
bear. For this reason moral realism ought to be rejected.

Let us concede for the sake of argument that commitment to
moral realism has as its condition acceptance of the ontology described. Does this concession force us to dismiss the realist's
claims in the way that the positivist suggests? It is hardly likely
that a reasonable answer to this question can be given in the abstract. True enough, heuristic principles of theory construction
do create a presumption against postulating the existence of entities with unusual characteristics. Yet unfamiliarity per se is not
sufficient reason for ruling against the existence of an object. If it
were, a good deal of microphysics would have to be rejected. The
point is that questions about the existence of objective values or
moral states of affairs, like questions about the existence of elec-
trons or quarks, cannot be assessed apart from the roles such entities play in some explanatory account. What we need to know is
whether a realistic ontology of the sort described constitutes an
indispensable feature of an explanatory component of general
moral theory. As I shall try to show in a moment, some version of
moral realism would appear to be necessary to account for the
fact of morality's normative force. If this is true, then theoretical
ground would be established for speaking of independent moral
states of affairs that in principle could provide solutions to conflicts between the rules of actual moral codes.

(3) The preceding reflections bring us to the third of the positivist's claims, namely, that postulating the existence of moral
states of affairs above and beyond the facts given in actual moral
codes is superfluous in any reasonable explanatory account of
moral convictions and moral practices. Taken as a thesis of *descriptive ethics* this claim is uncontroversial. In other words,
there is no need to appeal to an independent realm of moral fact in
order to explain certain empirical data related to moral institutions. Consider a phenomenon that might be thought to pose special problems for the positivist, the phenomenon of cross-cultural
moral agreement. It might be suggested that the fact of such convergence of moral belief is best explained on realist grounds. How
could one account, it might be asked, for the adoption of similar
moral principles by diverse cultures having little or no contact
with each other unless one assumed that human beings have epistemic access to certain transcendent moral facts? Yet the positiv-

ist certainly has an answer to this question: Moral codes are generated by communities to meet the problems of social life. These *problems* are universal. It is thus only reasonable to expect that the rules devised to solve them will be relatively constant in content. I shall not argue the point here, but it seems likely that most issues in descriptive ethics admit of similarly adequate treatment on positivistic grounds.

The difficulty arises for the positivist when it is time to account for the *normative force* of moral principles. The issue here is not one of descriptive ethics; it is not a matter of determining why individuals or groups *regard* their codes as normatively binding. This latter issue can be resolved quite easily by the positivist, as various sociological, psychological, and evolutionary theories attest. Rather, the issue I am raising has to do with accounting for the fact that morality *is* binding on human agents; it has to do with specifying, in a loosely Kantian sense, the conditions of the possibility of this moral normativity. Now in positivistic terms no nonreductive rendering of this normativity is possible. On these terms normativity is translated into accepted social standards, group demands, cultural mores, individual commitments, or some similar empirically determinable phenomenon. To speak of anything else is to speak of some mysteriously elusive moral fact above and beyond the humanly created circumstances surrounding concrete moral institutions. But if the positivist is correct, then normativity per se is a mystification, a useful fiction perhaps, but a fiction in any event. It is for this reason that J. L. Mackie is correct when he claims, *pace* Hare, that the rejection of realist moral ontology inevitably means the loss of normative backing for our moral discourse.[32] Normativity, if it is anything more than a useful fiction, is precisely the sort of fact the realist wishes to acknowledge and the positivist wishes to reject. The consequence of all of this for the present discussion should be clear. If the positing of nonreducible moral facts is necessary to account for normativity in general, then no *special* ontological problem is created by claiming there is a moral fact of the matter that in principle may serve as grounds for resolving conflict resulting from a clash between the rules of a moral code.

Of course, the foregoing, as a response to the defender of the moral dilemmas thesis, begs the question against moral nihilism, the view holding that the concept of a nonreducible moral normativity *is* a fiction. In the present context, however, this *petitio* is not serious. Proponents of the dilemmas thesis may attempt to salvage their thesis by embracing such nihilism, but in doing so they could no longer take seriously many of the phenomenological facts that probably motivated the thesis to begin with. As we have seen, many adherents to the dilemmas thesis argue to the existence of irresolvable moral conflict from the phenomenological structure of such situations, that is, from the fact of the agent's typical experiences in such situations. This argument presupposes that the experiences in question have some normative foundation. But if nihilism is true, such emotive expressions are unquestionably pathological since the entire range of moral emotions is without any genuinely normative grounding. The preceding reflections suggest the essential difficulty in the acceptance of moral nihilism by the proponent of the moral dilemmas thesis. For the defender of that thesis, situations of moral perplexity are not merely instances of moral indeterminacy. On the contrary, they are instances of indeterminacy constituted by conflicting moral requirements that are *actually* binding. It is this fact that putatively renders such situations excrutiatingly difficult. In the nihilist's view, however, no moral requirements are genuinely binding since the notion of normativity per se is a fiction. In other words, the nihilist can admit moral dilemmas of a sort, dilemmas without normative bite, simple indeterminacy. But this would hardly seem to be enough to satisfy adherents of the dilemmas thesis.

In the final analysis, then, a full-fledged salvaging of the moral dilemmas thesis will require the rejection of moral positivism and the nihilism it presupposes. And this means, of course, that the thesis will need as its foundation some form of moral realism, in particular, one whose distinctive ontology allows for the existence of moral dilemmas. Such a realism could depict moral reality as irreducibly fragmented or pluralistic. Moral perplexity, then, at least in a good number of cases, would be seen as a function of this irreducible fragmentation and thus as irresolvable in principle. In what follows I shall attend to considerations impinging on the decision to construe moral reality in this manner.

The Fragmentation of Moral Reality (I)

One pluralistic version of moral realism has been presented recently by Mark Platts, who characterizes his theory as a refurbished ethical intuitionism.[33] Platts's theory is distinguishable from classical intuitionist thought in two important respects.

First, it makes no claim regarding the intuition of moral reality via some *special cognitive faculty*. On the contrary, moral facts are recognized in the way ordinary facts are recognized, "by looking and seeing." Second, as opposed to a tendency in classical intuitionism, we can never be absolutely certain, in Platts's theory, either that our moral beliefs are correct or that we have completely understood the moral concepts used to express those beliefs. "Our moral language, like all the realistic part of that language, transcends our practical comprehensions in trying to grapple with an independent, indefinitely complex reality."[34] In addition to these negative features, Platts's theory is marked by three distinctive positive characteristics: (1) It holds moral statements to be realistic in the sense of factually cognitive. This is to say that it regards such statements as making claims about the world, claims that are either true or false and whose truth or falsity is a function "of the (independently existing) real world."[35] (2) The realism advocated by the theory is an *austere* realism; that is, it is not tied to determinate naturalistic interpretations of the meanings of basic moral terms. Thus, the theory denies the possibility of reducing moral facts to nonmoral (natural) facts. Nonetheless, moral facts are said to be consequential or supervenient on nonmoral facts. The relation is presumably akin to that between an arrangement of dots on a card and a face that is to be seen on the card. "The dot arrangement *fixes* . . . whether or not there is a face to be seen. Still, we do not *see* the face by attending to that dot arrangement, where that arrangement is characterized in terms free of picture and face-vocabulary—say, by a mathematical grid system."[36] Nonmoral facts *fix* moral facts in the same way, but the presence of moral facts is not inferred simply from an examination of the nonmoral facts. Because moral facts are independent of nonmoral facts in the sense described, moral concepts have the property of *semantic depth*. We can never be completely satisfied that we have understood their meanings, and, therefore, we can neither be sure that we recognize instantiations of them nor be secure in our applications. It is for this reason that the classical intuitionist's doctrine about the certainty of our moral knowledge is ill-founded. (3) The theory depicts moral reality as irreducibly pluralistic. According to Platts, ethical monism, which reduces all moral reality to one property (e.g., the Good), is false. There are, rather, a number of distinct ethical properties (e.g., sincerity, loyalty, honesty) that constitute the fundamental stuff of the moral universe, have no common denominator, and thus may conflict with each other. Here, then, we have a moral metaphysic compatible with the view that genuine moral dilemmas exist.

But why is pluralism preferable to monism as an account of moral reality? Platts gives three separate answers to this question, all of which, I think are ultimately unsatisfactory.[37] First, pluralism is said to be called for as a way of explaining the "brute fact" that moral dilemmas exist. Platts claims that any denial of this putative fact bespeaks of moral laziness or moral blindness. Second, ethical pluralism supposedly accounts best for a linguistic fact, namely, that the "interesting, basic terms of moral description" are terms like 'sincere', 'loyal', and 'compassionate', and not some overarching term such as 'the Good'. That these terms are basic is signified both by the fact that the identification of properties denoted by them is a condition of determining goodness and by the fact that "we have a grasp of these ideas independent of . . . our grasp of 'good'." Thus, there are no grounds a priori for suggesting either that the basic ideas cannot conflict or that subsumption of them under some more comprehensive term will eradicate the conflict. Third, embracing ethical pluralism and the implied thesis about moral dilemmas will disabuse us of any simplistic belief that morality provides a procedure for determining what ought to be done in every given case. While morality does provide action-guidance in a good number of instances, it falls short of completeness in this respect. The fundamental job of moral discourse, according to Platts, is not to prescribe but to describe the moral structure of the world.

Attractive as these arguments may be on their face, they suffer from deficiencies that, in part at least, are the result of a failure to consider the possibility that moral perplexity is fundamentally a problem of moral epistemology rather than a function of conflict in the moral universe. This omission is especially evident in the first claim asserting the existence of moral dilemmas as an unquestionable datum of the moral life. True, we are, often enough, perplexed about what morality requires in any given case; such perplexity is, to use Platts's terminology, a *brute fact*, and any refusal to acknowledge this fact betrays, if not moral blindness or moral laziness, an unwarranted confidence in our powers of moral discernment. Yet an ethical monist can easily account for this feature of the moral life simply by locating the difficulty in an inadequacy of moral perception. Needless to say, an epistemological explanation of this sort does not in itself impugn the tenets of ethical monism, which is a thesis about moral reality, not moral knowledge. But if treating moral perplexity as a problem of knowledge is admitted as a genuine possibility, then Platts's subsequent claims about basic terms and decision procedures lose much of their force. Even if the terms he identifies as basic *are* basic in the stipulated respects, we may still speak of an *ordering* (from the moral point of view) of the properties they denote, an ordering that constitutes *the* Good or *the* Right and that we might have difficulty discerning in any given instance of conflict. Similarly, decision procedures for adjudicating such conflict may be unavailable to us simply because of deficiencies in our cognitive capacities, deficiencies that inhibit our perception of the Good or the Right (i.e., the *one* moral reality). It seems, then, that one can do justice to all the features of moral perplexity cited by Platts without embracing ethical pluralism.

Of course, none of the foregoing counts as an argument for ethical monism, but it does show that monism, as a doctrine of moral ontology, is consistent with an appreciation of the moral data isolated by Platts provided that the explanation of those data takes an epistemological turn. The issue then becomes one of justifying such a turn in one's explanatory scheme. And, ironically enough, it is Platts's own theory of *semantic depth* that at least renders plausible, even if it does not fully justify, the epistemological account. This consequence of the theory is suggested in his treatment of another form of moral indeterminacy, the fact of intercultural and intracultural moral disagreement.[38] Now the moral relativist, as represented by Platts, focuses on this fact in order to show that moral realism is false. Given that there is no external standpoint from which to adjudicate such disagreement, the relativist maintains, the realist's claims about objective moral reality are implausible. Platts's general response to this relativist argument is one we have anticipated in our earlier discussion and one any realist will appropriately make: The mere fact of moral disagreement does not show that realism is false since the realist can always account for such disagreement as a function of mistaken belief. What is especially important for our purposes, however, is Platts's further claim that, given the tenets of an *austere* realism, the indeterminacy cited by the relativist is precisely what we should expect. If moral concepts are characterized by semantic depth, that is, if their meanings, instantiations, and applications lack transparency, then disagreement should be the norm rather than the exception. This explanation is unequivocally epistemo-

logical and thus wholly consistent with the position that moral
indeterminacy between persons of the same culture or of diverse
cultures is adjudicable in principle. But, if this sort of account is
available as a response to the ethical relativist, it is likewise available as a response to the ethical pluralist, a fact Platts fails to acknowledge. For the monist can argue that the concept of, say, 'the
Right', which picks out *the* proper course of action in cases of
conflict, has the property of *semantic depth*. The meaning, instantiation, and application of the concept are epistemically elusive. It is thus hardly surprising that agents are often morally perplexed. The perplexity is quite simply a function of the fact that
human beings "are tawdry, inadequate epistemic creatures strug-
gling with an indefinitely complex world."[39]

At this stage, the purpose of the discussion is not to suggest
that ethical monism is true but merely to show that an austerely
realistic philosophy of moral language provides the semantic
equipment necessary to explain the epistemic difficulties forming
part of the monist's account. Hence, Platts's adoption of pluralism
is premature. His analysis, however, does serve to illustrate a pair
of points made in the previous chapter about compatibility between dilemmatic judgments. I suggested that whether or not one
regarded such judgments as incompatible would depend on one's
interpretations of basic deontic concepts (e.g., 'ought' and 'ought
not') and that these interpretations were bound to be affected by
certain background beliefs about the nature of morality. Now an
implication of Platts's account is that all such concepts, if they are
to be understood properly, will require translation into the so-
called *basic* terms of moral discourse. Thus, to say, for instance,
that an act which is both the keeping of a promise and the telling
of a lie ought to be done and ought not to be done would be to say
in essence that the act possessed the property of fidelity and the
property of insincerity. There is, of course, no intrinsic incoherence in such a description, and therefore dilemmas will pose no
problem on this score. Yet to accept this translation as the appropriate one would almost certainly reflect some *prior* commitment
to ethical pluralism. For what else would dictate this acceptance
were it not the judgment that such a translation most accurately
depicted a pluralistic state of moral affairs and depicted it without
incoherence? Despite Platts's remarks about basic terms, there is
certainly nothing about the structure of moral language per se
that requires the translation. One could just as easily interpret the
concepts in terms of 'the Right', as the monist is likely to do, an

interpretation yielding the inconsistent judgment that the act in question is both an exemplification of the Right and not an exemplification of the Right. Most assuredly, any decision against this latter translation would reflect either of two considerations, that the resulting inconsistency undercut the attempt at coherent representation of a fragmented moral reality or that the category of 'the Right' had no reference, that there existed no moral properties apart from the properties denoted by basic moral terms. Yet both of these considerations presuppose a commitment to some form of pluralism. Thus, what was putatively an issue of logic (consistency between 'ought' and 'ought not') now turns on a question of metaphysics. Does ethical pluralism accurately depict the structure of moral reality?

If my assessments up to this point have been correct, Platts's arguments in support of this doctrine are inconclusive. The rejection of pluralism is compatible with a recognition of the moral phenomena highlighted by those arguments, and his own austerely realistic theory provides a semantic foundation for that rejection. Of course, none of the foregoing clinches the case against ethical pluralism. In concluding my discussion of philosophical defenses of the moral dilemmas thesis I want to consider one final argument, presented by Thomas Nagel, which grounds that thesis in a pluralistic conception of moral reality.[40]

The Fragmentation of Moral Reality (II)

Nagel's point of departure is the phenomenon of practical perplexity or what he calls a "basic conflict," that is, a situation in which each of two incompatible practical choices "seems right for reasons that appear decisive and sufficient."[41] According to Nagel, basic conflicts are generated by collisions between fundamental types of value, which, he claims, are five in number: (1) *obligations* to persons or institutions, obligations that are incurred by deliberate undertaking or in virtue of special relations to the persons or institutions in question (e.g., obligations to promisees, family, or country); (2) *general rights,* which are not dependent on deliberate undertakings or special relations and which give rise to constraints on action (e.g., the duty not to infringe on another's liberty); (3) *utility* or consideration of the effects of one's actions on the welfare of all, including welfare considerations unrelated to special obligations or general rights; (4) *perfectionist ends* or intrinsic values of projects apart from their instrumental values to individuals (e.g., scientific knowledge having little or no practical import); and (5) *commitments* to one's own projects, commitments that constitute values above and beyond those reflected in the reasons for undertaking the projects in the first place. Now as Nagel sees it, these fundamental values resist both *general* ordering and commensuration, the former because it is "absurd" to rule out the possibility of setting aside any ordering in a given case, the latter for theoretical reasons having to do with the sources of values. The claim about absurdity is especially obscure, and I shall leave discussion of it until later on. For the moment I want to concentrate on the theoretical grounds for suggesting that basic values are incommensurate.

Nagel's argument in support of incommensurability rests neither on the fact that no single standard of value has met with universal acceptance nor on the fact that utilitarianism, the one serious attempt at construction of such a standard, leads to counterintuitive moral judgments. Rather, the conclusion that basic values lack a common measure is grounded in his doubt "that the source of value is unitary—displaying apparent multiplicity only in its application to the world."[42] The basic values have, according to Nagel, irreducibly different sources, and this fact, presumably, is reflected in certain *formal* distinctions among the values themselves. For instance, both general rights and obligations are distinguishable from both perfectionist ends and utility inasmuch as the former are relatively personal or agent-centered—that is, they relate to what the agent does—while the latter are relatively impersonal or outcome-centered—that is, they relate to ends or results of actions, to what happens. In fact, each of the basic values can be distinguished from all the others by locating the position it occupies on this personal/impersonal continuum. Thus, obligations, because they are constituted by deliberate agent undertakings or special relations, are, relatively speaking, more personal than general rights, which abstract from individual undertakings and particular relations. Similarly, perfectionist ends, since they do not make reference to the interests of persons at all, are more impersonal than utility, which has to do with the aggregate welfare of persons. Of course, commitments are the most personal of the values for obvious reasons. As noted already, for Nagel these formal distinctions among the basic values point to the irreducibly different sources of the values themselves, sources that are tied to distinct ways of looking at the world. The utilitarian outlook, for instance, consists of a detachment allowing us to survey the world with an eye that incorporates—at least theoretically—everyone's view of that world. The outlook associated with obligations, on the other hand, is a perception of the world from the perspective of particular situations related to deliberate undertakings and special relations. The examples could be multiplied. The general point is that the various perspectives that generate the basic values cannot in principle be assimilated to one another, and therefore any reductionistic program such as utilitarianism is bound to fail. The value world is multifaceted, or, as Nagel sometimes seems to suggest, there are many value worlds, and the terms used to describe these worlds are not intertranslatable.[43] For this reason much (though, as we shall see, not all) practical conflict, including moral conflict, is beyond resolution.

The crux of Nagel's argument, of course, is his presupposition that a category or set of categories generated by a particular mode of inspecting the world does not admit of translation into another category or set of categories born by an alternative mode of inspection. The presupposition is both unargued for and, needless to say, controversial. Its general truth would imply, for instance, that the findings of physics could never be translated into the terms of ordinary language since the physicist's perspective on the world is different from the ordinary perspective. While this conclusion may be true for many areas of microphysics (e.g., quantum mechanics), as a claim to general truth it is certainly false (e.g., a table admits of description in the language of elementary particle physics). The point is that divergence of perspective need not imply lack of intertranslatability. Thus, Nagel's argument falls short of demonstrating genuine incommensurability between the basic values. I shall not press this point further, however, since it may still be the case that the basic values are incommensurate despite the shortcomings of Nagel's argument and what I want to determine at this juncture is the consequence of such incommensurability for the moral dilemmas thesis.

Interestingly enough, Nagel himself admits that, while the incommensurate nature of the basic values does produce moral dilemmas in a number of instances, we need not conclude that all conflicts between such values are irresolvable. The reason cited is that there can be "good judgment" in cases of conflict without there being "total justification" for a chosen course.[44] *Judgment*, which is said to be equivalent to an Aristotelian practical wisdom, is the faculty exercised in an agent's individual decisions over time and not in appeals to and formulations of general prin-

ciples. It takes over when *total justification* comes to an end, that
is, when principles generated by the basic values fail to yield a determinate conclusion. While the exercise of judgment may have as
its source some prereflective acceptance of general principles and
while we may come to discover such principles through a systematization of particular decisions, such systematization is not
essential to judgment's implementation. And this state of affairs is
a good thing since any hope for a comprehensive systematization
of what is right and what is wrong is futile given the radically distinct natures of the basic values. Ethics presumably is like our
general theoretical knowledge of the empirical world. Just as it is
mistaken to believe that history, psychology, philology, and economics can be reduced to physics, it is likewise mistaken to think
that the various subdivisions of our moral knowledge, subdivisions designated by the basic values, can be integrated into a comprehensive whole. In view of this inescapable fragmentation of
our moral knowledge, judgment is an indispensable feature of our
practical lives.

In general, I do not think that this picture of practical reasoning
is coherent. If "good judgment" in situations of conflict is to mean
anything more than arbitrary decision, then it must be grounded,
at least implicitly, in some standard of evaluation, however difficult the articulation of that standard might be. What is the nature
of this standard? It cannot involve a principle of commensuration
since *ex hypothesi* the basic values are incommensurable. The
only alternative explanation would appear to be that the standard
reflects a *primitive* ordering of the values, primitive in the sense
that it does not rely on the possibility of translating the competing values into some common currency. Such a primitive ordering
would state merely that for a given situation value *a* has precedence over value *b* without suggesting that the order of precedence can be given expression in terms of some property shared by
the values. But, if standards of judgment can reflect *primitive*
orderings in the sense described, it is not at all clear why there
cannot be a *general primitive ordering* of the basic values, that is,
one making possible in principle the resolution of all moral conflict. The belief that such a general ordering exists is wholly consistent with the incommensurability thesis, and it is for this reason that Nagel's analogy between ethics and our general empirical
knowledge is misleading. While it may be true that, like our
knowledge of the empirical world, our knowledge of the moral
world, because of incommensurability, resists *reductionistic* inte-

gration, it does not follow that the latter is beyond the integration of primitive ordering. This conclusion is an important one; for it highlights the fact that a rejection of the moral dilemmas thesis is entirely compatible with an acceptance of incommensurability as long as the possibility of primitive ordering remains open.

Much rests, then, on the reasons given by Nagel for dismissing this possibility. As mentioned earlier, his claim is that any *general* ordering of the basic values is absurd because there will always be circumstances in which the ordering must be overturned, in which a value lower on the hierarchy will take precedence over a value higher up. The implausibility of a general ordering, therefore, is presumably a function of the claim to absoluteness implicit in the ordering itself. To take one of Nagel's own examples, although obligations will often override utility, "it is absurd to hold . . . that utility, however large, can never outweigh obligation."[45] Yet even if this last judgment is correct, it does not yield the conclusions that Nagel suggests it does. For the judgment does not demonstrate the impossibility of an absolute general ordering of obligation and utility; it merely shows that, if there is an absolute ordering between the two values, that ordering is more complicated, more sensitively attuned to circumstances, than may have been thought at first. Nagel's argument holds only if one assumes that an ordering of the values must be simplistic, and this assumption is certainly false. The point may be generalized. There is nothing about the notion of a primitive general ordering per se that rules out the possibility of one basic value's sometimes giving way to and other times overriding some other basic value, given variation in circumstances.

In the final analysis, then, Nagel fails to provide any substantial reason for rejecting the view that the values constituting moral reality are primitively ordered in a comprehensive whole. To repeat, as long as the possibility of such an ordering remains open, we can deny the existence of genuine moral dilemmas while admitting the fundamental incommensurability of the basic values. For our purposes, therefore, most of the important questions are left unsettled.

Conclusion

I have tried to show in this chapter that recent philosophical attempts to demonstrate the existence of moral dilemmas are unsuccessful and, moreover, that the moral dilemmas thesis requires a version of moral realism whose ontology is compatible with the stipulations of that thesis. I have attempted to demonstrate, furthermore, the failure of two recent philosophical accounts of such an ontology, accounts designed in particular to justify a depiction of moral reality as irreducibly fragmented or pluralistic. At this juncture my intent has not been to suggest that ethical pluralism is false but only to show that ethical monism remains as an alternative even in the face of certain philosophical counterarguments. But where does all of this leave us?

Most directly, it leaves us with the matter of adjudicating between competing moral ontologies. Yet how in principle is such adjudication possible? It is often suggested that ontological schemes should be evaluated in accordance with their capacities to render intelligible ranges of human experience. But if my conclusions in this chapter are correct, then the experiential data generated by situations of moral perplexity can be accounted for by theories that either allow or disallow the existence of moral dilemmas, and this would imply that the competing ontologies are underdetermined by the phenomena we are trying to explain. Moreover, if we assented to the view now commonly held, that the representations of our experiences, moral or otherwise, are already *theory-laden*, then any phenomenological grounding of a metaphysical claim is bound to be suspect as an instance of begging the question. To take an earlier example, a proponent of the dilemmas thesis might suggest that the perplexed agent is pathologically anxious about having taken *the* wrong course of action (pathologically because there is no one wrong course) or that that agent's distress is the distress of nonpathological moral remorse. But either of the characterizations of the agent's experience depends on the truth of the dilemmas thesis. And it is only reasonable to expect that the phenomenological account offered by an antidilemmas position will suffer from the same difficulties.

If representations of moral experience are themselves theory-laden or if, less controversially, phenomenological arguments are otherwise inconclusive, then we are faced once again with the question of the comparative strengths of competing interpretive schemes and their attendant ontologies. Is there anything more to be said? Though I cannot prove the point, I suspect that no decisive philosophical resolution of the controversy is forthcoming. Yet I think that a good deal more can be said if one takes the position that a picture of moral reality ought to be judged holistically, that is, from the perspective of one's general view of the world and of morality's place in that world. Given this way of looking at the matter, an interpretation of moral perplexity should be assessed against the background of those beliefs constituting the nodal points of a general world view. In this regard the following remarks of Bernard Williams are suggestive:

> Someone might argue on larger metaphysical grounds of some kind that such situations [moral dilemmas] could not arise, that it was impossible that any agent should meet such a situation; but, if there were such an argument, it would have to yield metaphysical impossibility, or, in some way, a moral impossibility, and not a proof that the judgments involved in such a situation were contradictory. There is a substantial and interesting question: "What would have to be true of the world and of an agent that it should be impossible for him to be in a situation where whatever he did was wrong?" I doubt in fact that there is anything that could produce such a guarantee short of the existence of an interventionist God, or else the total reduction of moral life to rules of efficient behavior—two extremes which precisely leave out the actual location of moral experience. But it is at any rate a real question, which it would not be if the correct thing to say were: nothing has to be true of the agent or of the world for this to be so, it is guaranteed by the logic of moral expressions.[46]

Williams's point is that there is nothing in the logic of moral discourse that renders the raised question vacuous. I would go one step further and suggest, *pace* Williams, that there is nothing about "the actual location of moral experience" that makes the question any less substantial. Indeed, I am claiming that one cannot properly locate that experience until the question or some variation of it has been answered. This means that moral perplexity is a phenomenon that cannot be assessed fully apart from certain fundamental beliefs about the world. For the religious believer these will include beliefs about the nature of God, the relation between God and the world, and the way in which this relation impinges on the moral life. The remainder of this study will deal with the consequences such beliefs have for the construal of moral perplexity.

3

THOMISTIC NATURAL LAW AND THE ORDER OF VALUE

In this chapter and the next I shall consider how a Christian theistic perspective on the world might affect the matters that have been raised thus far. More particularly, I shall try to assess how a vision of the moral life grounded in such a theism might shape the way moral perplexity is construed. The term 'theism' is employed here to denote the view that there exists a unified, perfect being (God) who, though wholly separate from it, has created the universe, sustains it, and providentially directs it. This characterization of theism is, admittedly, quite austere. Thus, nothing is said, for instance, about the specific content of the doctrine of providence or the manner in which God's perfection and unity are to be interpreted. The objective at this point is simply to articulate a conception of God that is formally distinguishable from the traditional alternatives (e.g., pantheism, deism) and that is roughly identifiable as the conception deemed normative by the Christian philosophical and systematic theological traditions. Of course, as the discussion proceeds, greater specification will be required. Indeed, we shall see that how one assesses the relationship between an ethics of theism and the interpretation of moral perplexity will depend in large measure on the detailed explication of the doctrine of God and related notions.

For the purposes of analysis I distinguish between two types of theistic ethic, *theological voluntarism* and *theological essentialism*, each of which represents a dominant strain in the Christian tradition and both of which taken together arguably exhaust the possible alternatives of that tradition. Put in the simplest of terms, theological voluntarism holds that moral requirement is foundationally constituted by divine volition or divine command.[1] In other words, the claim that *a* is morally required (whether '*a*' denotes a particular act or a general act type) signifies in some fashion that God wills or commands *a*, and it is this latter fact of God's willing or commanding *a* that establishes or grounds the fact of *a*'s being morally required. Alternatively, theological essentialism has it that moral requirement is foundationally constituted by a moral order that structures the universe and that in some way reflects God's essence or nature.[2] In this view, to say that *a* is morally required is to say that *a* is required by the moral order, which in turn is congruent with the essence or nature of God's being. Of course, in principle it is possible for the theological essentialist to hold that God always wills what morality requires (e.g., because God's will is always in conformity with God's nature). Yet what distinguishes the essentialist from the voluntarist is the former's denial that the divine will per se foundationally constitutes moral requirement in the sense described above. Again, for the essentialist, it is the moral order reflective of God's nature that grounds such requirement.

Extended discussion of theological voluntarism and the implications of the position for interpretations of moral perplexity will occupy the next chapter. The present chapter will concern a species of theological essentialism, namely, Aquinas's doctrine of natural law. There are at least two reasons for focusing on the Thomistic doctrine. First, apart from its being the richest and most elaborate variant of theological essentialism available, Aquinas's theory shows some sensitivity to the problem of moral perplexity and thus provides an occasion for reflection on matters central to this study. Second, inasmuch as it has served traditionally as a normative point of departure for Roman Catholic moral theology, the Thomistic doctrine of natural law affords an appropriate perspective from which to view the debate about moral conflict in which Catholic ethicists have been engaged during the past twenty years or so. The lines of the debate are drawn as follows: Over against a particular strain of Catholic natural-law thinking, certain revisionist theorists have argued that any adequate moral theology must acknowledge the existence of genuine moral dilemmas.[3] In contrast, others have contended that a proper understanding of the natural law should lead one to reject the possibility of insoluble conflict between moral principles.[4] Various ethical and theological justifications have been advanced on both sides. Yet, more often than not, the arguments have proceeded with insufficient attention to metaphysical implications, most notably the consequences of either position for the doctrine of God. Examination of Aquinas's moral theory, developed as it is within the context of a philosophical theology, affords an opportunity for tracing connections between metaphysical suppositions and particular readings of moral conflict. Indeed, I shall conclude that, given classically Thomistic assumptions about the relation of God to moral requirement, it would be exceedingly difficult, if not impossible, to accept the revisionist thesis. While there are theoretical resources in Aquinas for explaining moral perplexity epistemologically, that is, as the function of limitations on moral knowledge, the metaphysical rudiments of Thomistic doctrine create a framework in which the existence of moral dilemmas could not be admitted in any ordinary sense of the term.

The argument will take the following course. First, as a way of setting the stage for further discussion I shall outline the basic features of Aquinas's natural-law theory, including its relation to the doctrine of eternal law, which provides the theological context of his moral theory. I shall suggest that, when wrenched from that theological context, the Thomistic theory of natural law is indeterminate with respect to the question whether genuine moral dilemmas exist. Next, I shall consider a standard interpretation of Aquinas on moral dilemmas. According to this interpretation, Aquinas rules out the possibility of dilemmas *simpliciter* but allows for their existence as consequences of specific wrongdoings by moral agents. My conclusion will be that this rendering of his position is misleading, that Aquinas's apparent admission of dilemmas is merely apparent, and that there is reason for believing his overall treatment of the question is determined substantially by his metaphysics—more precisely, by his teleological conception of divine providence and his understanding of the good's unity in the unity of the divine being. Third, I shall give an account of what an epistemological explanation of moral perplexity would look like on the terms of a Thomistic theory of moral knowledge. This sort of perplexity, I shall suggest, would have to be regarded as a function of the depth structure of moral concepts, a depth structure that is only partially accessible to human reason. Finally, I shall discuss how Thomistic theism would have to be modified so as to admit the possibility of genuine moral dilemmas. Generally speaking, then, my concerns are both exegetical and constructive. While I wish to determine what Aquinas said and why he said it, I also want to assess what constraints, if any, Thomistic natural-law theory imposes on the construal or moral perplexity as a matter of principle.

The General Theory

The theological foundation of Aquinas's ethical system manifests itself at the point of convergence between his theories of natural and eternal law. The former theory grounds his understanding of moral requirement; the latter is integral to his doctrine of God. The term linking the two components in the system is the notion of participation (*participatio*). Natural law, the foundation of moral requirement, is, as Aquinas puts it, the "participation of the eternal law in the rational creature"; this is to say that the natural law consists in that portion of God's eternal law directing rational activity.[5] The eternal law in its entirety is the principle of ordering by which God providentially directs the universe. All creatures are subject to this directing operation, though each in its appropriate mode. The directive principle in any given instance includes the creature's unreflective, natural inclination or dispositional tendency toward its unique fulfillment, that is, toward the realization of its proper end or good. In the case of irrational creatures the eternal law exerts its influence exclusively through such dynamic tendencies. Rational creatures, on the other hand, while partaking of the eternal law through unreflective inclination, in addition can conform their activities to this law through cognition and obedience. In other words, rational creatures can come to know a measure of the eternal law's content (though, as we shall see, a less than exhaustive measure) and govern their behavior intentionally on the basis of this knowledge. The substance of the knowledge relevant to the moral life is given in the so-called precepts (*praecepta*) of the natural law, and it is on these precepts that the Thomistic doctrine of moral requirement is founded. In short, for Aquinas those human acts required by morality are precisely those acts called for by the precepts of the natural law.

As is well known, the rational appropriation of these precepts, according to Aquinas, consists in a process combining practical reason's insight into the structure of rational activity with reason's discernment of the various goods constituting human nature. His explicit discussion of this process occurs in his treatment of the question whether the natural law comprises one or several precepts, and his overall strategy in answering the question involves the drawing of a parallel between the principles of speculative reason, whose general role is the ascertainment of truth, and the principles of practical reason, whose central function is the direction of human action.[6] In the cases of both the speculative and the practical reason, a first principle is generated by the primitive object of reason's apprehension. As far as speculative reason is concerned, this primitive object is *being*. In other words, whatever reason apprehends particularly in its speculative function, it apprehends being as its formal object. This fundamental apprehension serves as a formal constraint on all assertions of truth. The constraint is specified in speculative reason's first indemonstrable principle, which amounts to Aquinas's version of the law of non-contradiction ("the same thing cannot be affirmed and denied at the same time"). More precisely, Aquinas claims that this first principle is founded on the sense or meaning (*fundatur supra rationem*) of the concept of being and that all other principles of speculative reason are based on this first principle (*supra hoc principia omnia alia fundatur*).[7] What he means by the latter is not that all other principles are deduced from the first principle but rather that no other principle can violate the first principle's dictates. No principle of speculative reason, that is, can violate the law of noncontradiction.

As noted already, this general account of speculative reason and its principles is presented by Aquinas as a structural analogue to the account of practical reason and its principles. Just as being constitutes the primitive or formal object of reason in its speculative role, so *good* is apprehended by practical reason as its primitive or formal object. Good serves in this capacity inasmuch as every rational agent, whatever her particular purpose, acts for an end perceived to be good. Now the sense or meaning (*ratio*) of good is "that which all things tend toward" (*quod omnia appetunt*), and it is this sense or meaning that grounds a formal constraint on all practical principles.[8] The constraint is implicit in practical reason's first precept, which states "that good is to be done and followed, and evil is to be avoided." On this precept of practical reason all practical principles are based, again, not in the sense of deducibility, but rather in the sense that all practical precepts are limited formally by this first precept. Only that which is perceived as good can constitute the object of a practical precept, and, given the *ratio* of good, this means only those objects that can be grasped as objects of general tendency can serve as foundations of practical precepts. What is more, all objects that practical reason does identify as objects of tendency will in fact give rise to practical precepts. Since practical reason discerns via experience that human beings are governed by natural inclinations or dispositional tendencies toward particular objects, it grasps these objects as intrinsically valuable goods to be pursued and, accordingly, as bases of practical precepts. Thus, reason discovers that human beings are inclined toward self-preservation, sexual intercourse, the rearing of children, living in society, and coming to know the truth about God.[9] These findings provide the substance of the primary precepts of the natural law and therefore determine the particular contents of moral requirement. Generally speaking, persons are morally obliged to preserve human life, educate their children, live cooperatively, and so forth. From all of this Aquinas's answer to the initial question follows appropriately. The precepts of the natural law are several, though they are founded ultimately on one formal, practical precept.

My purpose here is neither to evaluate Aquinas's substantive remarks pertaining to the specific contents of human good nor to assess the cogency of his argument leading to the formulation of the primary precepts. What I am concerned to determine at this juncture is how a moral dilemma would look from the vantage point of a natural-law theory having this formal structure (i.e., a theory that ties moral requirement to intrinsically valuable human goods in the manner of Aquinas) and whether, apart from theological considerations, there is anything about such a theory per se that would demand either ruling out or leaving open the possibility of such dilemmas arising. The answer to the first question is reasonably straightforward and prepares the way for addressing the second problem. If a dilemma is understood as an irresolvable conflict between binding moral requirements and if moral requirements are products of precepts anchored in intrinsically valuable human goods, then a moral dilemma would have to be taken as a sign of irremediable conflict among these goods. And this would mean that the goods in question, while laying unqualified claim on human action, were either unambiguously equal in value or both quantitatively and qualitatively incomparable. It would mean, moreover, that no normative principle of ordering existed by which one might resolve these conflicts. Are there features of a natural-law theory's formal structure that either exclude or permit the possiblity of such irresolvable conflicts?

In response to this last query it might be argued that any set of subsidiary principles grounded in one common principle of higher

generality must be internally ordered and that, therefore, no irresolvable conflict could occur between members of the set. Indeed,
Aquinas himself is careful to note that, while the precepts of the
natural law are many, they have the character of *one* natural law
(*habent rationem unius legis naturalis*) inasmuch as they follow
from one fundamental precept, and this position of his has been
taken by Germain Grisez to imply that the set of primary precepts
"is not a disorganized aggregation but an orderly whole. The precepts are many because the different inclinations' objects, viewed
by reason as ends for rationally guided efforts, lead to distinct
norms of action. The natural law, nevertheless, is one because
each object of inclination obtains its role in practical reason's legislation only insofar as it is subject to practical reason's way of determining action—by prescribing how ends are to be attained."[10]
These are difficult remarks to interpret precisely, but their import
would appear to be that the relation of the primary precepts to the
first precept of the natural law guarantees an ordering that excludes irresolvable conflict among those primary precepts. The
ordering manifests itself as practical reason's limitation of the
claims that goods can make on human activity for their realization. In cases of conflict, that is, certain goods will give way to
others in accordance with some determinate organizational principle of practical reason.

However one evaluates it as a representation of Aquinas's thinking on the matter, one could not possibly accept the foregoing line
of reasoning as an argument demonstrating the impossibility of
irresolvable conflict between the primary precepts.[11] Whether or
not it can be said that these precepts and their corresponding
goods are mutually ordered in the sense suggested, it is clear that
such an ordering cannot be *guaranteed* by the mere fact of common origin in one fundamental principle. It is one thing, and undoubtedly true, to say that two inconsistent propositions cannot
be deduced from a single, self-consistent proposition. It is quite
another thing to suggest that from a unitary practical precept
only mutually ordered precepts are derivable. And it is still another to claim, as the argument under consideration apparently
does, that a unitary practical precept in conjunction with a range
of separately derived specificatory premises (those propositions
specifying the particular goods constituting human nature) can
yield only sets of precepts that are ordered among themselves. To
be certain these precepts were ordered, one would have to be assured on independent grounds that a principle of mutual ordering

conditioned the set of specificatory premises, or, less abstractly, one would need to determine independently that the goods of human nature were unified or ordered in some relevantly significant way. Such a determination cannot be ensured by the fact that all precepts are limited by one fundamental first principle.

If common origin in a unitary first principle is not in itself sufficient to establish an ordering of fundamental goods and their corresponding precepts, are there further considerations that bear on the matter? Interestingly enough, it has been argued by John Finnis, a recent proponent of Thomistic, natural-law theory, that the possibility of at least one type of ordering must be dismissed outright given a proper understanding of the fundamental goods or what he calls the *basic values* of rational practice.[12] There are, according to Finnis, three points that are crucial to such an understanding. First, each basic value is "self-evidently a form of the good" in the sense that each will be perceived by a rational agent as providing a sufficient reason for action and in the sense that each can serve as a sufficient explanation of rational behavior.[13] Second, no basic value can be analyzed or explicated in terms of any other value, be it basic or derivative, and this means, of course, that the basic values are incommensurable in relation to one another. Thus, conflicts between primary precepts grounded in basic values could not be adjudicated by appealing to some common standard of exchange, whether utilitarian or otherwise. Third, and most significant for our purposes, the basic values do not admit of hierarchical ranking or what I have referred to previously as primitive ordering. None can be regarded as qualitatively superior or inferior to any other; each is equally fundamental and important. It is often the case, to be sure, that a particular basic value will become an object of focus and thus assume the appearance of priority. Yet at best this appearance is provisional since any of the basic values may become the primary object of concern:

> If one focuses on the value of speculative truth, it can reasonably be regarded as more important than anything; knowledge can be regarded as the most important thing to acquire; life can be regarded as merely a pre-condition, of lesser or no intrinsic value; play can be regarded as frivolous; one's concern about 'religious' questions can seem just an aspect of the struggle against error, superstition, and ignorance; friendship can seem worth forgoing, or be found exclusively in sharing and enhancing knowledge; and so on. But one can shift one's focus. If one is drowning, or, again, if one is thinking

about one's child who died soon after birth, one is inclined to shift one's focus to the value of life simply as such. The life will not be regarded as a mere pre-condition of anything else; rather, play and knowledge and religion will seem secondary, even rather optional extras. But one can shift one's focus, in this way, one-by-one right round the circle of basic values that constitute the horizon of our opportunities.

Since all of the basic values can become objects of focus in the sense suggested and, therefore, since all can assume a place of preeminence in the mind of the contemplator, it must be concluded, as Finnis sees it, that "there is no objective priority of value amongst them."[14]

The force of this argument is questionable. It is hardly a surprising psychological fact that, when focused on, each of the basic values can appear to occupy a place of preeminence, especially in instances where the focus has been prompted by the loss or imminent loss of the good in question. Indeed, Finnis's remarks about the power of death or imminent death to effect a shift in focus to the value of life are quite plausible in this respect. Yet it is less than clear that this psychological fact alone yields any interesting conclusions regarding *objective* priority relations among the values themselves. To suggest without further argument, as Finnis does, that *any* of the basic values can "reasonably" be held as most important simply begs the question against the claim that some basic values are, objectively speaking, always more important than others or at least that some basic values, again objectively speaking, always override others in certain circumstances no matter what the subjective focus. And it is important to add that issuing this last claim does nothing to impugn the status of a basic value as one that affords sufficient justification for rational action or sufficient explanation of rational behavior. It is one thing to suggest that a basic value is *intrinsically* good and thus is an intelligible object of rational pursuit even if it possesses no further *instrumental* value. It is another thing to say that all intrinsic goods are objectively of equal importance in every conceivable circumstance.

Despite the inconclusiveness of Finnis's discussion, let us assume for the moment that basic values are beyond the possibility of objective hierarchical ranking. The assumption's implication, of course, is that a conflict between moral requirements anchored separately in distinct basic values could not be resolved by appealing to some principle of relative importance. Are we then to conclude that conflicts of this type must be interpreted as moral dilemmas? According to Finnis, this is not the conclusion to be drawn since resident in practical reason itself is another sort of ordering principle that serves to adjudicate conflicts between goods.

The principle in question is Finnis's version of the Thomistic doctrine of double effect. In brief, the principle states "that one should not choose to do any act which *of itself does nothing but* damage or impede a realization or participation of any one or more of the basic forms of human good."[15] The self-evidence of this principle putatively becomes apparent on consideration of the nature of rational practice. Rational activity is tied to the pursuit of basic values in the sense that any intelligent action will be grounded in a choice to realize one basic value or another. Given the nature of the world and the finitude of human capacity, however, such a choice will inevitably issue in a second effect, namely, the failure to realize some other basic value or values. Thus, a scholar chooses to pursue truth with the indirect consequence that human lives which might otherwise have been saved (by entering medical practice, for instance) will most assuredly be lost. Despite the unfortunate nature of this sort of side effect, choices to pursue basic values are, according to Finnis, certainly reasonable and *ceteris paribus* unequivocally moral. In this respect such choices differ from choices to perform acts that in themselves (apart from their consequences) do nothing but damage or impede the realization of some basic value (e.g., choosing to kill an innocent person in an experimental procedure that is sure to lead to the acquisition of significant knowledge about the human condition). One could construe this latter type of choice as reasonable only if it were possible to determine that the beneficial consequences *outweighed* the loss of good. Yet granted incommensurability among the basic values, this determination is impossible *de jure*. The upshot is that any act describable as one which directly damages a basic value is beyond the limit of moral justification. Given the previously stated presumption that choices to promote basic values are always rational and *ceteris paribus* morally justifiable despite deleterious side effects, it follows that all conflicts between the basic values are resolvable, not by maximization of the good in some utilitarian or otherwise consequentialist sense, but rather by ensuring that no act is performed that *directly* damages a basic value.

This general position raises a host of questions that cannot be treated here.[16] What is important to note for present purposes is that the argument's conclusion rests on the normative assumption that in cases of conflict the *indirect* consequences of an act, including the realization or loss of basic values, are irrelevant to the moral assessment of that act—no matter how foreseeable those consequences, no matter what the degree of agent control over those consequences, and no matter how grave those consequences may be. According to this assumption, that is, the only information relevant to such assessment in these cases is that having to do with which basic values are *directly* promoted or impeded. The point that needs to be registered here is that, whatever one makes of this normative canon, its validity cannot be substantiated merely by appealing to the formal structure of natural-law theory. To say the basic values present themselves exclusively as sufficient reasons for actions, as intrinsically valuable goods to be pursued, is to say nothing whatsoever about *how* such values are to be realized, that is, whether they will be realized directly or indirectly. If this last claim holds true, then it is open for the natural-law theorist to argue that *any* realization or loss of basic value is relevant to the assessment of human acts in conflict situations. And if such is the case, then it is also possible for the natural-law theorist to acknowledge the existence of genuine moral dilemmas, at least as far as the theory's formal structure is concerned. Citing the distinction between direct and indirect realization would simply be insufficient in this account to resolve a conflict between fundamental goods since in this sort of situation both the performance of a particular act *and* its omission could be regarded as morally wrong, the former in virtue of its direct damaging of a basic value, the latter in virtue of its indirect contribution to the damaging of a basic value.

As an illustration, take the well-worn example of the small-town judge who determines that she must unjustly convict and harshly sentence an innocent person in order to avoid the wrath of a group that demands the conviction and threatens large-scale destruction of innocent human life if the guilty verdict is not returned. Let us assume for the sake of argument that both *justice* and *human life* are basic values in the sense described. It would be possible to argue that the judge is faced with a genuine moral dilemma since she is bound to commit a moral wrong no matter what she decides to do. A conviction would damage the value of justice; a failure to convict would issue in destruction of the value of human life. The fact that the second choice would contribute only *indirectly* to the loss of a basic value could be regarded in all consistency as simply irrelevant to the moral analysis of the act in question. None of this is to say, of course, that the formal structure of natural-law theory *demands* this normative reading of the situation. The point is rather that there is nothing about the formal structure per se that rules out such an interpretation. More generally, there is no self-evident connection between a theory of natural law and the principle of double effect, Finnis's arguments notwithstanding.

In the absence of further considerations, the reasonable conclusion to be drawn from discussion up to this point is that the Thomistic theory of natural law, abstracted from its theological setting, provides no unambiguous determination of the question whether situations of moral perplexity are ever to be interpreted as genuine dilemmas. Even granting incommensurability among the intrinsically valuable goods of human existence (an incommensurability more often stated than argued for), the possibility of an ordering of these goods, whether hierarchical or otherwise, remains open from the perspective of the theory's formal structure. At the same time, such an ordering is not guaranteed by that structure. If there are resources for resolving the issue in Aquinas's moral theory, then those resources are most likely to be found in the metaphysics of the system.

In seeking the optimal reading of moral perplexity on Thomistic principles, therefore, it would make for intelligent strategy to look to Aquinas's doctrine of God. We have seen already that, in virtue of the connection between natural law and eternal law, the Thomistic explanatory account of moral requirement includes this doctrine as a constituent feature. It is important to add that the precise terminus of that explanatory account is the notion of God's essence or nature. Moral requirement, this is to say, as a function of the eternal law, is, according to Aquinas, primitively grounded in that nature. This conclusion follows from his general view that, when properly understood, the concepts of eternal law and divine essence or nature are fully coextensive.[17] The claim that they are coextensive is founded in turn on Aquinas's account of the eternal law as an idea or exemplar (*ratio*) resident in the divine mind and on Aquinas's understanding of the divine intellect's primary object. Put simply, because the eternal law is

equivalent to an exemplar in the divine mind, it must be equivalent to the divine essence since the primary object of God's intellect is his essence.[18]

Acceptance of this general position carries with it certain important implications. It rules out the possibility, for instance, that
the divine will *simpliciter* could ever be cited as a sufficient explanation of the existence, content, or character of moral requirement. This is not to say, of course, that Aquinas denies the fact of
congruence between God's will and moral requirement. Quite the
contrary, on his terms the entire range of consequences associated
with the eternal law's operation forms an object of divine volition.
But this last statement needs to be set against the background of
the Thomistic account of the divine personality, an account holding that God's will is determined by his intellect, that the primary
object of his intellect, as we have seen, in his essence, and that his
will is therefore necessarily limited by his nature. God wills, in
other words, according to what he knows, and what he knows is
his own essential structure.[19] The point is that such a conception
of the divine personality preserves the primacy of God's nature in
any explanation of moral requirement, even given the perfect
coordination of God's will with the details of the eternal law. Admittedly, the matter is complicated somewhat by Aquinas's view,
following on his denial of genuine composition in the deity, that
the divine will, intellect, and essence are unambiguously united
in reality.[20] It is on the basis of this doctrine of divine simplicity
that Aquinas will sometimes suggest that the divine will is metaphysically coextensive with the eternal law.[21] Nonetheless, the
possibility of issuing this claim in the Thomistic system is always
dependent on the conceptual link afforded by the notion of God's
essence. We can say that the divine will and the eternal law are
metaphysically equivalent only because there is a certain sense in
which we can say that the divine will *is* the divine essence.

The preceding reflections provide an important reference point
for subsequent discussion. Given the characterization of moral
perplexity as an apparent conflict between moral requirements and
given that such requirements in the Thomistic system are ultimately metaphysical functions of the divine nature (thus Aquinas's
theological essentialism), any account of perplexity shaped by
the system will have to be compatible finally with what can be
known about God's nature as it is tied theoretically to the substance and structure of moral claims. Indeed, we shall see eventually that certain of the details that Aquinas provides vis-à-vis

the divine nature will present obstacles to countenancing the existence of moral dilemmas.

Aquinas on Dilemmas

As a way of moving toward this conclusion, I turn now to consider the aforementioned standard interpretation of Aquinas on moral dilemmas. To repeat, this interpretation asserts that Aquinas concedes the possibility of a dilemma's resulting from a specific misdeed (dilemma *secundum quid*) but dismisses the possibility of a dilemma's arising apart from this condition (dilemma *simpliciter*).[22] In the account attributed to Aquinas by this interpretation, morality consists of a range of binding requirements, each of which can be obeyed without difficulty in every actual circumstance, provided no one requirement is ever willfully violated to begin with. Consequent on such a violation, however, a situation could arise in which one or more of the binding requirements *would have to be* disobeyed. Such a picture of the moral life is certainly imaginable and perhaps even compelling when one focuses on particular sorts of moral predicaments. Take a case of conflict between strictures forbidding the breaking of promises and the doing of harm to innocent persons. It might be suggested with some plausibility that such a conflict could not arise *unless* some other moral requirement were violated first. For example, an agent might face this kind of conflict as a result of having promised to avenge a friend by harming the innocent family of the friend's enemy. If the making of such a promise is regarded as morally wrong and if the strictures against breaking promises and harming innocents are taken as binding without exception, then one would need to conclude that the agent in question generated a moral dilemma through a specific misdeed. The view under consideration generalizes on instances such as this one. Moral dilemmas can arise in this way and no other. Is such a view attributable to Aquinas as the standard interpretation contends?

The answer to this question must be partially yes and partially no. While Aquinas does appear to rule out the possibility of dilemmas *simpliciter* and while he speaks about situations of unavoidable sin that arise from a prior condition of sin, the examples he gives of such situations could be regarded as dilemmas in only the most attenuated of senses. This last point becomes clear on close examination of a *locus classicus* of the standard interpretation.[23] The context of Aquinas's discussion here is the issue of whether a mistaken conscience morally obliges an agent to obey its dictates. According to a position that Aquinas wishes to refute, a mistaken conscience cannot so oblige the agent for the following reason *inter alia:* It is possible that a false conscience will direct an agent to contravene God's law. For instance, an agent may conscientiously decide that she must commit fornication. Such a contravention is never permissible; on the contrary, it is always sinful. Yet if a false conscience always required obedience, then an agent whose conscience mistakenly dictated disobedience of God's law would be faced with a dilemma since both disobeying that law and disobeying one's conscience would be sinful. Because situations of unavoidable sin are impossible as a matter of principle and because divine law always binds, one must conclude that a mistaken conscience cannot oblige the agent morally. It is this conclusion and the argument leading up to it that Aquinas rejects. His reasoning is as follows:

> One whose conscience tells him to commit fornication is not in a dilemma *simpliciter* because he can do something by which he can avoid sin, namely, change the false conscience. But he is faced with a dilemma to some degree, that is, as long as the false conscience remains. And there is no difficulty in saying that, if some condition is presupposed, it is impossible for a man to avoid sin; just as, if we presuppose the intention of vainglory, one who is required to give alms cannot avoid sin. For if he gives alms, because of such an intention, he sins; but, if he does not give alms, he violates the law.[24]

Thus, Aquinas's answer to the general question is that the antagonist raises a false issue. An agent whose conscience directs disobedience of God's law is not faced with a dilemma without qualification since there is a way out. The agent, that is, can correct the false conscience. The situation is presumably analogous to the case of an agent who fulfills a duty to give alms with the wrong intention. Here the agent can dissolve the putatively dilemmatic circumstances by putting aside the sinful intention. In both instances, however, the conflict will remain as long as the problematic condition is not removed. For this reason, then, "there is no difficulty in saying that, if some condition is presupposed, it is impossible for a man to avoid sin."

There are, of course, grounds for quarreling with Aquinas's response to the disputed position. After all, it is hardly satisfying to suggest that an agent with a mistaken conscience is not in a real dilemma because the error can be corrected. Presumably, the problem arose in the first place out of the agent's decided and irreversible conviction that the mistaken conscience was accurate. Be that as it may, the issue before us is not the success or failure of Aquinas's response but rather the extent to which his remarks support the standard interpretation of his views about moral dilemmas. In this regard, the striking feature of his discussion relates to the precise character of the moral predicaments permitted theoretically. Despite the contentions of the standard interpretation, Aquinas does not say that an agent can ever be faced with a genuine moral dilemma, that is, a situation in which all available alternatives for action are morally wrong. His claim is more modest. What he does say is that an agent in certain circumstances is bound to sin unless she makes use of the morally permissible way out. Unless the mistaken conscience is changed, and according to Aquinas it can be changed, sin is unavoidable. Unless the corrupt intention is set aside, and presumably the intention can be set aside, the almsgiver is bound to sin whether the required alms are given or not. If these sorts of situations are all that Aquinas allows for, it is fair to conclude that he does not allow for genuine moral dilemmas at all!

The evidence certainly warrants this conclusion. All of the passages cited by the standard interpretation to show that Aquinas admits moral dilemmas conditional on prior misdeeds are passages we are forced to read in the manner suggested above.[25] As a result, there is room for attributing to Aquinas a much stronger antidilemmas thesis than the one permitted by the standard interpretation. According to this revisionist interpretation, Aquinas always proceeds dialectically as though the admission of a moral dilemma of any sort by an ethical theory were a mark against that theory. Thus, his response to the charge that his own system leads to this admission is typically to show that the charge is mistaken, that on closer examination what may look like an authentic dilemma generated by his theory turns out not to be one after all. We have seen an instance of this maneuver already in his discussion of the false conscience. There Aquinas accepted the presumption that moral dilemmas were impossible in principle, and he went on to suggest that assuming the bindingness of a mistaken conscience did not force one to acknowledge the possibility of dilemmas in any full-fledged sense of the term. This manner of proceeding indicates, I think, that for Aquinas dilemmas are not phenomena that can be countenanced by moral theory. Accordingly, I shall assume, henceforth, that his intended position excludes the possibility of dilemmas *in any form.*

On what grounds are dilemmas excluded by the Thomistic system? I have already argued that nothing distinctive about the formal structure of natural-law theory demands such an exclusion, and I have suggested, moreover, that the resources for a Thomistic interpretation of moral perplexity are rooted, most likely, in the metaphysics of the system. This last suggestion, however, might be countered with the claim that the move to metaphysical matters is much too quick since Aquinas himself provides a rationale for rejecting dilemmas that is independent of the system's metaphysical substructure. Indeed, it has been put forth by Alan Donagan that the motivation behind the Thomistic rejection of dilemmas is *logical* rather than *metaphysical.*[26] More particularly, Donagan suggests that Aquinas's central concern is the preservation of consistency. According to this account, Aquinas regards a genuine moral dilemma as a sign of inconsistency in one's system of moral principles and thus as a symptom of theoretical inadequacy. Yet the textual support that Donagan provides for his reading is unconvincing.[27] And this is a significant point. For, if Aquinas did regard dilemmas as signs of inconsistency, his position would require further defense. As should be clear from previous discussion, the acknowledgment of a dilemma's existence need be regarded neither as a sign of inconsistency in one's system of moral principles nor as a mark of incoherence in the set of one's general moral beliefs and one's particular non-moral beliefs about the world.[28] Before one could resolve the issue of consistency, one would first have to provide an interpretation of the deontic concepts ('ought' and 'ought not') constituting pairs of judgments that structure conflict situations. And this would mean in the present instance that one would need to determine which interpretations of the concepts were demanded by the Thomistic moral theory.

At first glance the following deontic analysis might recommend itself. Given the terms of natural-law theory, to say that some particular act, x, ought to be performed is to say that x is required by some primary precept of the natural law, and to say that x is required by a primary precept is to say that the performance of x will promote some intrinsically valuable human good. Similarly, to say that x ought not to be performed is to say that x violates some primary precept, and this is to say in turn that the performance of x will damage or impede the realization of some good, that the performance, in other words, will promote evil. If this analysis is correct, then to assert that some particular act, x, both ought to be performed and ought not to be performed is to imply that the performance of x would promote some good and at the same time impede the realization of some good. Is there an inconsistency in this implication? Surely not. Whatever might be said on other grounds, there is certainly no logical contradiction in the claim that a particular act will simultaneously promote good and evil. According to this rendering, then, there would be no inconsistency in suggesting that a particular act both ought to be performed and ought not to be performed. A dilemma, that is, would pose no threat to the coherence of the system.

Now in response to the foregoing line of reasoning it might be argued that Aquinas implicitly maintains the logical incoherence of dilemmas when he claims that 'morally good' and 'morally evil' are contrary concepts, that they denote, presumably, mutually exclusive properties and thus cannot be attached simultaneously to a single act. "If therefore we consider an action in the moral order, it is impossible for it to be morally both good and evil."[29] The point of this response would be to offer textual evidence supporting the position that Aquinas's rejection of dilemmas is motivated by logical concerns. In assessing this response, two questions ought to be raised. First, in light of the deontic analysis of the preceding paragraph, how could Aquinas claim that 'morally good' and 'morally evil' are contrary concepts? Second, given his remarks about contrariety, must we conclude that Aquinas rejects dilemmas on logical grounds?

The answer to the first question must be that Aquinas would refuse to accept the terms of the deontic analysis offered above because it fails to distinguish nonmoral good and evil from moral good and evil, a failure resulting in misleading interpretations of the deontic concepts.[30] For Aquinas, in contrast to that analysis, saying that a particular act promotes an intrinsically valuable human good could not be all there is to saying that the act is morally good or that it ought to be performed from the moral point of view. Analogously, for Aquinas, claiming that an act is one that promotes evil or impedes the realization of some good could not exhaust the meaning of the suggestion that the act is morally evil or that it ought not to be performed, morally speaking. To put the matter another way, moral good and moral evil must be, in Aquinas's view, second-order predicates. Understood in this fashion, their application to a particular act would have to be taken as a reflection of the second-order judgment that the act in question ought to be performed or ought not to be performed given a complete rendering of *all* the goods and evils it generated. If this is an accurate reading of his intentions, Aquinas could concede the internal consistency of the statement that an act promotes good and evil simultaneously (a concession that he must surely make) without admitting the consistency of the statement that the act is *both* morally good and morally evil. On the basis of what has been said so far, then, he could still contend that moral dilemmas were logically impossible.

The issue before us, of course, is whether Aquinas does exclude the possibility of dilemmas on logical grounds. Granted the Thomistic position that the concepts 'morally good' and 'morally evil' are contraries, there might appear to be little to quarrel with in Donagan's presumption that Aquinas's theoretical aversion to dilemmas is prompted by the concern to preserve consistency. But the appearance would be misleading because the claim expressing the relation of contrariety will not stand on its own. It does not follow simply from the laws of logic that 'morally good' and 'morally evil' denote mutually exclusive properties. And there is no indication that Aquinas thought such did follow. The upshot is that Aquinas's remarks about contrariety do not demonstrate that he regarded the theoretical dismissal of dilemmas as a position required by logic and logic alone. This conclusion leads us to still another question. If Aquinas's rejection of dilemmas is not grounded in logic, what is its basis? Why does he hold that 'morally good' and 'morally evil' denote mutually exclusive properties? As far as I am able to determine, Aquinas provides no explicit answer to this question in either of its forms. Nonetheless, an implicit rationale can be reconstructed, I think, one founded on substantive, metaphysical considerations rooted in the Thomistic system.

There are two parts to the reconstructed account, one based on the Thomistic doctrine of divine providence, the other on Aquinas's understanding of the radical unity of God's nature. Let us begin with the argument from providence. This argument takes as its point of departure Aquinas's remark that "it is proper to man to be inclined to act according to reason."[31] Given the theoretical constraints of the general system, this remark carries with it several important implications: (1) Conformity of an agent's actions to the dictates of reason constitutes a *good* for that agent. This conclusion follows from Aquinas's analysis of the sense or meaning (*ratio*) of good as that which forms an object of general tendency or inclination. (2) As a *good* of the agent, conformity of action to the requirements of reason contributes indispensably to the agent's perfection or self-realization. What warrants this inference is Aquinas's further explication of the notion of good as "something which perfects another as an end."[32] (3) An agent's performance of what is morally required contributes to that agent's perfection or self-realization. This conclusion follows from Aquinas's idea, noted earlier, that the content of moral requirement is made known to the agent through the dynamic of practical reason's insight into the structure of rational activity combined with reason's discovery of the specific goods constituting human existence. In other words, the pursuit and achievement of moral rectitude in action is for Aquinas a rationally governed process and therefore contributes substantially to human flourishing. Of course, this connection between moral rectitude and human flourishing is precisely what should be expected given Aquinas's view that the principles of moral requirement, the precepts of the natural law, are part and parcel of the eternal law through which God providentially directs the universe. Properly understood, the promulgation of the content of moral requirement is a way that God guides rational creatures toward the fulfillment of their proper ends. (4) An agent's failure to perform what is required morally obstructs, if it does not annihilate, her movement toward self-realization. This point is a corollary to that expressed in (3). To neglect the demands of moral rectitude is, so to speak, to abandon the divinely chartered path leading to human flourishing.

What, then, would dilemmas mean on these terms? They would mean minimally that the divinely ordained providential scheme was disordered at various points. To maintain that agents were faced with irresolvably conflicting moral requirements would be to admit that in these circumstances no unproblematic path to human fulfillment availed itself to the agent, that divine providential guidance in such cases was marked by an internal tension. For a moral dilemma would entail a situation in which an agent paradoxically impeded her own progress toward perfection by engaging in the very activity that the perfection demanded. Such a state of affairs would signify a defect in the created world to the extent that the necessary conditions of human fulfillment could not be met. The implication expressed here is not merely that human nature is sinfully corrupt and consequently incapable of ac-

tualizing its potential without the aid of divine grace. If this sort
of defect were what dilemmas entailed, there would be little problem in Aquinas's acknowledging their existence since he never denies the necessity of grace in this sense.[33] The point being made is
more radical than that. It suggests that even with the help of divine grace self-realization would be impossible objectively. Neither is the implication simply that human nature in this life lacks
the capacity for achieving *ultimate* perfection or happiness. If acknowledging such an incapacity were the theoretical outcome of
positing dilemmas, then once again, Aquinas would have no difficulty admitting their existence since, as is well known, he regards
ultimate fulfillment or self-realization as inaccessible to human
beings in their earthly lives.[34] The issue at stake in the admission
of dilemmas rather involves denying the possibility of the provisional perfection that for Aquinas is the result of moral achievement. In other words, the existence of moral dilemmas would
mean that human beings would be incapable of attaining that
measure of flourishing appropriate to them in their *natural* states.

This theoretical consequence is in itself sufficient to explain
why Aquinas would regard dilemmas as *metaphysical* impossibilities and thus why he would interpret the concepts 'morally
good' and 'morally evil' as contraries. Nonetheless, there is perhaps an equally compelling reason for his exclusion of dilemmas,
a reason rooted in his general, metaphysical account of the character of good. According to Aquinas, when we use the term 'good',
we signify a property whose essence is fully captured only in the
divine nature. The claim is not merely that God is the sole being
perfectly *instantiating* the property of goodness. To put the matter
this way is to suggest that God's nature, like that of finite beings,
is conditioned by participation in an ontologically independent,
universal entity—goodness—and such a suggestion jeopardizes
the notion of God's aseity. The claim is rather that God *is* goodness itself and that finite beings are good inasmuch as *they* participate, albeit imperfectly, in the goodness that God is. This general
line of reasoning informs Aquinas's view that the *primary* referent of the term 'good' cannot be a property possessed by finite
creatures in any unqualified way but must be a property perfectly
resident in the divine nature alone.[35] As a result, our predications
of goodness in finite contexts at best are predications with a secondary sense, a sense, in other words, that does not fully compre-
hend the essence of the concept's primary referent. Employment
of the predicate in its fully proper sense is possible only in appli-

cation to God. This is not to imply, of course, that in our attribution of goodness to God we work with a predicate whose proper sense is wholly transparent to us. On the contrary, for the sense of good to be transparent in this context we would require a complete understanding of the divine nature. Yet such knowledge, according to Aquinas, transcends the limits of human cognition.[36]

What all of this yields, of course, is a concept of goodness whose proper sense is at best austerely grasped by finite, rational consciousness. Still, the content of that concept is not entirely opaque to human cognition, as we have seen. Thus, we can meaningfully explicate the *ratio* of good as that which forms an object of tendency or as that which perfects its subject. For our purposes it is important to note the formal correspondence between these senses and certain descriptions applicable to God. In the precise meaning of the terms, it is God and only God that finally constitutes the object of dispositional tendency for all finite beings, and it is God and God alone who perfects subjects. Such a correspondence between the proper senses of 'good' and descriptions applicable to God is to be expected, naturally, given the supposition of metaphysical equivalence between goodness and the divine nature. More generally, the supposition establishes a rule of analysis. In principle, any metaphysical account of goodness must be consistent with what is known about the goodness constitutive of the divine nature. This rule generates in turn a constraint on the interpretation of moral perplexity. Put simply, we must reject any rendering of moral perplexity whose consequence is a general conception of goodness that collides with what we know about the goodness of God.

Now what can we know about this divine goodness? Admittedly, Aquinas's account is sparing in its details, a fact that is hardly surprising given his stipulations regarding limitations on finite, rational comprehension of God's essence. Nevertheless, one formal feature of the divine goodness, Aquinas implies, admits of intelligible description, and this feature pertains especially to the matter before us:

> For the divine goodness is simple, being, as it were, all in one. Because the divine being contains the whole fullness of perfection, as we proved in the First Book. Wherefore, since a thing is good so far as it is perfect, God's being is His perfect goodness: for in God, to be, to live, to be wise, to be happy, and whatever else is seen to pertain to perfection and goodness, are one and the same in God, as

though the sum total of His goodness were God's very being. . . . In yet another way the creature's goodness falls short from God's. For, as we have stated, God, in His very being, has supreme perfection of goodness. Whereas the creature has its perfection, not in one thing but in many: because what is united in the highest is manifold in the lowest. Wherefore, in respect of one and the same thing, virtue, wisdom, and operation are predicated of God; but of creatures, in respect of different things: and the further a creature is from the sovereign goodness, the more does the perfection of its goodness require to be manifold.[37]

The main thrust of these remarks is certainly to acknowledge limitations on the creature's capacity for imitating God. Perfect imitation would entail, among other things, that the creature's goodness conformed perfectly to the divine goodness, and this would mean that the former, contrary to fact, would have to shed its manifold character. The critical factor from our point of view is the picture of the divine goodness rendered. As a function of the divine simplicity, God's goodness is unified, both in the sense that it is equivalent to his being and in the sense that its constituents are reducible without remainder to a single property. But if God's goodness is unified in this manner, then goodness itself, when properly understood, must be seen as unified likewise. The structure of goodness, therefore, is *essentially* one of unity. Inasmuch as we speak of particular goods, then, that are distinct from one another and that ostensibly lack the potential for reductive unity, we are using the term 'good' with a deficient sense, one that does not accurately reflect the essence or nature of goodness itself.

The implications of this conclusion for the construal of moral perplexity may now be traced. Situations of perplexity interpreted in Thomistic terms are situations in which an agent must directly damage or fail to realize some value or values in the course of performing an action whose purpose is the realization of some other value or values. To assume that these situations were genuine dilemmas would be to assume that the separate values constituting the range of options in any particular instance were essentially disparate or divided, that they could not be combined or ordered in a manner making it possible to speak of the *one* good for the agent. The assumption would entail, in other words, that the good for the agent was not unified in principle, that the term 'good' in such a case did not denote a single, undifferentiated property, that the structure of goodness was irreducibly pluralistic. Yet we have seen that from Aquinas's perspective to talk about goodness in this fashion is to employ the concept with a sense that fails to capture what goodness is essentially. Goodness is by its very nature undivided. To speak of an agent's achieving good, even in the limited way this is possible for finite creatures, is to speak of her participation in a single property that finally lacks genuine composition. Such is not to deny, of course, that a human agent partakes of the good in a variety of ways. Indeed, it is precisely this variation in participation that Aquinas underscores in his remarks about the manifold character of human goodness. Human beings, that is, typically partake of the good by becoming courageous, benevolent, faithful, truthful, and so on. Still, saying that the way to the good is manifold is not to say that the good itself is varied in character. And given the essential nature of goodness as depicted by Aquinas on philosophical-theological grounds, one would have to presume the ultimate unity of the goal toward which the manifold way leads. Similarly, one would need to postulate the ultimate unity of the basic human values inasmuch as they represent modes of participation in the one, utterly simple good. What this means is that in cases of conflict among these values one would need to presume in principle the possibility of an ordering that served to resolve the conflict. To exclude this possibility is to imply that the good is fundamentally fragmented, an implication that on Aquinas's terms would suggest further the fragmentation of God's very nature.

If the foregoing is an accurate reconstruction, what we have in Aquinas is a value ontology that contrasts markedly with pluralistic ontologies such as the Nagelian conception reviewed earlier. For Nagel, it will be recalled, the fundamental values of human existence are, in the final analysis, disordered. Moral reality, on his terms, consists in an array of competing value worlds, each apprehended by a different human perspective. For Aquinas, on the other hand, there is, so to speak, *one* radically simple value world constituted by the divine perspective as it apprehends the divine nature. From God's point of view, therefore, the detailed resolutions of all moral conflicts will be readily apparent. This is to say nothing, of course, about what can be discerned from the human point of view. Consequently, while we are forced to conclude that genuine moral dilemmas must be ruled out as a matter of principle on Thomistic grounds, we are still left with the question of why finite, rational creatures experience difficulties in coming to know just what morality requires in situations of conflict. If conflict resolution is always possible *de jure,* how is the phenomenon of moral perplexity to be explained? Any attempt to discover Aquinas's answer to this question will need to begin by examining his remarks concerning the limitations of practical reason.

The Limitations of Practical Reason

Aquinas's most extended treatment of practical reason's limitations is to be found in his discussion of the question whether the natural law is the same for all human beings:

> In the case of the practical reason . . . which is concerned with contingent matters, such as human actions, even though there be some necessary truth in the common principles, yet the more we descend to what is proper and peculiar, the more deviations we find. Therefore in speculative matters the same truth holds among all men both as to principles and as to conclusions, even though all men do not discern this truth in the conclusions but only in those principles which are called axiomatic notions. In active matters, on the other hand, all men do not hold to the same truth or practical rectitude in what is peculiar and proper, but only in what is common. And even among those who hold to the same line of rectitude in proper and peculiar matters, such rectitude is not equally known to all. It is clear, therefore, that as far as common principles are concerned in the case of speculative as well as of practical reason the same truth and the same rectitude exists among all and is equally known to all. In the case, however, of the proper or peculiar conclusions of speculative reason, the same truth obtains among all, even though it is not known equally to all. For it is true among all men that the three angles of a triangle are equal to two right angles, even though not all men know this. But in the case of the proper or peculiar conclusions of the practical reason there is neither the same truth and rectitude among all men, nor, where it does exist, is it equally known to all. Thus it is true and right among all men that action proceed in accordance with reason. From this principle there follows as a proper conclusion that deposits should be restored to the owner. This conclusion is indeed true in the majority of cases. But a case may possibly arise in which such restitution is harmful and consequently contrary to reason; so, for example, if things deposited were claimed so that they might be used against the fa-

therland. This uncertainty increases the more particular the cases become: as, for example, if it were laid down that the restitution should take place in a certain way, with certain *definite* precautions; for as the limiting particular conditions become more numerous, so do the possibilities decrease that render the principle normally applicable, with the result that neither the restitution nor the failure to do so can be rigorously presented as right.[38]

These remarks suggest the following general picture of practical reason. Although the fundamental precepts or common principles of the natural law (e.g., one ought to act in conformity with reason) are the same for all, the particular conclusions drawn from them will vary from person to person in accordance with varying circumstances. Thus, while it is possible and useful to formulate more specific precepts (e.g., one ought to restore deposits) based on what the fundamental precepts ordinarily require in particular circumstances, these more specific precepts at best will serve as general rules of thumb, applying only in "the majority of cases" (*ut in pluribus*); for a situation could arise in which a specific precept dictated a course of action that collided with what is actually required by the fundamental precept in that situation. The consequence is that our general knowledge of moral requirement, codified in sets of workaday moral principles, is not unfailingly reliable. Exception-making circumstances can always arise.

Thus, the sort of moral uncertainty that Aquinas emphasizes here is that which relates to a certain level of our general moral knowledge. We cannot say that this knowledge is indefeasible, though it does establish a range of presumptions. What is important to note is that the acknowledgment of such uncertainty will not account for the kind of moral perplexity with which we have been concerned. To deny that our workaday moral principles represent a body of necessary moral truths is not to deny that we are certain about what morality requires in particular situations. To admit, for example, that the principle 'one ought to restore deposits' fails to hold in every case is not to suggest that we cannot know for certain whether it applies in a specific case. Yet moral perplexity of the sort we have considered is the perplexity an agent experiences in a *particular* instance. Such perplexity cannot be explained by citing the less than universal applicability of general principles.

Is there anything implicit in Aquinas's position that would account for an agent's uncertainty in particular cases? In order to answer this question we need to form a clearer picture of how the contingencies of particular situations complicate the determinations of practical reason and how such complications could contribute to another type of moral uncertainty. For the purposes of analysis let us elaborate on the example presented by Aquinas. The issue before us is the question of when it is reasonable, that is, moral, to return to the owner property held in trust. We shall assume with Aquinas that in the largest number of instances the property ought to be returned. Yet the judgment that it ought to be returned does not hold of necessity; it may be the case that the goods in question will be put to immoral use. Thus, in a particular situation it is essential for the agent to determine just how the property will be utilized. Perhaps, as Aquinas suggests, it will be employed as part of a plan to attack the agent's country. Again, we grant Aquinas's presumption that in ordinary circumstances this fact would provide sufficient moral reason to withhold the goods. Still, the matter is not yet settled since now the agent needs to judge whether the owner has a just grievance against the agent's country. Perhaps the owner is a citizen of a nation that has suffered unjust aggression at the hands of the agent's country. Perhaps the owner is a leader of a just revolution. Assuming certain criteria of moral relevance (bracketing for present purposes the question whether Aquinas would accept such criteria), either one of these facts could constitute sufficient moral grounds for aiding the owner by returning the goods. Nonetheless, exceptional circumstances could falsify even this judgment. Suppose the owner intended to prosecute the just cause with immoral means (e.g., terrorizing innocent noncombatants) and suppose the goods in question were to be implemented as a feature of this plan. Given such details in conjunction with certain normative presuppositions, it could be judged that the morally appropriate course of action is to withhold the property. One could go on multiplying hypotheses. What all of this illustrates is the potential for complexity in situations requiring moral decision. Such a potential can only lend a measure of uncertainty to the formulation of singular moral judgments. For one could never be sure that one has accounted for all the facts of the case. The possibility always remains that a morally relevant fact, sufficient to falsify one's decision, will have gone unnoticed or is otherwise beyond one's ken. Moral uncertainty in particular situations, then, could be regarded as a function of the contingent nature of practical reason's subject matter combined with the fallibility of human knowledge about what is the case.

It should be clear, however, that this account will not explain how an agent can experience moral perplexity of the sort that involves a seeming conflict between binding moral requirements. All the account can establish is that moral uncertainty is possible inasmuch as the *factual* circumstances of particular situations are often enormously complex. Yet cases of moral perplexity, understood as apparent moral dilemmas, are possible in principle even assuming that all of the relevant facts are known. An agent, for example, who must either lie or break a promise can remain uncertain about the proper course of action even though she is aware of the entire range of circumstances bearing on the moral decision. Uncertainty in such cases is *normative* uncertainty, and normative uncertainty is not in these instances reducible to *factual* uncertainty. The general point is that, while the contingent nature of practical reason's subject matter might be appealed to as a way of explaining the moral uncertainty related to factual indeterminacy, it cannot be cited as a way of explaining how an agent can be normatively perplexed about the proper course of action in situations of conflict.

Are there other features of Aquinas's account that would provide data for explaining how it is that an agent can be perplexed in this latter sense? In addressing this question it is interesting to note that, when Aquinas discusses the limitations of practical reason, he cites, in addition to the contingent nature of its subject matter, the fact of human sinfulness and its potential for obscuring moral determinations. While the primary precepts of the natural law "can no wise be blotted out from men's hearts," an individual may be prevented from applying these precepts correctly by concupiscence or some other sinful passion. "Sin blots out the law of nature in particular cases, not universally, except perchance in regard to the secondary precepts of the natural law. . . ."[39] Indeed, it is precisely this state of affairs that supposedly explains in part the existence of the divine law (the prescriptions of the Old and New Testaments). For example, Aquinas argues that one of the reasons for God's supplemental revelation of the Old Law was that "natural law began to be obscured on account of the exuberance of sin."[40] Because of human corruption, practical reason left to its own resources cannot unfailingly determine the content of moral requirement.

At this point the central consideration is whether the condition

of human sinfulness can serve to explain an agent's perplexity in
instances of conflict between moral principles. What would such
an explanation look like? Aquinas himself does not attend to this
particular question, so we shall have to go beyond his explicit discussion. Take the example of two individuals, A and B, who are
running for separate political offices. Attracted by B's moral stands
on various issues, A pledges support for B's candidacy in the
course of the general election campaign. As time goes on, however, A discovers that B's public rhetoric is not matched by an appropriate moral scrupulosity in campaign practice. Unseemly
deals are cut. Promises are issued that knowingly cannot be kept.
Plans are made to circumvent the democratic process in an assortment of ways. Candidate A concludes that the endorsement of B
was mistaken and considers publicly repudiating B's candidacy.
Yet A knows that a public retraction will damage irretrievably her
own election chances and will probably mean the end of her own
political career. Self-interest sets in motion a process of moral ra-
tionalization. She begins to assign undue weight to the initial
pledge of support. "Promises made have binding force," she reasons. "I have an obligation to keep steadfast in my allegiance."
Still, she remains sensitive to the countervailing moral considerations. "Political dishonesty cannot be countenanced." "Truth
must be told." And so forth. From all of this A infers that whatever course of action she chooses she will be guilty of a moral
transgression.

Assuming for the sake of argument that the normative resolution of A's problem is clear objectively (she ought to withdraw the
support), the foregoing example does illustrate how a corrupt inclination could unconsciously cloud an agent's moral reasoning to
the degree that moral perplexity is the outcome. Generally, it is
reasonable to propose as a psychological fact that human beings
can and will be tempted to appreciate or depreciate the normative
status of a moral principle in unwarranted ways whenever such
manipulation is convenient. Thus, apparent moral dilemmas in a
number of instances might be explained away as functions of sinfully prompted agent misperceptions. Yet it should be obvious
that this sort of explanation can be extended to cover at best only
a limited range of situations. Quite often cases of moral perplexity will arise when sinful motivations are absent. We need not
search far for illustrations. Consider the example of the doctor who
determines that her patient is not psychologically equipped to
face the fact of terminal illness. The doctor must decide whether

the truth is to be told. Here we have a conflict between the principles enjoining truth-telling and promoting the patient's well-being. Let us presume that the doctor's self-interest will not be significantly affected by either choice and therefore that she suffers from no temptation to exaggerate or undervalue the status of either of the principles. Even granting this presumption, it would hardly be surprising that the doctor remained uncertain about the proper course of action. What this shows, naturally, is that appeals to sinful propensities will not always suffice as adequate explanations of moral perplexity. Now in response to this last claim it might be argued that, while we are frequently unable to identify a sinful disposition on the part of an agent in situations of perplexity, we must still attribute the source of that perplexity to the *general* sinfulness of the human condition. According to this account, an effect of sin is the *systematic* distortion of moral perception, and one manifestation of this effect is the persistent inability of agents or observers to discern the normative resolutions of moral conflicts. Yet it seems to me that this maneuver preserves the general line of argument by depriving it of genuine explanatory force. Unless they can be tied to specific instances of agent or observer corruption, appeals to the doctrine of sin remain vacuous as accounts of moral perplexity.

The conclusion to be drawn from all of this is that the remarks of Aquinas cited thus far will not provide the theoretical resources for a complete account of the phenomenon under consideration. Neither the contingent nature of practical reason's subject matter nor the fact of human sinfulness is sufficient to explain in every case how it is that human beings often fail to discern what morality requires in situations of conflict. If there is a resolution to the problem in Aquinas, it will have to be reconstructed systematically from other elements of the general theory.

We have already encountered features of the theory that suggest a line of approach. Implicit in Aquinas's understanding of moral obligation and its relation to the good is a portrayal of moral discourse as language having a depth structure conditioned by the referent of moral concepts. This depth structure, given Thomistic metaphysical suppositions, is at best only partially accessible to finite, rational creatures in this life. The reason for this state of affairs is that all moral concepts, to greater or lesser degrees, denote the property of goodness, a property whose full nature transcends the worldly capacities of human comprehension. As we have seen, the restricted accessibility of the referent of moral con-

cepts is in Thomistic thought a function of limitations on finite
cognition of the divine esssence. Goodness, the ultimate referent
of moral terms, is a property constitutive of God's nature, and
God's nature cannot be perfectly known in this life. What this entails theoretically is a notion of the good whose nature is at best
imperfectly grasped by human beings in their present lives, a general condition that could create a measure of tentativeness or uncertainty in the particular applications of moral concepts. Indeed,
it is precisely this point that Aquinas appears to articulate in
terms of the relation between eternal and natural law:

> The human reason cannot have a full participation of the dictate of
> the Divine Reason, but according to its own mode, and imperfectly.
> Consequently, as on the part of the speculative reason, by a natural
> participation of Divine Wisdom, there is in us the knowledge of
> certain general principles, but not a proper knowledge of each
> single truth, such as that contained in the Divine Wisdom; so too,
> on the part of the practical reason, man has a natural participation
> of the eternal law, according to certain general principles but not as
> regards the particular determinations of individual cases, which
> are, however, contained in the eternal law.[41]

The eternal law, which, as we have seen, is coextensive with the
divine essence, includes in principle every particular moral determination. But these particular determinations are not compre-
hended by the natural law, which represents the point of contact
between the eternal law and human cognition. The "proper knowledge" given in the natural law is knowledge at a relatively advanced level of generality. What this suggests, of course, is that
human knowledge of the good does not extend unproblematically
to particular instantiations. To assume otherwise is to assume
that finite, rational creatures are capable of exhaustive insight
into the eternal law or God's essence itself. Needless to say, for
Aquinas none of this would imply a radical skepticism at the level
of singular moral judgment. Working with a concept of the good
whose sense is austerely grasped, practical reason is able to discern connections between general principles and singular judgments. Yet reason's hold on these connections is a tenuous one,
subject to varying degrees of certainty and always falling short of
absolute certainty.[42]

On the basis of the foregoing, it is now possible to reconstruct a
Thomistic account of moral perplexity in epistemological terms.

From this perspective apparent moral dilemmas are describable as particular situations in which an agent is unclear about the course of action picked out, so to speak, by the concept of the good. The unclarity in such cases is a function of the concept's depth-structure, which is grasped by the agent in limited ways at best. More precisely, what remains indiscernible in these instances is a principle that would provide an ordering among seemingly disparate values and that would thereby resolve the perplexity. Given Thomistic metaphysical constraints, such a principle, despite its epistemic inaccessibility in the particular case, would have to be regarded as an implicit feature of the concept's depth-structure. The good is essentially ordered, though the nature of the ordering often stubbornly evades cognitive apprehension.[43] In short, while dilemmas are ruled out *de jure*, their apparent existence is accounted for as a function of limiting conditions on human powers of moral perception.

Concluding Reflections

At the beginning of this chapter I noted the existence of a particular strain in Catholic, natural-law thinking, a strain that has supposed a proper understanding of the moral order should lead one to reject the possibility of insoluble conflict between binding moral principles. I noted in addition that certain revisionist Catholic ethicists have challenged this view in arguing that any adequate moral theology must acknowledge the existence of genuine moral dilemmas. As representative of this challenge, consider the following remarks of Nicholas Crotty:

> One's overview of Christian moral life is at issue here. If we believed that our moral task as Christians is to steer clear of evil situations or, when this proves impossible, to keep ourselves "innocent" in such situations, it would make some sense to be exclusively preoccupied with our conformity to the order and hierarchy that we saw embodied in moral law and to devise a moral theory, however intricate, which would permit this conformity even in conflict situations. If, on the contrary, moral life is conceived in terms of our response to our situation and its creative potentialities for human welfare, if our situations are sin-filled situations and sin-disrupted situations, and if our moral task is not to withdraw from such situations but to "redeem" them to the extent that is or can be made possible, our emphasis and preoccupations will be otherwise.

What will count now is that actual implications and consequences are detrimental to persons and community, the behavior is to this extent morally evil behavior. The evil implications and consequences may be unavoidable. They may be unintended side-effects of our behavior. They may be outweighed by other implications and consequences that are favorable to human welfare. But they are there and morally they are evil. As such, they need to be recognized and deplored in true Christian repentance.[44]

Crotty appears to suggest that the theoretical dismissal of dilemmas is intelligible only against the background of an unchristian preoccupation with preserving moral innocence. Sufficient appreciation of the world's sinful character presumably requires the acknowledgment that certain situations exist in which no unequivocal moral resolution is possible. In the last chapter of this essay, I shall address the claim positing a connection between the doctrine of sin and the moral dilemmas thesis. What needs to be underlined at present is the misleading character of Crotty's assessment. Our reflections on the Thomistic theory of natural law point to the fact that, quite apart from concerns expressed in his analysis, genuine metaphysical issues are at stake in the debate about moral conflict. As we have seen, any natural-law theory developed within the framework of Thomistic metaphysics will have enormous difficulties countenancing moral dilemmas, though there will be theoretical resources for explaining moral perplexity in epistemological terms. Given this state of affairs and assuming for the moment that there are compelling independent theological reasons for acknowledging the existence of dilemmas, there would seem to be two options open to the Catholic revisionists. Either they will have to abandon the Thomistic theory of natural law altogether and replace it with some other account of the relation between God and morality, or, less radically, they will have to revise the metaphysical substructure of the theory in such a way as to permit the positing of dilemmas.

It is not entirely clear to me which course the revisionists would take, but what I want to consider here is the possibility of the less radical approach. Can the metaphysical underpinnings of Aquinas's natural-law theory be modified so as to leave room for the revisionist's claims? What would the consequences of such modification be? Needless to say, in addressing these questions we must keep in full view the precise metaphysical determinants that constrained the interpretation of moral perplexity. Our reconstructed account suggested, it will be recalled, that the theoretical dismissal of dilemmas was grounded in the Thomistic conceptions of God's simplicity and God's providence. Can these conceptions be revised in a way that renders the moral dilemmas thesis a theoretical possibility for a theistically grounded theory of natural law?

Let us take first the claims about the simplicity of God's nature and the way such claims impinge on the construal of moral perplexity. Granted this simplicity and granted the equation of God's goodness with goodness itself, Aquinas is compelled, I have argued, to depict the good as essentially undivided, the result being a presumption that the intrinsic goods of human existence are ordered in a manner that permits in principle the resolution of all moral conflict. Now it might be thought that one way of avoiding this conclusion and allowing for a fragmented moral reality that could explain the existence of dilemmas would be to assign the realm of value an ontological status that is independent of God's being. In this view, the axiological order could be characterized, presumably without threat to the unity of God's nature, as irreducibly pluralistic, consisting, that is, of a range of separate fundamental values that are both incommensurable and beyond the possibility of primitive ordering. Given such an ontology, of course, and given the proper combination of worldly circumstances, dilemmas could arise. Yet it is not at all clear that this metaphysical picture affords a satisfactory solution to the problem. What would it mean, in this view, to say that God is good? It would mean apparently that God participates somehow in this ontologically independent, axiological order. To say that God is *perfectly* good, moreover, would be to say that God instantiates maximally all of the value there is. But on the terms of the present analysis it is difficult to see how one could speak of such instantiation without jeopardizing the notion of God's simplicity. If being perfectly good entailed instantiating a wide range of radically discrete value properties (e.g., being faithful, truthful, benevolent, etc.), then it would also entail exemplifying a complex nature. Yet such a complex nature in God's case is precisely what is excluded by the doctrine of divine simplicity. The result is that the idea of God's perfect goodness is rendered problematical. There is an additional difficulty with the present proposal, a difficulty I alluded to briefly in earlier discussion. Simply put, to divorce the realm of value from God's being in the manner suggested would be to compro-

mise the notion of God's aseity. If God has a nature and if having
this nature involved participation in an ontologically independent
realm, then, as Alvin Plantinga has made clear, God's existence,
as well as his nature, is dependent on that realm in a significant
way. For, indeed, in this view God could not have existed unless
this realm existed, and furthermore, God could not have been
what he is (he could not have had the nature he has) were it not for
the existence of this realm.[45] The point is that the concern to preserve God's self-sufficiency theoretically would seem to militate
against the theological essentialist's adopting any proposal that
rendered the value world independent of God's being.

Thus, there are strong reasons for suggesting that, if the notion
of divine simplicity is to be preserved, an irreducibly pluralistic
value ontology will have to be rejected. The obvious conclusion to
be drawn from this is that any advocacy of axiological pluralism
most likely will require jettisoning the simplicity thesis. Now it
might be claimed at the outset that such a modification could be
accommodated theoretically with minimal difficulty. Indeed, the
revision might even be welcomed on grounds independent of the
concern to advance axiological pluralism. After all, the doctrine
of divine simplicity entails not only the notion that God's value
properties are unambiguously united; it entails also the idea that
all of God's attributes, as well as his *existence*, coalesce in undifferentiated unity. In some mysterious sense, that is, God's power
is putatively indistinguishable from his goodness; his power and
goodness are indistinguishable from his intelligence; all of these
are indistinguishable from his existence; and so forth. One can
only wonder about the intelligibility of such a view. Thus, one
might suggest that it is best to treat the simplicity thesis as a historical curiosity, having its ultimate roots in the Parmenidean
conception of reality as that beyond all differentiation, a thesis
that can hardly be sanctioned by the modern mind. But before we
dismiss the doctrine of divine simplicity, we ought to determine
just what, if anything, is at stake in the matter *theologically.*
What are the grounds for suggesting that God's nature is without
composition?

Along with Plantinga, I think that the most important motivation lying behind the simplicity thesis, at least as articulated by
Aquinas, is, interestingly enough, the aforementioned concern to
protect the idea of God's aseity.[46] This concern is given expression
in the following of Aquinas's remarks: "Every composition requires a compounder: for if there be composition, it results from

several things: and things that are several in themselves would not combine together unless they were united by a compounder. If then God were composite, He would have a compounder: for He could not compound Himself, since no thing is its own cause, for it would precede itself, which is impossible. Now the compounder is the efficient cause of the composite. Therefore God would have an efficient cause: and thus He would not be the first cause, which was proved above."[47] Aquinas's point, of course, is that the divine self-sufficiency is implicitly called into question by any talk of God's having a composite nature. A being constituted by a collection of distinct properties is presumably dependent on an extrinsic causal force sustaining the union of elements. In this view, then, saying that the divine nature is complex would imply that God could not have existed were it not for the existence of such an independent causal force.

This line of reasoning is certainly suspect. It has been suggested by one commentator that Aquinas's argument holds only if one assumes that complexity entails an amalgamation of parts on the order of a physical compound.[48] But is all complexity to be analyzed in these terms? True enough, a physical compound is dependent for its existence on an extrinsic causal force. Yet must we posit the existence of such an extrinsic force in an account of God's attributes? For instance, if it is meaningful to claim, as many have, that God's having a nature does not entail the existence of a realm of ontologically independent properties, that such properties may be seen in some sense as primitively resident in God, then why could it not be said that the causal force uniting God's elements is itself primitively constitutive of God's nature in some analogous way? Similar questions can be raised regarding the putative connection between the doctrine of divine simplicity and the doctrine of divine aseity, questions I cannot possibly resolve here. The point is simply that these kinds of considerations will have to be attended to by any theistic, natural-law proponent who wishes to advance a theory of axiological pluralism.

Let us assume for the sake of argument that the problems bound up with admitting complexity in God's nature could be resolved in a way permitting assent to a pluralistic value ontology that accounted for the existence of dilemmas. Such assent presumably would involve appropriating the following picture: Moral reality consists of a range of separate fundamental values that are both quantitatively and qualitatively incomparable. As a matter of principle, in other words, conflicts among these could not be adjudi-

cated. There are possible worlds, moreover, in which such conflicts occur. In these cases one or more of the basic values fail to
be realized. None of this is to suggest, of course, that God could
ever be faced with such a conflict. The reason is that all of the
fundamental values *per definitionem* are primitively constitutive
of God's nature; there is no possible world, that is, in which God
fails to express all of the value there is. With human beings, of
course, the situation is different. Circumstances can and do arise
in which persons, responding to the claim of some basic value,
must fall short of satisfying the acknowledged claim of some
other basic value. In order to prevent harm, for example, promises
must sometimes be broken. In order to save lives, lies must sometimes be told. And so forth. Genuinely binding moral requirements are inescapably violated in such instances. One might put
the point by saying that moral reality, according to this view, is
unambiguously prescriptive only in an ideal world, the possible
world in which conflicts between the basic values do not arise. Yet
this possible world is not the actual world that human beings find
themselves in. As a matter of fact, there exist certain conditions
under which the action guides of morality conflict in a way that is
beyond resolution.

There is certainly no question that the foregoing presents a consistently describable picture of morality. The issue is whether
such a picture can be incorporated by a natural-law theory that
ties moral requirement to the doctrine of providence in the manner of Aquinas. And, of course, this point brings us to the second
consideration that, as I have argued, serves to explain Aquinas's
theoretical aversion to dilemmas. To reiterate, the Thomistic theory of natural law compels us to interpret statements of moral obligation as implicit directives guiding rational creatures along the
path leading to self-realization. Given this rule of interpretation,
to suggest that morality is unequivocally prescriptive solely in an
ideal world is to suggest by implication that God's providential design is perfectly suited only to such an ideal world, that it contains no provisions for a range of circumstances in the actual
world. It is to suggest, furthermore, that God has created beings
whose capacity for fulfillment (in the provisional sense denoted
by moral achievement) is limited by the conditions of the actual
world and that such beings could flourish without qualification
only in a world that does not exist. Indeed, as I have mentioned,
these are serious theological consequences, an appreciation of
which seems to lie behind the following remarks of the contemporary, natural-law proponent Richard McCormick:

If it is truly moral values that are conflicted, our worldly situation is hopeless. We have no choice at times but to be unjust, unfaithful—to sin even amidst our best efforts. That is, of course, a strong Protestant tradition—but unabashedly Catholic as I am, I shall protest it here. And I think on good grounds. Ramsey complains that I cannot "conceive of conflicts of nonmoral goods or evils that are not resolvable by commensurate reason." That is correct. But why? Because I believe in a providential God in whose world the conflicts we do experience have a resolution. The difficulty in resolving these conflicts should not be identified with "no resolution" and the terribly black conclusion that our only choice is to choose *between* being either just or faithful. Proportionate reason will settle these claims between conflicted moral goods and suggest to us what is, indeed, just, faithful, and so on. Our struggle is to know what is truly proportionate.[49]

One need not agree with McCormick's normative conclusion that moral conflicts are to be resolved by *commensurate* or *proportionate* reason (whose principles have a decidedly utilitarian cast) in order to recognize the force of his metaethical supposition that any moral theory forging a connection between obligation and providential design is going to have problems accounting for the existence of genuine dilemmas.

Short of denying the connection between providence and moral requirement—a connection that affords the theological rationale of the moral life in Thomistic, natural-law theory—can the Catholic revisionist maintain the dilemmas thesis? Perhaps so. Yet it is difficult to see how the thesis could be preserved without admitting the existence of significant limitations on God's creative power. If part and parcel of creation's purpose is a human flourishing tied to the fulfillment of moral obligation, then any obstacle to that fulfillment would have to be regarded as an impediment to realization of that purpose. The finitude of the divine power would be manifest in its inability to create conditions that made self-realization possible in an unambiguous way. It is important to note just how serious a limitation this would be. A process theist, for instance, who admitted limitations on God's power in principle, could argue that situations of moral perplexity were occasions for the exercise of divine resourcefulness. In such an account, while solutions to moral problems might not be immediately obvious to the divine reason, God would be unsurpassable in his capacity for discovering solutions to these problems as they appear. According to the process theist, then, situations of moral perplexity could be construed as occasions for hope that God in his un-surpassable wisdom would discern ways in which human flour-ishing might be effected despite initial signs suggesting that this is impossible. Yet it should be clear that genuinely dilemmatic in-stances of perplexity could not conceivably be occasions for hope in this sense. To say that a conflict between moral requirements is irresolvable as a matter of principle is, of course, to dismiss any hope that a way out might be found. And inasmuch as human self-realization is bound up with fulfillment of moral requirement, this is to suggest that even God, who might be resourceful beyond compare, could not conceivably discover ways in which moral agents might flourish in such situations. The very intelligibility of hope in these circumstances depends on interpreting instances of moral perplexity as open to resolution at least in principle and not as genuine moral dilemmas (situations in which there is *no* unambiguous moral solution).

What the foregoing establishes, I think, for the natural-law theo-rist is a strong theological presumption against the possibility of genuine moral dilemmas. At this point, certainly, it would be pre-mature to suggest that the presumption is indefeasible. Whether a systematic connection between the dilemmas thesis and the ad-mission of significant constraints on the divine creative power provides the natural-law theorist with a decisive reason for deny-ing the thesis is a question that cannot be decided in isolation from other theoretical considerations. Much, if not all, will de-pend on the weightiness of the theological claims typically ad-vanced in support of interpreting moral perplexity in dilemmatic terms. These claims will be the subject of the final chapter. Before considering them, however, we must consider the position of theological voluntarism and the implications of that position for the questions we have been raising.

4

DIVINE COMMANDS AND
MORAL DILEMMAS

IN this chapter I consider the relationship between theological voluntarism, or what is often called the divine command theory of ethics, and the interpretation of moral perplexity. To repeat, theological voluntarism holds that moral requirement is constituted foundationally by divine volition or divine command. In this view, the fact that a is morally required (whether 'a' denotes a particular act or a general act type) signifies in some way that God wills or commands a, and it is precisely this latter fact of God's willing or commanding a, according to the theory, that constitutes the fact of a's being morally required. Similarly, the voluntarist contends, the fact that a is morally prohibited signifies in some fashion that God forbids a, and it is this very forbidding that grounds or establishes the prohibition in question. Under the heading of theological voluntarism I include both its metaethical version, which claims that the connection between moral requirement and divine will is one of meaning ('a is morally required' *means* 'God commands a') and its normative version, which holds that the connection is evaluative in nature ('God commands a' *justifies, warrants,* or *validates* 'a is morally required'). For present purposes the distinction between the two versions is unimportant, and, consequently, I shall not be concerned, for the most part, with assessing their comparative strengths and weaknesses. Neither shall I be concerned with the general question of theological voluntarism's adequacy as an ethical doctrine.[1] My purpose is simply to determine the limitations that theological voluntarism imposes on the construal of moral perplexity, granted the theory's adequacy for the sake of argument.

My ultimate contention will be that, given even the barest of rational constraints on the divine activity, it would be extraordinarily problematic for the theological voluntarist to admit the existence of genuine moral dilemmas. The reason for the difficulty is that such an admission, on the terms of the theory, would amount to accepting the fact of God's issuing conflicting commands and that issuing conflicting commands violates certain canons of rationality. Of course, this position raises a number of questions about the relation between reason and the issuing of imperatives, questions I shall attend to in some detail later on. In any event, the overall discussion will proceed as follows: First, I shall consider three analyses of moral conflict offered by three theological voluntarists. The first analysis allows for moral dilemmas, the second rules out certain kinds of dilemmas, and the third excludes dilemmas altogether. I shall try to show that each of these analyses begs important questions about what God can or cannot command and, more generally, about how the theological voluntarist must interpret moral perplexity. Next, I shall attend more directly to the issue of rational constraints on the divine activity. Drawing on a well-known account of the logic of imperatives, I shall propose that an individual who issues conflicting commands is irrational, though the irrationality in such a case differs from the irrationality of one who issues inconsistent assertions. Given this account of imperatival logic, I shall conclude provisionally that the theological voluntarist who assents to the moral dilemmas thesis commits herself to the position that God is irrational since a moral dilemma must be taken on the theory's own terms as signifying the existence of incompatible divine imperatives. Finally, I shall consider an alternative account of the logic of imperatives, one that allows for the *rational* issuance of conflicting commands. If such an alternative account turned out to be acceptable, then it might be argued that the voluntarist could allow for the existence of moral dilemmas without impugning the divine rationality. Over against such an argument, I shall try to show (a) that the alternative account is misleading and (b) that, even given the alternative account as a general theory of imperatival logic, accepting the moral dilemmas thesis will be problematic for the theological voluntarist. The result, I shall contend, is that the theological voluntarist has compelling, if not indefeasible, reasons for rejecting the moral dilemmas thesis.

A Causal Divine Command Theory

The first position to be discussed is one proposed by Philip Quinn.[2] In response to metaethical constructions of theological voluntarism, constructions he regards as deficient, Quinn wishes to formulate and defend what he calls a causal divine command theory, which "presents God as an agent bringing about moral obligations and prohibitions by means of his legislative activity."[3] According to this view, there is no *logical* connection between divine command and moral obligation, but there does exist a *necessary* and *sufficient* causal connection between the two. Put simply, God's commanding p (where 'p' represents some state of affairs picked out by an English declarative) is depicted by Quinn as both a necessary and a sufficient causal condition of p's being morally obligatory. Given this principle and given the appropriate definitions, two other principles follow. The first states that God's commanding not-p is a necessary and sufficient causal condition of p's being morally forbidden. The second states that God's not commanding not-p is a necessary and sufficient causal condition of p's being morally permitted. These principles make it possible to account for the fundamental deontic concepts in terms of divine commands without embracing controversial tenets about the *meanings* of those concepts. Thus, Quinn's theory escapes the sorts of criticisms often lodged against metaethical divine command theories.

The major philosophical question raised by Quinn is whether his theory can stand up to other kinds of objections. From our perspective the most important of these objections argues that the causal theory of divine command morality is unacceptable inasmuch as it leaves open the possibility of God's commanding both the performance and the nonperformance of an action. Of course, given the conditions of the theory, such a command would generate conflicting moral obligations, and because the theory contains no principles that allow for one obligation's overriding another, conflicts between obligations would have to be judged irresolvable. Furthermore, permitting the possibility of conflicting obligations violates a commonly accepted axiom of deontic logic stating that if p is obligatory then it is not the case that not-p is obligatory. According to the objection, then, since 'God commands p' and 'God commands not-p' are compossible propositions and since there cannot be conflicting obligations, the only conclusion is that the causal divine command theory must be rejected.[4]

One way of responding to this objection is to deny the compossibility of 'God commands p' and 'God commands not-p'. If these propositions cannot both be true, then on the terms of the theory conflicting obligations cannot arise. But Quinn refuses to take this approach. He argues that "no obvious considerations suffice to show that these propositions are not compossible" and that therefore the response "would appear to be counterintuitive and wildly ad hoc."[5] Rather, he suggests, the more fruitful strategy for the divine command theorist is to reject the deontic axiom that excludes the possibility of irresolvable conflicts between moral obligations. As Quinn sees it, there are three reasons for rejecting this axiom. First, a number of modern secular moral philosophers reject it, at least implicitly. Second, some systems of deontic logic do not include the axiom. Third, there are counterexamples to the axiom; that is, we can point to instances in which a particular action is both obligatory and forbidden. Granted that such reasons are sufficient to render the axiom problematic, Quinn argues, the objection under consideration is inconclusive. In other words, that the divine command theory allows for moral dilemmas is no mark against it since there is good reason to believe that such dilemmas do exist.

It should be clear that Quinn's response to the stated objection begs several crucial questions. In the first place, the fact that a number of secular philosophers reject the deontic axiom in question is not in itself a reason for the rejection. The issue turns on just what arguments these philosophers propose in support of their view. Furthermore, in Quinn's case it is important to be sure that the positions cited are compatible with the divine command theory of morality. The one philosophical position Quinn mentions explicitly is that of Joel Feinberg.[6] Quinn quotes the following passage from Feinberg's account: "Moreover, it is quite possible to be committed in two or more directions at the same time, so that, whatever you do, you will fail to discharge one of your duties. Clearly, in such a situation there is one best thing to do, one thing, which you ought to do, even though there are several incompatible things you have an obligation to do." Feinberg continues the analysis:

> It will not help to introduce the strange notion of a prima facie duty or obligation. If a student borrows a thousand dollars from his brother to help finance his graduate education and solemnly pledges to repay the money within ten years, he thereby puts himself under

an obligation—not an apparent obligation or a probable or a tendency to be an obligation—to pay the debt. And if during the course of the next decade unforeseen hardships occur—if, for example, he should prove more fecund or less resourceful than he had anticipated—and if his brother should suddenly strike it rich, then perhaps the best thing for him to do is to inform his brother, with all due reluctance, that he will not be able to discharge his obligation. I submit that he would quite naturally describe his failure as a *renunciation of an obligation.* We would not necessarily claim that he had done the wrong thing, nor need we necessarily blame him. After all, sometimes people *ought* to renounce their obligations.[7]

In the present context, the significant feature of this position is that, while it allows for the existence of conflicting obligations, it also suggests that such conflicts are morally resolvable. Doing the "one best thing" in conflict situations putatively involves the violation of a genuine obligation but calls neither for the attribution of blame nor, more importantly, for the *ascription of wrong.* Perhaps this position admits of philosophical defense granted certain normative or metaphysical principles. Yet how can we make sense of such a view from the perspective of a *divine command theory of morality?* Given that theory, what would it mean to say that an action violated an obligation and thus a divine command but at the same time involved no moral wrong? Presumably, the divine command theorist wants to account for rightness and wrongness in terms of God's commands. But if this is the case, then to say that performing a particular act in conflict situations involved no moral wrong is to imply the absence of a divine command forbidding the act; and this implication denies precisely what Quinn wants to affirm, namely, that in conflict situations there exists a divine command prohibiting any course of action that might be taken. The general point is that Quinn can hardly appeal to a position like Feinberg's in the course of responding to the stated objection since such a position is inconsistent with the divine command theory of ethics.

Similar claims can be made regarding Quinn's reference to systems of deontic logic that do not include the disputed axiom. Once again, he provides a single citation, in this instance to the work of Bas van Fraassen.[8] Van Fraassen rejects the axiom that excludes the possibility of dilemmas, quite simply because he believes that genuine moral dilemmas do exist. But on close inspection we discover that he holds this belief precisely because he adopts a version of the position I referred to earlier as *moral positivism*.[9] To repeat, in this view, moral codes, like legal codes, are systems embodying rules or principles *created* by human beings over time for the purpose of meeting the problems endemic to community life. Given the inability of human beings to conceive of every practical circumstance likely to call for adjudication, it is sometimes the case that these principles will conflict in the absence of explicitly created metarules designed to resolve such conflicts. For this reason, the positivist contends, moral dilemmas exist.[10] Now, as I argued earlier, *any* appeal to such a conception of morality will be problematic as a justification of the moral dilemmas thesis.[11] But whatever the score on that matter, it is difficult to see how Quinn in particular could make such an appeal. After all, for the divine command theorist moral obligations are the product of God's imperatives and not simply a function of human contrivance. At the very least, then, the proponent of a position such as Quinn's would need to reconstruct the positivist explanation of moral conflict by arguing that the rules *God* created through his commands are incomplete in the relevant sense and that *this* incompleteness accounts for morality's irresolvable conflicts. Needless to say, such an explanation of moral perplexity relies on a series of assumptions regarding limitations on God's powers of foresight, assumptions that are, at a minimum, theologically controversial. At any rate, Quinn's invocation of a deontic system like van Fraassen's cannot stand without further discussion since the philosophical foundations of such a system are incompatible with the divine command theory of morality.

What we are left with, then, is Quinn's own argument for rejecting the axiom in question. According to him, the divine command theorist has good reason for the rejection because there seem to be genuine counterexamples to the axiom: "Antigone's conflict of obligations, as Sophocles tells the story, is perhaps the clearest among them. Her moral dilemma is that she has an obligation to bury a dead brother and an obligation not to bury a dead brother, and there is no clear sense in which one of them overrides or removes the other. Sartre's example of the young man who must choose between joining the resistance and caring for the aged relative is a similar case."[12] Granted that such instances count as genuine moral dilemmas, the considered objection to the divine command theory loses its force.

The issue, naturally, is whether these cases are most plausibly interpreted as authentic moral dilemmas. And given our previous discussion, we should recognize that matters are not as clear as Quinn makes them out to be.[13] Could it not be argued, for instance, that Antigone found herself in *extraordinary* circumstances that rendered whatever she did unequivocally permissible, even though under *ordinary* conditions she would have been obliged to bury her brother and bound to obey the dictates of the state? Similarly, might it not be said that, while one typically ought to resist evil political forces and care for special relations, Sartre's young man is in an *extraordinary* situation and that in such situations whatever one does is unambiguously permissible from the moral point of view? Indeed, could it not be claimed that a range of our moral obligations are conditional in this sense and thus admit of suspension in special contexts? Of course, Quinn might counter with the argument that interpreting conflict situations in this manner fails to do justice to their phenomenological character (e.g., the agent's experience of guilt or our normative intuitions that the victims of the course taken have a just complaint). Yet as I tried to show earlier, such an argument begs important questions and simply fails to establish the dilemmatic structure of these kinds of cases.[14]

What this means for the present discussion is that Quinn cannot unproblematically affirm the existence of moral dilemmas as a way of defending the divine command theory against the stipulated charge. At best he can claim that the proper interpretation of conflict cases is unclear enough to render the status of the deontic axiom uncertain. Perhaps this uncertainty is all that is needed to defeat the considered objection. Nonetheless, it is important to emphasize what Quinn himself acknowledges, namely, that this defense of divine command morality can succeed only at the expense of admitting the possibility of conflicting divine imperatives. As noted already, Quinn does not regard such an admission as a liability. Indeed, he states that anyone who denies the compossibility of 'God commands p' and 'God commands not-p' "seems to be on weak ground."[15] But certainly the argument moves too quickly here. True enough, there is no *formal* contradiction in the complex proposition 'God commands p and God commands not-p'. Neither is there a formal contradiction in the proposition 'God asserts p and God asserts not-p'. Still, there might be good reasons for rejecting the second proposition, and if so, perhaps there are good reasons for rejecting the first. Of course, the reasons in either case would more than likely be theological in nature, the outcome of reflection on the doctrine of God. And such considerations do take us beyond the realm of formal logic *simpliciter*. Yet theological matters are no more substantive than any argument that could be advanced in support of the dilemmas thesis. The general point is that Quinn fails to take seriously enough the possibility that theological factors make the acceptance of conflicting divine commands much more problematic than any dismissal of the dilemmas thesis. If such factors do exist, then the appropriate response of the divine command theorist to the criticism in question is that instances of moral perplexity are always resolvable *de jure* no matter how difficult such resolution is *de facto* since God does not issue incompatible imperatives.[16]

Perplexity, Divine Reason, and Providence

The second position to be considered is that of Peter Geach, who believes that certain moral dilemmas must be exluded theoretically by any divine command doctrine linked to a particular conception of God.[17] Geach's general concern is to establish, in opposition to modern philosophical trends, that the content of one's moral code ought to be constrained by one's beliefs about God's commands. The claim is not that all moral knowledge depends on revelation. Indeed, Geach argues, such a view is "logically impossible" since some moral knowledge is requisite to determining the authenticity of revelation. The point is rather that we need knowledge of God to have knowledge of the principle 'Evil ought not to be done so that good may come' and that this principle actually follows from a certain understanding of God. If these claims are correct and if the relevant theological assertions are true, then a particular kind of dilemma could not arise, namely, one involving a conflict between the prohibition of an *act* falling under the description 'evil' and the principle of utility, which requires the maximization of beneficial *consequences*. Such a dilemma could not materialize because utility considerations would always have to give way to the prohibition.

Why is possessing a set of theological beliefs necessary for rational adherence to the principle of not doing evil that good may come? In answering this question, Geach considers what reasons might be given for refraining from an evil act such as adultery. He concludes that any rational justification would have to appeal to the agent's wants and that this sort of appeal will take one a long way in moral theory since "an action's being a good or bad thing for a human being to do is of itself a fact calculated to touch an agent's inclinations."[18] Of course, such an account of moral justification is controversial inasmuch as it rules out the Kantian alternative, but we need not address that issue here. What is important is that for Geach moral virtue or the *general* disposition to perform good acts and avoid evil ones is a desirable capacity for any agent. At the same time, Geach contends, the appeal to agent desire or inclination is insufficient to warrant a principle *absolutely* forbidding the doing of evil: "But somebody might very well admit that not only is there something bad about certain acts, but also it is desirable to become the sort of person who needs to act in the contrary way; and yet *not* admit that such acts are to be avoided in all circumstances at any price." In order to justify the absolute prohibition of evil acts, presumably one must resort to theological propositions.[19]

The argument from theological premises goes as follows: Given an interpretation of moral requirement in terms of divine command, we may still ask whether God, in the manner of a human legislator, has established general laws prohibiting certain classes of actions. At first glance it might seem that God has not done so, and this position would be grounded in an examination of the analogy between human and divine legislation. On the one hand, because of their finite capacities for anticipating contingencies, human beings need to construct laws that are general in nature. God, on the other hand, is free of such limitations and thus can command as specifically as the contingencies require. Yet the issue here turns, according to Geach, not on God's abilities but rather on the capacities of humans. Human beings can come to know that certain actions (lying, infanticide, etc.) are generally undesirable, but because of prejudice, limited knowledge of present relevant circumstance, and inability to predict consequences, individual human agents are incompetent to determine when exceptions are warranted in particular instances. It is improbable, according to Geach, that in these cases individuals receive singular divine commands. "So unless the rational knowledge that these practices are *generally undesirable* is itself a promulgation of the Divine law *absolutely forbidding* such practices, God has left most men without any promulgation of commands to them on these matters at all: which, on the theological premises I am assuming, is absurd."[20] But is it rational to obey such commands? Geach answers in the affirmative on the grounds that it is irrational to attempt to defy an almighty God.[21] Granted the soundness of the argument, then, believers in the sort of God depicted have rational justification for refusing to perform evil acts no matter how bad the consequences of such a refusal may be.

Two curious features of this argument should be noted at the outset. First, it is not entirely clear why Geach regards as unlikely the possibility of God's issuing *singular* imperatives in situations of conflict between a prohibitory rule and the principle of utility. Of course, given this possibility, the argument for absolute principles fails since it could now be claimed that God might command ad hoc the maximization of beneficial consequences at the expense of violating the prohibition. The point in such a claim need not be to suggest (if this is Geach's worry) anything like a mysterious experience of divine intervention on the part of the agent but only to affirm that a conscientious decision to override a prohibition on consequentialist grounds may in fact reflect the presence of divine command. Second, even excluding this possibility, the force of Geach's argument against consequentialism is questionable. For if it is reasonable to think that human beings will recognize the general undesirability of certain actions such as lying or infanticide, it is likewise reasonable to believe that they will recognize the general desirability of promoting good where feasible and that this latter recognition will give rise to a general rule of beneficence. Now one could just as easily argue that since human agents are for various reasons incompetent to judge when exceptions to *this* rule are warranted and since God has provided guidance on these matters, one must regard the rule as an absolute divine law. But taking this rule as an absolute means rejecting the principle of *never* doing evil that good may come, because whether evil ought to be done will now depend on which course of action will be judged to promote the most good overall.

Despite the inconclusiveness of Geach's account, let us assume its success for the sake of further discussion. As noted already, granted the argument's conclusions, dilemmas involving a conflict between a prohibitory rule and the principle of utility could not arise. Could other sorts of dilemmas materialize? For instance, might there be an irresolvable conflict between two of the absolute prohibitions? Consider the following line of argument advanced in the early part of this century by the Anglican moral theologian Kenneth Kirk:

> But the number of clearly-defined principles, of which it can be said that *in no conceivable circumstances* may the breach of them be

thought of as in any degree allowable, must at the best be very small. Indeed, if we followed out this line of thought to the end (as has rarely been done in Christian ethics), there could strictly speaking be only *one* such principle. For if any principle had an inalienable right to be observed, *every* other principle would have to be waived if the two came into conflict in a given case. It is only because such conflicts between primary moral principles are in most cases almost inconceivable that we are able to speak loosely of a *number* of laws whose breach would be "wrong in itself." But the conception *is* a loose one.[22]

Kirk's main point is that theoretically there could be no moral system (such as Geach's) containing a multiplicity of absolute or exceptionless principles because we could conceive of conditions under which any one of the principles would conflict with any one of the others. Thus, all but one of the principles would have to admit of exceptions. Of course, Kirk's position tacitly presupposes that genuine moral dilemmas cannot exist and thus that there *must* be a hierarchical ranking of all the principles of a moral code. This presupposition naturally calls for further discussion. But for present purposes the most important assumption of his argument is that, if a moral system contained an authentic set of *exceptionless* principles, irresolvable conflicts among these principles would be conceivable.

Needless to say, this conclusion is hardly surprising if the issue is conceivability in some formal logical sense. The truly interesting question, however, is whether factors of a more substantive nature render such conflicts impossible in a sense other than strict logical impossibility. Donagan has argued, for example, that "it is not hard to imagine systems of mores, each consisting of several nonequivalent exceptionless principles, which can be informally exhibited as admitting no conflict."[23] Take the case of a system containing absolute principles forbidding lying and the direct killing of innocent human beings. Given the meanings of the relevant moral species terms and given the conditions of the world, these two principles could not generate moral conflict. For one thing, each principle is compatible with itself. There are no circumstances in which refraining from killing one innocent can count as directly killing another. Similarly, there are no conditions under which not lying with respect to one matter can count as lying with respect to another. Neither can the two principles conflict with each other. Not lying can never count as direct killing, and not killing can never count as lying. Admittedly, there can be no question of strict *logical* impossibility here since we can imagine counterfactually a causal world in which, for instance, one could kill an innocent by refusing to lie. The idea is rather that a system of absolute prohibitions having a determinate content combined with a world having a determinate structure could make for conditions that preclude the possibility of moral conflict, where 'possibility' denotes something other than logical possibility.

It is difficult to know exactly how such considerations bear on Geach's position. What the foregoing discussion demonstrates is that a system of absolute prohibitions might be informally displayed as conflict-free by exhibiting the content of all its principles against the background of beliefs about the world's structure. Whether Geach's system admits of such display is impossible to tell since he does not specify exhaustively which principles with what content the system contains.

At the same time, Geach does argue that with one qualification irresolvable conflicts must be excluded a priori on theological grounds:

> "But suppose circumstances are such that observance of one Divine law, say the law against lying, involves breach of some other absolute Divine prohibition?"—If God is rational, he does not command the impossible; if God governs all events by his providence, he can see to it that circumstances in which a man is inculpably faced by a choice between forbidden acts do not occur. Of course such circumstances (with the clause 'and there is no way out' written into their description) are consistently describable; but God's providence could ensure that they do not in fact arise. Contrary to what unbelievers often say, belief in the existence of God does make a difference to what one expects to happen.[24]

There are a number of points to be made about this position.

First, Geach's appeal to providence in precluding dilemmas requires further elucidation. As we have seen, from premises such as those of Thomistic natural law one might appeal to the doctrine of providence in arguing for the theological impossibility of dilemmas. In that view, dilemmas are problematic precisely because the principles of moral obligation are part of the eternal law through which God providentially guides rational creatures toward the fulfillment of their proper ends. Given such premises, to assume that dilemmas existed would be to assume that God had created a world in which unequivocal human flourishing was sometimes impeded. The issue, of course, is whether Geach links moral requirement to providential teleology in a relevantly similar way. Based on what he says in other places, there is every reason to believe he does.[25] What is important to note for present purposes is that the providential argument for the exclusion of dilemmas requires theoretical premises above and beyond those internally related to theological voluntarism per se.

Second, what are we to make of Geach's qualification that belief in providence ensures the impossibility of dilemmas "inculpably faced?" The point seems to be that *culpably* faced dilemmas could arise, that an agent's misdeed could generate an irresolvable conflict between moral principles. One implication of this position relates to the scope of God's providence. If Geach is correct, then while there are decisive theological grounds for believing that providence unequivocally guides the morally pure toward the fulfillment of their proper ends, there is no theological justification for believing that such guidance is made available to human agents guilty of moral transgressions. What this view suggests is that God's providential scheme directs completely and unambiguously only in a morally ideal world. Needless to say, such a view is perfectly coherent, but the question is whether the position is adequate to a theology that depicts God as one whose purposes include the redemption of sinners. In the abstract it could seem wholly adequate to believe that "a man who acts dishonourably, say in his married life, may indeed find himself in a situation where he cannot help wronging either A or B."[26] Yet, is it theologically feasible to assert that God's providential direction is absent in such situations, that even the repentant adulterer, for example, cannot hope for unequivocal divine guidance regarding the proper course of action *post lapsum*?

Even granting that such questions might be resolved, there are more serious difficulties with Geach's acceptance of the view that dilemmas are possible after the fact of wrongdoing. For such dilemmas would imply not only the absence of a clear providential direction but also, it would seem, the existence of conflicting divine commands. Is such a position compatible with Geach's stipulation that God's rationality precludes his commanding the impossible? Much will depend, naturally, on how the notion of commanding the impossible is construed. Geach may mean to rule out nothing more than God's issuing of general commands that conflict in every possible world (e.g., 'Keep your promises' and 'Do not keep your promises'). If this is all Geach wants to say and if he is correct, then there is nothing about God's rationality that would exclude the possibility of genuine moral dilemmas *post lapsum*. For instance, God might issue imperatives prohibiting lying and the breaking of promises, imperatives that clearly do not conflict in every possible world. Still, we can imagine circumstances in which an agent culpably generated a conflict between them (e.g., by "wrongly" promising someone to lie), and one might insist that in such circumstances God technically did not command the impossible since, after all, he issued imperatives that were jointly obeyable in *some* possible world.

On further reflection, however, we can see that the matter is not as simple as the previous discussion makes it. Take the case of a human monarch formulating the rules of a legal code. The monarch takes pains to ensure that the set of rules devised are conflict-free at the level of principle (i.e., they do not conflict in every possible world) and tries to anticipate conditions under which the rules might conflict in the actual world. Where such conditions are anticipated, provisions are made by attaching *ceteris paribus* riders or exception clauses to the appropriate rules. What the monarch does not do, however, is construct a *system* of metarules designed to adjudicate conflict resulting from some violation of the first-order rules. As it happens, just such a conflict arises, the consequence of a subject's transgression. Admitting guilt, the subject appeals to the monarch for guidance. Should p be performed in conformity with law x or should p not be performed in conformity with law y? The monarch responds with the command that p be performed and not be performed, and she declares that this command is not irrational since the two laws from which the judgment is deduced are jointly obeyable in some possible world. Assuming that the monarch's words are to be taken literally, this response would be puzzling because there is no possible world in which a particular act is both performed and not performed by some agent, and therefore, if commanding the impossible is irrational, the monarch's command is irrational. To make this claim, of course, is not to deny that a conscientious subject could have avoided the predicament. The point is simply that this possibility of avoidance *simpliciter* does nothing to defend the monarch against the charge that her imperative is irrational *in this specific instance*.

This conclusion is especially significant for the theological voluntarist inasmuch as it shows that the rationality of particular commands cannot be guaranteed by deducing those commands from a system of general imperatives that are conflict-free in some possible world. Thus, in response to the charge that moral dilemmas (whether culpably generated or not) impugn God's rationality, it is insufficient to argue simply that God has issued a set of *general* commands that do not conflict in every possible world. The question is whether God issues additionally *particular* commands that are incompatible under any conceivable circumstance. Now it might be suggested that God commands *only* generally and that, although we might deduce conflicting moral requirements from those general commands in certain contexts, God does not issue particular commands in those contexts. Yet this suggestion is problematic on at least two counts. In the first place, if we assume God's foreknowledge, we must assume that he will foresee every instance of conflict among his general commands in the actual world. Given this capacity of foresight and given *ex hypothesi* the absolute status of his general commands, we can only conclude that he issues conflicting commands in cases of irresolvable conflict. To assume otherwise would be to assume, more than likely, that God failed to understand the rules of inference by which particular imperatives are deduced from general mandates. But, in the second place, even if we conceded that God lacked the requisite foreknowledge, difficulties remain with the suggestion under consideration. Whatever the limitations on God's foresight, we could still presume that God would know of conflicts between his general commands *when they materialized.* And if he allows the implications of those general commands to stand in conflict cases, then the conclusion is inescapable that he issues incompatible commands in such cases. The only way to avoid this consequence without rejecting the existence of dilemmas and without sacrificing God's rationality is to hold that God issues a number of general commands that are compatible in some possible world, that these general commands conflict in the actual world, and that God never knows when they conflict. Once again, there is no strictly logical incoherence in such a view. Nevertheless, it is difficult to see just what sense can be made of a *providential* God who is so limited in his knowledge of historical events.

However that matter is resolved, we can say the following: The existence of moral dilemmas, whether culpably or inculpably originated, will be unacceptable theoretically to any position holding (a) that moral requirement is constituted by divine command, (b) that God is cognizant of the situations of human agents in the actual world, (c) that he is rational, and (d) that his rationality precludes his issuing incompatible commands. Thus, Geach is premature in his supposition that genuine moral dilemmas are possible after the fact of some wrongdoing. Of course, a crucial element in this general theological argument against dilemmas is the premise that a rational God cannot command the impossible. Geach himself, while accepting its truth, does not defend the premise, which, as we shall see later on, is more controversial than might be thought at first. Ultimately, I shall try to show that, despite possible objections, adoption of this premise is reasonable and that, consequently, the theological voluntarist has considerable justification for refusing to interpret moral perplexity in dilemmatic terms.

Creation, Redemption, and Moral Conflict

The third position to be analyzed is that proposed by the systematic theologian Emil Brunner.[27] According to Brunner, all moral requirement has its source in God's supreme commandment that the neighbor be loved. Given the proper account of how this commandment relates to the orders of creation and the realm of redemption, one can proceed to explain theologically the *appearance* of moral dilemmas. At the same time, Brunner contends, these dilemmas are merely apparent. Theological considerations, in his view, force us to conclude that there can be no irresolvable conflicts in the moral life. In order to understand precisely how Brunner comes to these judgments, it is necessary to attend to his theological scheme in somewhat greater detail.[28]

In Brunner's account, although every moral requirement is an instantiation of the command to love the neighbor, God does not simply issue this command with the expectation that human agents will interpret its content for specific cases. On the contrary, God himself provides the interpretations, so to speak, by issuing fully determinate commands to particular persons in singular contexts. These determinate commands cannot be anticipated through deduction from some abstract principle. Nevertheless, certain general theological considerations afford important reference points for the agent's proper hearing of the particular injunctions, considerations related to the economy of divine creation and redemption. More particularly, since God has revealed himself as both creator and redeemer of the world and since human beings are called on to imitate God, the key to understanding what God commands in specific situations is given in the divine creative and redemptive activities.

On the one hand, as creator, God affirms the world, including the so-called orders of creation (sexual differentiation, family, economics, culture, state, and law), through which human social life is made possible. Accordingly, the command of the creator requires a similar affirmation on the part of humans, and this means that an agent is obliged to fulfill the duties that attach to the stations she occupies in the various created ordinances. Thus, parents qua parents have certain obligations to their children, employers qua employers have certain obligations to their employees, citizens qua citizens have certain obligations to the state, and so forth. These duties are impersonal in character. Indeed, given the nature of the world, their fulfillment sometimes requires harsh, coercive measures, as evidenced, for instance, in a judge's assignment of criminal penalties. Still, from the perspective of creation, discharging these role-specific duties is essential to loving the neighbor since the orders contribute indispensably to the world's preservation. As redeemer, on the other hand, God wills the transformation of the world, which, because of sin, is not all that it ought to be. The command of the redeemer, then, enjoins humans to reform the world in various ways. Preeminently, this injunction calls on the agent to mitigate the harsh effects of the created orders by dealing with individuals in personal, noncoercive ways. From the perspective of redemption, the forging of such personal, noncoercive relationships is precisely what loving the neighbor means.

Given this theological account, one might identify at least two possible sources of moral dilemmas: (1) conflicts between the requirements of creation and the requirements of redemption and (2) conflicts among the various role-specific duties constitutive of the created orders themselves. An example of the first would be the case of a political authority whose role in the political order obliges her to employ coercive means (the waging of war, the punishment of criminals, etc.), an obligation clashing with the nonresistant requirements of redemption as manifested in the Sermon on the Mount. An instance of the second would be the aforementioned case of Sartre's young man who, as a participant in the familial order, also has the duty to defend his country. The question before us, of course, is whether these and similar conflicts are beyond the possibility of moral resolution.

As noted earlier, Brunner's answer is that there are no such insoluble conflicts. Take the case of the political authority whose official responsibility requires the use of coercive measures. While the authority may have the impression that she is faced with a genuine moral dilemma resulting from the incompatible requirements of creation and redemption, "this impression of being involved in a tragic conflict simply arises from the detachment which belongs to any process of abstract thought."[29] More precisely, the mistaken belief has its source in a failure to appreciate the proper scopes of the requirements in question. "The Divine Command requires us to break through the harshness and impersonality of the official order, so far as this is at all possible, without destroying the order itself."[30] Were authorities to dispense with coercive means altogether, the political order could not perform its divinely established function of preserving the conditions necessary for social life. Still, that order is not an autonomous realm whose inhabitants are emancipated from the requirements of redemption. In their extraofficial, personal lives, political functionaries are called on to express the principles of the Sermon on the Mount. But even in contexts covered by the duties of office the requirements of redemption play a role. If a judge must assign criminal penalties according to law, she is also free to attend personally to the criminal's needs by seeing to it, for instance, that the family of the condemned is provided for. Brunner's general point is that the demands of creation and redemption are wholly reconcilable in the unity of an individual life. None of this is to deny, however, the burden involved in deciding the precise limits of creation and redemption in a given situation:

> In reality, however, neither the claims of the "orders" nor the Divine Command of the Sermon on the Mount are "law" in the sense that they relieve me of the responsibility of making my own decision. Rather it is the very fact that in each situation it is necessary to stand between the official order and the Sermon on the Mount which constitutes the necessary space, which gives free scope for decision.
>
> At all times I must myself decide what are the respective claims upon me of love and of the order, at this particular moment; or rather, it would be better to say, not what "love" and the "order" say I ought to do, but what kind of service the command to love my neighbor requires from me both in my "official" capacity and in my personal and direct relation with my brother. Further; it is not *I*

who have to decide this, but the point is that, in faith, in this situation in which I have to decide, I am to hear the concrete Command of *God* Himself.[31]

The sense of isolation that may accompany decision making in cases of conflict between the requirements of creation and redemption cannot be taken as a sign that in such cases no unequivocal divine command is to be heard.

Brunner makes similar claims regarding possible dilemmas rooted in putative conflicts among the duties attached to stations in the order of creation itself.[32] According to him, the very notion of a conflict between authentic duties rests on a mistaken, "legalistic" picture of what an authentic duty is. Strictly speaking, *general* duties of the sort represented in legal formulations "do not exist." Indeed, talking about such general duties in particular contexts is merely a convenient way of organizing morally relevant considerations in the agent's determination of what her *actual* duty is:

> In a situation of this kind I must proceed as follows: with the help of my "schedule of duties" and in the light of the various claims which clamour for my attention and constantly overlap—all of them apparently justifiable and necessary—in the spirit of faith (and this means, too, in view of the actual situation) I must listen to the Divine Command in order that I may be able to do what I am really bidden to do, that is, my real duty.
>
> Then, however, I shall find that *one* thing and *one only* is really commanded, is really my duty, and that the "conflict of duties" is only apparent, and does not really exist at all.[33]

Once again, Brunner's point is not to deny the burden of decision making in such situations. Indeed, he goes so far as to suggest that the painful experience of being confronted with an *apparent* conflict of duties is a necessary condition of perceiving the divine command that resolves the matter. At the same time, he contends, once the divine imperative has been heard and the appropriate action has been taken, there can be no room for the agent's tragic regret, since it can never be tragic to obey the command of God.[34]

Thus, situations in which an agent commits some moral wrong no matter what the course taken would appear to be ruled out. Yet other remarks of Brunner's cloud the matter theoretically. It is suggested, for instance, that fulfilling the harsh requirements of the created order "might be called 'tragic' were it not for the fact that the Christian knows that in so doing he is bearing a share of his own guilt, and is thus cooperating with God in His gracious work of preservation."[35] What can "guilt" mean here? How can an agent bear guilt in obeying the divine command? The clearest explanation is given in Brunner's discussion of the *calling*. According to this account, discharging the duties of one's calling may be harsh. Indeed, this harshness reveals the sinfulness of the world. Nonetheless, the believer can engage in such activity with a "good conscience" since her life is "'covered' by forgiveness." In these cases, "God takes over all responsibility for our action in the world which in itself is sinful, if we, on our part, will only do here and now that which the present situation demands from one who loves God and his neighbour."[36] Now it is difficult to see how such an explanation could be reconciled with the rudiments of Brunner's theory. For if an agent in certain situations can act in good conscience only because she will be forgiven for what is done, then this suggests that in such situations some wrong is done that requires forgivenesss. But on the terms of Brunner's theological voluntarism this wrong could only denote the disobedience of a divine command. And given this analysis, one would have to conclude that God issued conflicting commands under the conditions depicted. Such a conclusion obviously collides with Brunner's stipulation that in circumstances of apparent conflict between genuine duties only one course of action is actually enjoined.

In sum, a system such as Brunner's cannot appeal to the fact of divine forgiveness as a way of demonstrating that moral dilemmas do not exist since the presence of conditions rendering forgiveness appropriate implies that in the relevant contexts a moral wrong is done even in the performance of what is morally required. On what other grounds, then, might Brunner exclude the possibility of dilemmas? As far as I can tell, he provides no explicit anti-dilemmas argument beyond the vague appeal to forgiveness heretofore noted. But a reasonable presumption is that he regards dilemmas as impossibilities precisely because they would entail the existence of incompatible divine commands and because such commands would jeopardize the notion of a unitary God with coherent purposes. It is important not to confuse this rationale with a second one that certain of Brunner's remarks might appear to suggest, namely, that incompatible divine commands and thus moral dilemmas are inconceivable because all of God's particular commands are instantiations of his one, internally conflict-free, general command to love the neighbor.[37] This second justification would be inconclusive since it is altogether possible that a general imperative conjoined with certain states of affairs will generate incompatible singular requirements. Thus, the rule that all members of class a precede all members of class b and all members of class b precede all members of class c is internally conflict-free; still, conflicts will arise from the rule in any world that contains members of b and individual objects having dual membership in both a and c. To rule out such conflicts one would need to guarantee on independent grounds either that there are no members of b or that dual membership in a and c does not exist. Analogously, it is conceivable that the general imperative to love the neighbor, though internally consistent, will have conflicting instantiations in the actual world. For instance, if love required both veracity and nonmaleficence without qualification, then the adulterer who knew that his wife would suffer immeasurably from learning the truth would be faced with a dilemma. Once again, to rule out this sort of conflict one needs an independent argument. The premises of such an argument could be supplied by belief in a God whose rationality precludes his issuing incompatible commands at any level.

For our purposes the important question is whether the idea of a practically rational God really does sustain the theological voluntarist's rejection of dilemmas. What sort of account can be advanced in support of the claim that the divine practical reason prevents God from issuing incompatible commands? To resolve this question it is necessary to consider more generally the relationship between rational volition and the logic of imperatives.

Imperatives, Logic, and Consistency

The general question to be raised in this section is whether, and if so, in what sense, the notion of consistency may be applied to imperatives. Given the supposition that it is a virtue of rational beings to avoid inconsistency, an answer to this question is especially important. For if imperatives can be inconsistent with one another and if God is a rational being, then we would have to conclude that there are certain limitations on what he will command. And granted the terms of theological voluntarism along with assumptions about God's knowing the particular situations of agents in the actual world, this conclusion would mean that moral dilemmas could not exist inasmuch as they reflected the existence of inconsistent divine imperatives.

As is well known, R. M. Hare has argued that certain features of the logic of imperatives may be unearthed by noting similarities and contrasts between imperative and indicative sentences.[38] According to Hare, one begins with the fact that an imperative may have the same content as an indicative. Thus, 'You are going to shut the door' and 'Shut the door' both refer to the same state of affairs, that is, your shutting the door in the near future. The distinction between the sentences is that they do different things with this content. The point can be illustrated schematically. In the present case the two sentences have the content:

Your shutting the door in the immediate future.

While displaying content, this phrase fails to render a sentence that is semantically complete since it does not depict what is being done with the content. For all we know, the sentence of which the phrase is a part may be either indicative or imperative. Consequently, we require a schematic device that will display the sentence's mood as well as its content:

Your shutting the door in the immediate future, please.
(Imperative)
Your shutting the door in the immediate future, yes. (Indicative)

Following Hare we may refer to the part of the sentence shared by the two versions as the *phrastic* (from a Greek word meaning 'to point out or indicate') and the part of the sentence that differentiates the mood of the two versions as the *tropic* (from the Greek word for 'mood').

Because both imperatives and indicatives have a common phrastic component, Hare claims, they are subject to common semantic and logical maladies associated with the phrastic elements of sentences. For instance, since the phrastics of imperatives and indicatives contain signifying terms and phrases, he argues, both imperatives and indicatives suffer from the same sort of reference failure illustrated in the sentences 'The present king of France is bald' and 'Bow to the present king of France'. The issue before us is whether self-contradiction is just such a phrastic malady suffered by imperatives as well as indicatives.

One might think that this question requires a positive answer simply because the conditions that make for self-contradiction are conditions associated with sentence phrastics and because phrastics fulfilling these conditions can be rendered with either indicative or imperative tropics:

There is another malady to which imperatives, like indicatives, are liable, owing to the presence of logical connectives in the phrastics of both of them. This is called in the case of indicatives, self-contradiction; and the term is equally applicable to imperatives. Commands as well as statements can contradict one another. Even if this were not a normal way of speaking, we might well adopt it; for the feature to which it draws attention in commands is identical with that which is normally called contradiction. Consider the following example, taken from Lord Cunningham's autobiography. The admiral and the captain of a cruiser which is his flagship shout almost simultaneously to the helmsman in order to avoid a collision, one "Hard 'a port" and the other "Hard 'a starboard". Lord Cunningham refers to these two orders as "contrary"; and so they are, in the proper Aristotelian sense. It follows that the two orders contradict one another in the sense that the conjunction of them is self-contradictory; the relation between them is the same as that between two predictions 'You are going to turn hard 'a port' and 'You are going to turn hard 'a starboard'. Some orders can, of course, be contradictory without being contrary; the simple contradictory of 'Shut the door' is 'Do not shut the door'.[39]

What Hare seems to be arguing in this passage is that since there can be contradiction between indicatives and since the logical properties that generate the contradictions are properties of sentence phrastics (e.g., 'Your shutting the door, yes' and 'Your not shutting the door, yes'), imperatives must also admit of self-contradiction inasmuch as they too can contain contradictory phrastics (e.g., 'Your shutting the door, please' and 'Your not shutting the door, please'). But the problem with this line of argument resides in its mistaken assumption that both the necessary *and sufficient* conditions for generating self-contradiction are conditions related to phrastic properties. Indeed, if the conditions sufficient for generating self-contradiction were related to sentence phrastics *simpliciter*, then phrastics qua phrastics could contradict one another, a consequent that careful consideration shows to be false.[40] For example, 'Your shutting the door' and 'Your not shutting the door' are phrastics that might be taken as contradictories. Yet when paired with different tropics no contradiction arises. 'Your not shutting the door, yes' is perfectly consistent with 'Your shutting the door, please.' What this example would seem to demonstrate is that the logical properties of phrastics afford at best necessary but not sufficient conditions for generating

contradictions. If so, then the fact that phrastic pairs are contradictory in indicative contexts does not prove that the same phrastics contradict each other in imperative contexts.

But why would anyone want to deny that imperatives can contradict each other while holding that self-contradiction is possible
among indicatives? After all, one can offer what seems to be a satisfactory definition of inconsistent imperatives, namely, that two
imperatives are inconsistent if it is logically impossible for both
to be obeyed. Furthermore, one can explain apparently how imperatives can be inconsistent by appealing to their connection
with indicatives.[41] All imperatives can be recast in the form 'Let it
be the case that' followed by an indicative sentence. Indeed, we
must be able to formulate imperatives in this way if it is possible
to determine what state of affairs fulfills the requirements of commands. Now, if the indicative components of two separate imperatives express contradictory states of affairs ('Let it be the case that
x' and 'Let it be the case that not-x'), what could be more natural
than to suggest that this pair of commands contradicted each
other?

What the foregoing line of reasoning overlooks are crucial differences between the way the notion of contradiction is explicated
for indicatives or propositions and anything that might be said
about inconsistency among imperatives. Two indicative sentences
are said to be contradictory if it is logically impossible for one to
be true without the other's being false, and vice versa. By definition, then, both members of a contradictory pair of indicatives
cannot be true. Naturally, to make this claim is not to deny that,
given paucity of evidence and so on, one might be equally justified
in holding either of two contradictory beliefs. For instance, one
might have equally compelling reasons for believing that Robert
was in Chicago last week or that he was not in Chicago last week.
Nonetheless, one must assume that the propositions forming the
contents of the beliefs cannot both be true. But if this is the sort of
implication carried by the notion of contradiction generally, it is
hard to see how we can speak of contradictory imperatives in any
straightforward sense of the term. For even in cases where two imperatives collectively enjoin contradictory states of affairs, the
question of truth value cannot arise since imperatives can be neither true nor false. Neither does it seem possible to construct a
truth-value analogue suitable to account for imperative contradiction. Consider the following: Robert is a member of two organizations, X and Y. X requires that its members perform acts of a cer-

tain type, and Y requires that its members refrain from acts of the same type. Let us assume that although occasions to perform or refrain from the relevant act hardly ever arise, Robert is faced with one such occasion. Undoubtedly, Robert is in a quandary; an imperative of one of the organizations will have to be disobeyed. Yet he could hardly claim in defense of his inevitable violation that the quandary per se showed that one of the strictures had to be false. Imperatives, as we have said, are without truth value. Still, it might be argued, though imperatives can neither be true nor false, they can be operative or inoperative, and here is the relevant analogue to truth value. Could Robert claim that the quandary rendered either stricture inoperative? It is difficult to see how he could, assuming that the imperatives were issued in accordance with the administrative canons of both organizations. In other words, both imperatives can remain in operation even though collectively they enjoin contradictory states of affairs. The point is that, even if we could construct an analogue to truth for imperatives, it does not appear that the analogue will serve to account for contradiction among imperatives in a sense relevantly similar to indicative contradiction.

There is an important corollary to all of this. In the case of indicatives the reason for avoiding inconsistency is relatively clear. To assert or believe inconsistent things is objectionable because doing so necessarily involves asserting or believing something that is false.[42] Given the fact that imperative inconsistency cannot be explicated in terms of truth, *this* reason for avoiding inconsistency is not available in the case of commands. As a result, if the consistency paradigm and the justification for avoiding inconsistency are set by what it means for indicatives to contradict one another (both members of an inconsistent pair cannot be true), then it is not enough to say that all sets of imperatives enjoining contradictory states of affairs are themselves inconsistent or that the reason for avoiding such imperatives is as clear as the reason for avoiding inconsistent indicatives.

From this one might be tempted to conclude that the notions of consistency and inconsistency should not be applied to imperatives at all. Embracing such a conclusion, however, would be a serious matter indeed. For if imperatives could not be inconsistent with one another, then there could be no general logic of imperatives. For example, there could be no question of deducing singular imperatives ('Do *this* act') from general mandates ('Do acts of this type'). There could be no deduction of this sort since a necessary condition of deductive relations is to be able to say that the denial of a conclusion is inconsistent with certain premises held fast. Yet if there can be no inconsistency among imperatives, any imperative conclusion will be logically compatible with any set of imperative premises. Given such a state of affairs, it would be impossible, for example, to speak of genuine deductive reasoning in legal contexts because any singular judgment would be compatible with any general law. The consequences for theology would be just as severe. For instance, God's general command to love one's neighbor would be vacuous since it would be compatible with *any* particular injunction. Other examples could be cited. The main point is that denying the possibility of inconsistency among imperatives would wreak havoc on our ordinary conceptions of practical reasoning. It is crucial, therefore, to provide *some* account of imperative inconsistency without blunting important distinctions between indicatives and imperatives.

The basis for such an account is afforded by what von Wright has called the "will-theory of norms."[43] In this general view, a key to understanding the logic of commands is the recognition that they are expressions of some agent's will. Why does an agent command that an act be performed or that it not be performed? Setting aside cases in which the command is itself the response to a prior order, the will-theory of norms provides the following answer:

> The giver of the order *wants* the result of the prescribed act to *happen*. Therefore he *wants* the subject of the prescription *to do* the act in question, i.e. to make the wanted change happen. By commanding the subject he may *make him* do the act. Therefore he gives the order. The normative act is a *means* to the norm-authority's *ends*. It is a means to making the norm-subject do something, and this in turn is a means to making a certain thing happen. If we wish to say, as we are, I think, free to do, that wanting to attain an end entails wanting to use the means which are actually used for the sake of attaining this end, then we may say that the norm authority *wants to command* the norm-subject and that he *wants to make* the subject *do* the prescribed act.[44]

The point is not to suggest that every utterance having imperatival form is issued *de facto* for a reason citing the issuer's wants. Indeed, it is entirely conceivable that such utterances will be issued for no reason at all. Nonetheless, this sort of activity, as von Wright puts it, would be "conceptually alien" to the practice of commanding. "One could perhaps call it a 'misuse' or a 'parasitic use' of this institution."[45]

Given this normative connection between commands and the will to make agents perform or refrain from performing certain acts, one can provide a general account of inconsistency among imperatives without denying the possibility of two or more imperatives remaining in operation while collectively enjoining contradictory states of affairs. The account rests on the distinction between imperatives issued by a single norm-authority and those issued by separate norm-authorities. Put simply, imperatives that can be obeyed in no possible world may be said to be inconsistent if their source is a single norm-authority but not if individually they have different norm-authorities.

This position is buttressed by the following set of reflections.[46] Though it is impossible to *make* an agent do and refrain from doing the same thing (since it is logically impossible for an agent to do something and refrain from doing the same thing), it is altogether possible for one person to *try* to make the agent do the thing and for another person to *try* to make the agent refrain from doing the same thing. But if this possibility exists, why is it not possible for *one person* to *try* to make an agent perform and not perform an act? Imagine the case of a parent who claims that he is trying to get his child both to perform p and not to perform p. The parent backs up his attempt with sanctions and implements the sanctions when the child (inevitably) fails. Even if we allowed that a concept of *trying* could be constructed to describe the parent's activity, we would still regard the behavior as purposeless, irrational, or insane. Or take the case of two individuals, A and B, walking along together. In one hand A holds a cane, and in the other, a rope, which is tied around B. At one point, A prods B with the cane in order to move him in a particular direction and simultaneously holds B back with the rope. The case is analogous to one where an individual pushes and pulls an object with different hands in different directions at the same time. If in this last instance the individual claimed that the point was to test which was the stronger hand, his activity would become intelligible. If, on the other hand, he claimed both that he wanted to move the object in one direction and that he wanted to move it in the opposite direction, "we should think that he was joking with us or was mad."[47] Our response would be similar if A claimed both that he wanted B to move in a particular direction and that he did not want B to move in that direction.

In such cases we are confounded by what appears to be an incoherence in the agent's will. We would not be troubled similarly
were the incompatibility of purpose a function óf two individuals
willing in opposite directions. And this insight, given the connection between command and will, forms the basis for saying that
imperatives obeyable in no possible world are inconsistent if their
source is a single norm-authority but not if the individual imperatives have different norm-authorities. When commands have different norm-authorities and together enjoin contradictory states
of affairs, there is no need to admit to an incoherence in the will of
a commander. When commands enjoining contradictory states of
affairs have a single norm-authority, however, we are compelled
to acknowledge such an incoherence. In this view, then, inconsistent imperatives "can be said to reflect an inconsistency (irrationality) in the will of a norm-authority. One and the same will
cannot 'rationally' aim at incompatible objects. But one will may
perfectly well 'rationally' want an object which is incompatible
with the object of another 'rational' will."[48] Such a characterization suggests a rationale for avoiding inconsistency that does not
blunt important differences between indicatives and imperatives.
If the reason for avoiding inconsistent beliefs or assertions is to
avoid believing or asserting false things, the reason for avoiding
inconsistent imperatives is that the point of commanding is to
achieve certain ends and issuing inconsistent commands involves
willing ends that knowingly cannot be satisfied.

Of course, this account of imperatival consistency carries important implications for our general question of the relation between theological voluntarism and moral perplexity. For if a rational will "cannot aim at incompatible objects" and if such an
aim is indeed constitutive of a single norm-authority imperatives
that command contradictory states of affairs, then a rational will
cannot issue such commands. But if a rational will is so constrained and if God is practically rational, then he will not issue
commands that can be obeyed in no possible world. Thus, granted
the terms of theological voluntarism along with certain presuppositions about God's knowing the affairs of human agents in the
actual world, we would have to conclude that genuine moral dilemmas could not exist. Now it would seem reasonable to suggest
that this general position captures certain intuitions we have
about the rationality of commands. Yet as it turns out, the argument just outlined rests on an assumption that is controversial
even if it appears unobjectionable. The assumption is that it is al-

ways irrational for a commander to issue sets of imperatives collectively enjoining contradictory states of affairs because doing so involves an incoherence in the will of the commander. As noted already, this assumption is a central feature of the will-theory of norms. In an alternative account of imperatival consistency and rationality, however, the close connection between practical reason and the refusal to issue incompatible commands is called into question. It is essential, therefore, to consider this alternative account in some detail.

Imperatives, Reason, and Pragmatics

The alternative view of imperatives, articulated by Bernard Williams, takes as its point of departure the comparison between imperatives and indicatives in the matter of consistency.[49] While we may grant, according to Williams, that imperatives can be inconsistent with one another and may define that relation as holding between any two imperatives that cannot jointly be obeyed, "the significance of consistency and inconsistency with respect to imperatives stands on a radically different footing from their significance with respect to indicatives."[50] For one thing, as we have already noted, consistency and inconsistency for indicatives are explicated in terms of truth value, and there is no entirely symmetrical way of rendering imperatival consistency and inconsistency. Yet as Williams sees it, there is another related assymetry between indicatives and imperatives, one that may be depicted as follows.

Imagine two sets of circumstances. In the first, speakers A and B assert the statements p and not-p, respectively. In the second, A and B issue, respectively, the commands 'do x' and 'do not do x' to the same agent. In the first case, up to the point where the inconsistency becomes apparent, A and B can both think they have the best possible reasons for asserting what they do in the sense that they can both think they have the best possible reasons for believing their respective assertions to be true. But once the inconsistency is brought to light we are forced to admit that A and B cannot both have the best possible reasons for their assertions since both of those assertions cannot be true. The point, apparently, is not to deny that inconsistent beliefs, given paucity of evidence and so on, may be equally reasonable to hold, but only to affirm that "ultimately" the reasons supporting one of the beliefs must be deficient simply because one of the beliefs must be false. In the case of inconsistent commands, however, the situation is differ-ent. There A and B each could have the best possible reasons for issuing the respective commands, even though the commands are inconsistent, since what counts as a good reason in such contexts has to do with the aims and desires of the commander. In other words, the fact that the commands are inconsistent does not in itself show that the reasons for issuing either are "ultimately" de-ficient. "Put extremely crudely, the point comes to this: when two people come out with inconsistent assertions, there must be some-thing wrong; when two people come out with inconsistent im-peratives, there need be nothing wrong—that is just how things have worked out."[51]

Of course, this account, as it has been elaborated thus far, poses no special difficulty for the analysis of imperatival logic afforded by the will-theory of norms since the example Williams describes involves incompatible imperatives *with different sources*. Sure enough, a proponent of the will-theory might argue, there need be nothing wrong, in Williams's sense of the terms, when one indi-vidual has issued a command that turns out not to be jointly obeyable with a command issued by some other individual. Yet such commands issued knowingly *by a single individual* are an entirely different matter. Certainly it might be said, there is some-thing rationally deficient about the latter state of affairs even if there is no problem with the former. And thus it might be claimed, there is an analogy between indicative and imperative consistency that ought to be noted. Just as a rational individual will avoid making assertions known to be inconsistent, so will such an indi-vidual refrain from issuing commands both of which, it is known, cannot be obeyed.

Williams's response to this line of reasoning is to argue that for the purposes of the issue at hand there is no significant difference between incompatible imperatives having a single source and in-compatible imperatives with divergent sources. Though, he con-cedes, a commander who frequently issues inconsistent com-mands is unlikely to serve much purpose and though, he admits, it is questionable whether a commander who systematically is-sues such commands is *genuinely* commanding, still, Williams claims, the rationality of issuing such commands in any particu-lar instance is to be assessed differently from the rationality of is-suing inconsistent assertions:

> A man may have the best possible reasons for issuing each of two
> inconsistent imperatives to an agent. He will probably refrain from

doing so, and opt for one rather than the other, or for some third imperative. But his recognition of the fact that he cannot for any good purpose come out with both does not in itself have any effect of making him reconsider the reasons he had for wanting to utter them in the first place. It is like any other practical choice, where one can't have everything; and the question of whether a man should school himself not to be disposed to issue such imperatives is rather like the question of whether a man should school himself not to have conflicting desires—or at least, it would be if it were a real question, and not a very artificial one. His problem is just that he has aims of obedience-securing which conflict; to what extent he feels obliged to sort these out is an application of the general question of to what extent he feels obliged to sort out conflicting aims. A man, however, who has a disposition to make inconsistent assertions just cannot, once he has recognized the situation, continue to think (if he did so before) that he has the best possible reasons for making both assertions as unqualified and sincere assertions; he has discovered that he has inconsistent beliefs, and the reasons for each of two inconsistent beliefs cannot in the end be the best possible reasons.[52]

But if there exist cases in which there are equally good reasons for issuing *each* of two incompatible imperatives, does this mean that it is rational to issue *both* in such cases? Not necessarily. All in all, there might be, and there probably will be, good reason not to do so in a particular instance. For example, if one's purpose in issuing the commands is to secure obedience, then joint issuance would be irrational. Such a rationale, of course, is *pragmatic* in character. Yet once one agrees that these matters are to be settled on pragmatic grounds, one has to raise the question whether some end might not be served in issuing both of two imperatives that cannot be obeyed jointly. According to Williams, the relevant considerations here are similar to those that apply in cases of conflict generated by a system of rules. In general, there are good reasons why such a system should be consistent. After all, the point of a system of rules is to guide behavior in various ways, and inconsistent rules cannot guide behavior. At the same time, action guidance is a pragmatic concern that could be balanced against other sorts of pragmatic concerns. Perhaps the infrequency of the conflict makes modifying the rules to cover the conflict cases just not worth the effort. Analogous things, Williams argues, are to be said about imperatives and indeed about all practical discourse. Consistency constraints on such discourse reflect only one of a number of pragmatic concerns, and practical reason requires that the urgency of such constraints be measured relative to the urgency of those other concerns.[53]

In this view, then, whether it is rational to issue inconsistent commands in any given instance will depend on the purposes one has. Thus, it might be rational to do so if one's primary purpose is to confuse the recipient of the commands. The implications of this view for our general discussion should be clear. If it could be rational for a commander to issue sets of commands enjoining contradictory states of affairs, then it would be possible for a practically rational God to issue such commands, assuming there are no independent grounds for believing the contrary. But if this is true, then there is nothing about God's rationality per se that would preclude the theological voluntarist's admission of moral dilemmas. The issue would turn on whether God's purposes rendered intelligible his commanding the impossible.

What sort of divine purposes would satisfy this requirement? Consider the following remarks of St. Augustine formulated in response to the proposals of Coelestius: "'Again,' he says, 'we have to inquire whether man is commanded to be without sin; for either he is not able, and then he is not commanded; or else because he is commanded, he is able. For why should that be commanded which cannot at all be done?' The answer is, that man is most wisely commanded to walk with right steps, on purpose that, when he has discovered his own inability to do even this, he may seek the remedy which is provided for the inward man to cure the lameness of sin, even the grace of God, through our Lord Jesus Christ."[54] Of course, the impossibility of which Augustine speaks here is the inability of the sinfully corrupt human agent to fulfill the demands of the law even when its dictates are unambiguous. Augustine's point is that God may issue commands he knows cannot be obeyed in order to bring human agents to the realization that they stand in need of divine grace. Now it might be argued that this Augustinian insight could be extended to provide a rationale for the existence of dilemmas. The explanation would go something like this: Moral dilemmas exist, and consequently, God issues commands enjoining contradictory states of affairs. Yet this fact does not impugn the divine rationality since the commands in question are purposeful. The reason God issues such commands is not because he expects obedience but rather because he wishes to make agents realize that righteousness is attainable not via conformity to the moral law but only through divine grace. The point of the moral law in these contexts is not to guide but to convict.[55]

We can note two peculiar features of this argument at the outset. In the first place, it assumes that the human inability to fulfill moral requirement in dilemmatic circumstances would be relevantly similar to the inability associated with sin and the need for divine grace. Discovering one's inability in the first sense, the argument presumes, will lead one to acknowledge one's inability in the second sense. Yet we can at least raise the question whether there are significant differences between the two sorts of moral incompetence, and if there are such differences, then it may be fallacious to reason from one inability to the other. But even if this problem were to be resolved, there is a second oddity about the argument under consideration. In particular, it is difficult to see how the divine strategy depicted could work once this explanation of moral dilemmas became generally known. If God issues inconsistent imperatives, not because he expects obedience but because he wants to instill in human agents the consciousness of sin, then it becomes a real question whether he is genuinely commanding in such instances at all. But if God does not genuinely command in these situations, it is hard to understand how an agent could discover her own moral inadequacy in the sense described since it would no longer be meaningful to speak of an authentic contravention of the divine will under these conditions.

This last point touches on the basic difficulty with any attempt of the theological voluntarist to explain moral dilemmas by appealing to Williams's pragmatic account of imperatival rationality. The difficulty may be brought to light by noting an important distinction that Williams's discussion obscures. It is one thing to say that for certain purposes practical reason may require an agent *to issue utterances having the form of inconsistent imperatives* ('Do x and do not do x'). In a certain sense we may speak of such an activity as rational, and thus, on this matter, Williams's analysis seems correct. Yet it is quite another thing to say that *inconsistent commanding* is a rational activity in this sort of context granted our ordinary understanding of what a command is, namely, a prescription whose author sincerely wills the subject of the prescription to perform the act prescribed. Williams's argument does not establish the rationality of inconsistent commanding in this sense. But once all of this is recognized, the distinction he draws between indicatives and imperatives dissolves. Just as we may speak of a rational agent's issuing utterances having the form of inconsistent imperatives, so we can imagine circumstances in which a practically rational agent will issue utterances having the form of inconsistent assertions, for example, if the agent's purpose is to confuse the hearer. Needless to say, to make this claim is to state nothing about the rationality of *inconsistent asserting*, where an assertion is understood to be a sincere statement by the speaker about what is the case. In sum, we may concede that issuing utterances having the form of inconsistent assertions is a rational activity in certain contexts without conceding that inconsistent asserting is ever a rational activity. Similarly, we may concede that issuing utterances having the form of inconsistent imperatives can be rational given certain purposes without conceding that inconsistent commanding is ever rational.

From the foregoing discussion we may draw two significant conclusions. First, if it is rational for God to issue utterances having the form of inconsistent imperatives, then it may also be rational for him to issue utterances having the form of inconsistent assertions. The upshot is that a theological voluntarist who attempted to explain moral dilemmas in terms of Williams's account would have to admit by parity of reasoning that God's propositional utterances on various matters could be inconsistent given certain purposes he might have. Perhaps this admission is theologically innocuous; yet it is difficult to avoid the feeling, though I shall not pursue the point here, that accepting such a view would pose serious problems for the doctrine of revelation. Second, and more important for our purposes, even if we found this theological consequence to be tolerable, it is not at all clear in the last analysis that the theological voluntarist could explain the existence of *genuine* moral dilemmas by appealing to Williams's account. For, as we have seen, all that account shows is that it may be rational for an agent with certain purposes to issue utterances having inconsistent imperatival form; it does not show that inconsistent *commanding* is rational, where 'command' denotes a prescription whose author sincerely wills that the action prescribed be performed. But if the position of theological voluntarism holds that moral obligation is a function of what God genuinely wills or genuinely commands, then on the terms of that position God's mere issuing of utterances having inconsistent imperatival form would not be sufficient to generate moral obligation. And if no obligations are generated by such utterances, then appealing to the fact of these utterances cannot explain the existence of genuine moral dilemmas, which by definition involve irreconcilable conflicts between *authentic* moral obligations.

The theological voluntarist who persisted in affirming the existence of dilemmas might respond to the preceding in either of two ways. First, she might argue, while it is true that God's inconsistent imperatives do not reflect his genuine commanding or willing, this fact in itself poses no insurmountable difficulty for the dilemmas thesis because God's issuance of pronouncements having imperatival form is per se sufficient to establish moral obligations. There is certainly no strictly logical incoherence in such a position. Yet it would be hard to deny the peculiarity of the version of theological voluntarism it assumes. For one would think that a crucial feature of theological voluntarism (perhaps its most attractive feature from the perspective of the religious believer) is its characterization of morally dutiful behavior in terms of responding to what God *genuinely* wills. But it is precisely this characterization that the argument under consideration abandons. The conclusion is irresistible, therefore, that this dialectical maneuver would merely be an ad hoc strategem designed solely to save the dilemmas thesis.

Conceding this point, however, the voluntarist might offer a second argument, namely, that in situations of conflicting moral requirements there is a sense in which God does genuinely *will* the mutually exclusive alternatives. Take a case of conflict between two strictures, one enjoining the keeping of promises, the other forbidding the telling of lies. Under these circumstances, it might be argued, God desires both that the promise be kept and that the lie not be told, in the sense that he prefers the possible worlds in which promises are kept and lies are not told. Thus, one might claim that in such instances it is meaningful to speak of an inevitable moral cost inasmuch as some desire of God's would have to be frustrated no matter which course of action is taken. What are we to make of this line of argument? Admittedly, the view preserves a way of talking about the *moral unsatisfactoriness* of conflict situations, presumably without impugning God's practical rationality. The question, however, is whether the account can allow for the theoretical affirmation of *moral dilemmas*. And it is difficult to see how it can do so without either equivocating on central concepts or admitting incoherence in the divine will. For it is one thing to claim that God wills the keeping of promises and the refusal to tell lies, in the attenuated sense that he prefers the *possible worlds* in which promises are not broken and lies are not told. It is quite another thing to claim that God wills in the *actual world* both the performance and the non-performance of a particular act, which is both the keeping of a promise and the telling of a lie. The establishment of this second claim, of course, is what is necessary in order for the theological voluntarist to interpret the case in question as a genuine moral dilemma. Yet the state of affairs reflected in this claim is exactly one that compels the ascription of irrationality to the divine will.

By now enough has been said, I think, to shift the burden of proof onto the theological voluntarist who would argue that genuine moral dilemmas exist but that God, nonetheless, is a practically rational being. Even if one grants the terms of the pragmatic account that allows for the rationality of utterances having inconsistent imperatival form, one is still left with the question whether genuine commanding of the impossible is rational; and, as we have seen, one would be hard pressed to deny that such commanding is irrational inasmuch as it involves the pursuit of ends that knowingly cannot be satisfied. But given the tenets of theological voluntarism along with certain beliefs regarding God's knowledge of actual circumstances, a moral dilemma would have to be taken as an indication that God issued genuine commands obeyable in no possible world. The consequence is that the theological voluntarist would appear to have compelling reasons for holding that situations of moral perplexity are resolvable in principle no matter how difficult it may be to resolve them *de facto*.

Concluding Reflections

At this point one might object that the discussion up to now has proceeded along contentious lines since the assumption has been that preserving God's practical rationality ought to be an overriding theoretical concern. Yet this assumption could be called into question. It simply might be the case that a theoretical commitment to God's practical reason will have to be abandoned in the way of yielding to other more important theological concerns. Indeed, one might suggest with some measure of plausibility that the very reasons that would lead one to embrace theological voluntarism in the first place are the same reasons that should allow theoretically for God's transcending the canons of practical rationality and, consequently, for his commanding the impossible. Granted this view, the way would be cleared for the theological voluntarist's admission of moral dilemmas.

There are several rationales for adopting theological voluntarism that also seem to support the view that God transcends the limits of practical reason. Generally speaking, the rationales in question relate to theoretical considerations bearing on a range of divine attributes. For instance, one possible defense of the divine command theory of ethics argues that this account is the inevitable consequence of taking God's omnipotence seriously. If the criteria of moral requirement are independent of the divine will, then there is at least one sort of thing God cannot do, namely, render morally obligatory an action that fails to meet these criteria. Similarly, one might argue that the divine command theory of ethics follows from a proper understanding of the divine liberty. For if the standards of moral right and wrong are independent of God's will and if God necessarily wills what is morally right, then God's freedom is constrained by these standards. There are other possible variations on this sort of defense. The general point is that, if divine attributes such as omnipotence and liberty are construed in a way that rules out *any* conceivable constraint on the divine will and if these attributes are cited as the fundamental justification for adopting the divine command theory to begin with, the theological voluntarist will have every reason apparently to deny that God's will is constrained even by the requirements of practical reason. But, of course, given God's freedom from these requirements, the implication that he commands or wills the impossible would pose no obstacle to the admission of dilemmas.

The foregoing objection is a serious one that touches on fundamental issues related to the doctrine of God. Two general considerations diminish its force, however. In the first place, there is no *necessary* connection between theological voluntarism and the idea of an absolutely unconstrained deity. Indeed, there are a number of justifications that might be given for the divine command theory of ethics that have nothing at all to do with attributes such as omnipotence and liberty.[56] Thus, one might argue that the theory follows from the religious premise that God ought to be the preeminent object of one's loyalty. Or one might hold, with Karl Barth, that grounding moral requirement in the divine will is a proper expression of the belief that God has been gracious to humankind through the work of Jesus Christ.[57] Or one might reason that assent to the theory is part and parcel of acknowledging that humans are radically dependent on God. Of course, the point here is not to deny that such alternative justifications raise problems in their own right but only to emphasize the theoretical independence of the divine command theory from the conception of God as a being beyond all constraint. Given that independence, the objection under consideration could be advanced at best by *certain versions* of theological voluntarism.

This brings us to the second problem with the objection, namely, that the conception of God presupposed by these versions in itself generates significant theological difficulties. For to speak in the sense needed of a God beyond all conceivable constraint almost certainly would require reducing the divine nature to the status of pure will since filling out the details of that nature with other attributes would seem to imply some constraint on the divine volition (God, then, *could not* will in a manner that was inconsistent with that nature). It is within reason to ask whether a depiction of the divine as purely volitional and wholly unconstrained can be adequate to any theology that wishes to ascribe agential characteristics to God at all. The problem is that "God, like man, cannot just act. He must act for a purpose and see his action as in some way a good thing. Hence he cannot do what he does not regard as a good thing. This is not a physical constraint, but a logical limit. Nothing would count as an action of God unless God in some way saw the doing of it as a good thing."[58] Yet if God cannot act unless he recognizes the goodness of the act, then he cannot act unless he constrains his willing by some standard, whether that standard is independent or constitutive of his own nature. Were this problem to be solved, a conception of God as unambiguously volitional and unlimited would still pose theological difficulties for any theist even remotely connected with the Christian tradition. For instance, given that conception, it would be hard to render intelligible a range of claims the tradition has typically advanced, including the claim that God has issued promises to and entered into covenants with his people and that he will be faithful to these promises and covenants without qualification. After all, if God can be bound by no constraint, it is difficult to see how he could be bound by promises and covenants. Of course, a standard response to this objection is that God binds himself in these circumstances and, therefore, that such commitments are not genuine constraints. But this response will hardly do; for if God literally transcends all limitations, then he also transcends any constraint that would hold him to the promises and covenants he has freely forged.

We need not press the line of argument further. The general point is that any attempt to preserve God's omnipotence or liberty by depicting him as a being who escapes all describable limitations will present enormous theoretical difficulties on other fronts. Consequently, any appeal to such a conception as a way of preserving God's freedom from the requirements of practical reason and thus as a means of ensuring the theological possibility of moral dilemmas will be an appeal that generates serious problems of its own. Whether such problems are ultimately resolvable is a question I cannot pursue here. What is essential to note for present purposes is that the difficulties posed by such a doctrine of God should make its acceptance a matter of last resort for the Christian theist. Of course, it could be argued that the theoretical conditions of last resort are in fact met precisely by a *theological* need to acknowledge the existence of irresolvable moral conflict; and the success of this argument would depend, naturally, on the forcefulness of the theological considerations proposed in support of the dilemmas thesis. Are there such considerations and do they compel assent? In the final chapter I address these and related matters.

5

THEOLOGICAL ETHICS AND
MORAL CONFLICT

Iғ the previous arguments are sound, then they establish for any ethic of Christian theism a theoretical presumption against moral dilemmas. In the case of Thomistic natural law, acknowledging moral dilemmas will pose problems for the doctrine of providence and for the idea that God's power is sufficient to realize his creative purposes. In the case of theological voluntarism, accepting the reality of dilemmas will mean attributing incoherence to the divine will and thus acknowledging God's practical irrationality. Assuming that an ethic of Christian theism will link moral requirement either to divine providence in the manner of Thomistic natural law or to divine command in the manner of theological voluntarism, we can claim with reasonable assurance that the indicated difficulties impose a burden of proof on the Christian ethicist who advances the moral dilemmas thesis. Of course, one might point to the possibility of a *tertium quid*, namely, a Christian ethic that grounded moral obligation neither in divine providence nor in divine command and thus avoided the theoretical problems posed by dilemmas. Yet the prospect of constructing such an ethic seems unlikely. The result would appear to be that the aforementioned burden of proof remains in place.

In this chapter I shall try to determine whether that burden can be borne. More particularly, I shall attend to a number of positions that have been or might be appealed to in Christian ethical arguments for the reality of irresolvable moral conflict. My conclusion will be that these positions, whatever general force they may carry and whatever implications they may hold for other matters, do not require the acknowledgment of genuine moral dilemmas. The discussion will divide roughly into two parts. In the first part I shall consider a series of normative ethical analyses that have been offered by Christian moralists and that may appear to provide support for the dilemmas thesis. I shall argue that these analyses are inconclusive and at best drive us to deeper reflection on possible connections between the dilemmas thesis and certain fundamental theological concepts (e.g., justification by faith, the sin of the world). In the second part I shall consider at length the position of the Lutheran ethicist Helmut Thielicke, a position arguably representing the most elaborate attempt in the history of Christian ethics to link the dilemmas thesis to points of basic theological doctrine. My contention will be that Thielicke fails to establish the sorts of connections he purports to establish and that allegiance to the theological doctrines he prizes is wholly compatible with belief in the solubility of moral perplexity. Thus, the overall thrust of the discussion in this chapter will be that arguments typically employed by Christian ethicists in the way of affirming the existence of dilemmas finally cannot bear the burden of proof described above.

Agape and Special Relations

Christian theological affirmations of insoluble moral conflict most often arise out of reflection on normative issues having varying degrees of generality, issues such as the nature of Christian love, the Sermon on the Mount and the use of coercion, Christian responsibility to the political order, and so forth. Specific normative assessments generated by such reflection are grounded in a wide assortment of normative principles and values, which in turn are tied explicitly to a rich variety of sources, some unambiguously theological in nature (e.g., scripture and tradition) and others not (e.g., reason and experience). A common proposal is that, when all of the relevant principles and values are given their due, one will need to recognize in a range of cases the inevitability of irresolvable moral conflict or the inescapability of moral guilt. Occasionally, this normative judgment is supported by appeals to theological notions such as the reality of sin in the world, though more often than not the appeals lack the sort of sustained analysis necessary to establish firm connections between the normative assessment and the theological construct. In any event, I shall focus on three normative issues that have prompted theological ethicists to affirm the existence of insoluble moral conflict: (1) the relation between the claims of special moral bonds (e.g., friendship, family) and the claims of humanity at large, (2) the bearing of Christian love on the use of coercion, and (3) the employment of morally dubious means to achieve morally praiseworthy ends.

The first issue is often cast by theological ethicists as the problem of competing loves—the love of special relations that naturally arises in the course of human existence versus the neighbor love enjoined by the New Testament and the Christian tradition at large. Discussion typically begins with recognition of the distinctive characters of the respective loves.[1] On the one hand, the love of special relations—whether it be love of spouse, child, parent, or friend—is in essence a preferential and, consequently, an exclusive love. One loves one's special relations precisely because they are the persons they are. To love in the manner appropriate to these relations is to set the object of love apart from the rest of humanity, to devote one's time and energy to the beloved in unique ways, to make extra sacrifices, bestow distinct affections, and most important for our purposes, to act upon a range of *special* moral obligations that have been incurred with respect to the beloved. On the other hand, neighbor love or agape abstracts from the particularities that the love of special relations prizes. Agape is universal in its scope rather than preferential; it attends to the other "qua human existent and not because he is such-and-such a kind of person distinguishing him from others."[2] If the love of special relations is tied to a set of dispositions, affections, attitudes, actions, and obligations constitutive of particular associations, then agape is linked with a series of attributes and requirements that pertain to one's life as it relates to the whole of humanity. This impersonality that marks neighbor love is reflected preeminently in the moral principles it is often said to generate, principles calling for equal consideration, fairness, impartiality, and the like. In this respect, of course, the basic moral orientation of agape contrasts significantly with that of special-relations love, which intends the duties we have to some rather than the conditions that ought to govern our dealings with all. As will become clear later on, it is this contrast especially that gives rise to the problem of moral conflict.[3]

In any event, a question immediately raised by the foregoing is how these two kinds of love are to be drawn together generally in the unity of a human life. There have been numerous responses to this question, of course, in the history of Christian theological ethics. Yet for our purposes a recent account offered by Gilbert Meilaender is of particular interest since it acknowledges a systematic connection between the two loves but insists, nonetheless, that collisions will occur.[4]

According to this view, the love of special relations, because it exists in tension with the universal thrust of agape, must finally be reckoned a partial, inadequate love. At the same time, this love remains a good of creation, a divinely bestowed gift, and as such it may be justly received and enjoyed. Thus, within limits it is morally permissible to forge and maintain our special bonds—so long as we resist elitist tendencies and refuse to harm those beyond the pale of our special concern. Indeed, given the conditions of human existence, the love of special relations may profitably be regarded as a training exercise for and a finite intimation of the universal love in fellowship, which is fully realizable only in ultimate fellowship with God himself. For while the constraints of time and space make it impossible to achieve genuine fellowship with all, through love of our special relations we may come to understand what it means to love any person. "We may learn, that is, a love which is implicitly universal."[5] In this respect, then, the network of special relations can be seen as an aspect of God's providential economy preparing his creatures for the universal communal love to be attained in the final consummation.

Still, under the conditions of earthly existence, the love of special relations retains its preferential character. What, then, is to be said about the requirement of universal love in *this* life? According to Meilaender, there are at least two responses to this question afforded by the Christian tradition, one prescribing a life that is incompatible with social existence as we know it, the other commending an activity that remains consistent with natural forms of social interaction.[6] The first response calls on persons to sacrifice all particular attachments for the sake of serving the neighbor at large. Such "Franciscan love," while a permissible alternative for some, as Meilaender sees it, cannot be affirmed as a moral obligation binding on all human beings, most of whom rightly live and flourish in the midst of family and friends. The second response accepts this conclusion and attempts to do justice to the claims of universal love without disrupting the special connections that structure created life. According to this account, one's moral responsibilities to the outside world may be satisfied in good measure through fulfillment of the duties related to one's calling or

vocation in the workplace. Such an assessment is made possible
by a general understanding that characterizes the larger system of
callings as a divine ordering whose fundamental purpose is to provide for universal human need. In fulfilling the responsibilities of
vocation, then, one participates in God's providential activity and
thereby contributes, at least indirectly, to the well-being of persons who fall beyond the scope of one's special moral considerations and efforts. Thus, "the calling is a way of recognizing the
legitimate claims of distant neighbors without imagining that any
of us is responsible for meeting all of them and without driving
out of life any place for special, preferential bonds of love like
friendship. In this way, and unlike the Franciscan love which
breaks through all normal bonds of life, the concept of calling
makes it possible for love to be universal yet 'fitted for society.'"[7]

To a significant degree, then, the demands of agape can be co-
ordinated with the requirements of our special commitments.
Nonetheless, in particular instances conflict is possible or even,
as Meilaender sees it, inevitable. The problem is partly due to the
conditions of modern society where vocational responsibilities
characteristically necessitate considerable expenditures of time
and intermittent geographical dislocations. Under such conditions it is difficult and sometimes impossible to satisfy the claims
of personal relationships. Moreover, as vocational activity increases its share of the whole of social life, the canons governing
personal relations give way more and more to the norms of official
interaction. "We do not hire and fire people on the basis of friendship; indeed, to do so strikes many of us as more than a little suspect. Thus, in the world of vocation . . . we purchase fairness at
the price of impersonality."[8] At the most profound level, however,
the clash between special commitment and vocation is to be
understood less as a function of modern social circumstances
than as a reflection of conflict in the divine will itself:

> God gives both the creaturely bond of friendship, which enriches
> life, and the calling, which serves the neighbor. Theories which
> rest content in preferential loves or, alternatively, which glorify the
> calling above all else fail to appreciate the paradox of the divine will
> which Anselm discerned. The tensions between bonds of particular
> love and a love which is open to every neighbor (in the calling) can-
> not be overcome by any theory, however intricate. Our thinking can
> only warn against certain mistakes, certain wrong turnings which
> we might take. But this central problem of the Christian life must

be lived, not just thought. . . . The tension between particular
bonds and a more universally open love—of which tension between
friendship and vocation is an instance—cannot be eliminated for
creatures whose lives are marked by the particularities of time and
place but who yet are made to share with all others the praise of
God. The tension between particular and universal love is "solved"
only as it is lived out in a life understood as pilgrimage toward the
God who gives both the friend and the neighbor.[9]

In sum, to seek an unambiguously unified life that satisfies all
the demands of special relations and "distant" neighbors is, in
Meilaender's account, a task fundamentally misconceived.

What are we to make of this analysis? Given our earlier discussion of rational constraints on the divine volition, the central
point of interest is Meilaender's observation regarding the character of God's purposes as they are reflected presumably in the experienced tension between the two loves, and the first thing to be
said here is that the author leaves unclear the precise reason for
suggesting that the phenomena described call for an ascription of
"paradox" to the divine will. Indeed, we may agree that special relations are a gift bestowed by the Creator, that the flourishing of
these relations involves the participants' general recognition and
fulfillment of certain special obligations, and that God also imposes a range of general requirements bearing on our service to
the distant neighbor. We may even grant that the exact moral
boundaries of the two kinds of love are difficult to determine in
specific instances and that, furthermore, satisfying the rightful
claims of either love can strain relations in the other sphere. Yet
none of this commits us to admitting a paradox in the divine will
itself. Such an admission would be necessary only if we could
be certain that in particular situations, where the claims of the
two loves appeared to clash, God in fact did enjoin incompatible
courses of action. Nothing that Meilaender has given us suggests
that this is the case.

Now in response it might be argued that the problem is not in
God's commanding incompatible courses of action but rather in
his willing behavior whose outcome conflicts with other purposes he has. For example, we can readily imagine situations
where fidelity to genuine vocational responsibilities breeds resentment among family members, resentment eventually resulting in significantly damaged, if not entirely severed, family rela-

tions. Such situations may elicit the judgment that God requires actions (the fulfillment of vocational duties) that ultimately frustrate the realization of a good (familial flourishing) he intends his creatures to enjoy. Indeed, I believe it is this sort of assessment that Meilaender actually has in mind. Yet acknowledging that vocational commitments may interfere with thriving family relations need not imply paradox in the divine will even in the theological scheme depicted here; for the resentments at the root of the problem simply may be unjustified. After all, while it is eminently reasonable to claim that God gives the gift of special relations for the general purpose of their realization, it is also reasonable to submit that he intends the gift to be enjoyed within the limits established by the entire range of moral obligations, including the obligations of vocation. If ruptured family bonds are the consequence of a failure to respect these limits, then the coherence of God's purposes is maintained. Of course, it could be claimed that in some cases the dissolution of family relations is the result of no such failure but rather the outcome of simple finitude. Factors of time and space alone may be the cause of dissipated affections and withered commitments. In such instances one might say that God would prefer *ceteris paribus* the possible but counterfactual world in which these relations are kept intact but that he wills in the actual world fulfillment of vocational responsibilities, which erodes familial bonds *de facto*. Yet once again there is no paradox in God's willing here. For there is no paradox in willing a course of action one foresees as having some undesirable consequences. What would raise serious questions about divine coherence would be a situation in which meeting the *authentic moral demands* of vocation conflicted with the *genuine moral responsibilities* to family. In this sort of situation, it reasonably could be argued, God wills incompatible states of affairs in the actual world.

This amounts to saying that Meilaender's remarks about divine paradox are intelligible only on the assumption that the experienced tensions between special relations and neighbor love actually signify, at least in some instances, genuine moral dilemmas. Perhaps this assumption underlies his position. But if so, then its validity will rest on independent considerations establishing that the respective canons governing special relations and agape in fact do conflict irremediably under certain conditions. Meilaender provides no such considerations explicitly, but he might contend that an adequate explanation of the moral phenomena simply requires the dilemmatic interpretation. As I noted in earlier discussion, crucial questions are begged by such a contention. Still, it may be instructive to reflect at some length on one particular issue suggested by Meilaender's own analysis.

Take the matter of how canons of friendship relate to professional norms of impartiality. It is trivially true to claim that friendship generally involves an active concern for the friend's welfare, and this concern quite understandably might include making special efforts, if the need arose, to assist the friend in securing gainful employment. There may be occasions, however, when one's professional role puts one in an especially privileged position to advance the friend's interests in this regard, for example, when one is part of an establishment reviewing applicants for a job the friend seeks. Of course, as Meilaender makes clear, we harbor serious moral reservations about basing hiring judgments on preferential considerations since such considerations collide with principles of fairness we deem appropriate to decision making in the vocational world. And it may be reasonable to argue that in the largest number of cases where a friend is involved a professional ought to exempt herself from the review process. Yet Meilaender also suggests that the gains represented in such procedural integrity are achieved only at the expense of sacrificing something else of great value, namely, the quality of personal relationship that marks the friendship bond. The question before us is whether this loss should ever be regarded as a *moral* one, and particularly whether we are ever forced to conclude that in *rightly* conforming to principles of justice in these matters we are guilty of *wronging* the friend.

Suppose, having formally removed oneself from a review process involving a friend, one discovers through happenstance that the hiring committee has missed a crucial feature of the friend's qualifications, a feature that, if brought to the committee's attention, would substantially enhance the friend's chances of getting the job. Assume also the hardest of cases—that the job market is tight, that applicants would be pressed to find positions elsewhere, that one is convinced the friend would perform with excellence, and so forth. Should one take special measures to inform the committee of its omission? Of course, to do so would be to violate some principle of procedural impartiality since other applicants would not enjoy similar opportunities to have mistaken impressions rectified. Still, were one not to correct the oversight and were the friend to discover the fact, would it not be plausible to suggest that she might justly complain about one's behavior? Perhaps so. Yet it is equally plausible to argue that any *moral* force the complaint might have would derive not simply from its appeal to canons of special loyalty but also from its tie to a deeper conception of justice than that expressed by mere procedural impartiality. This deeper conception would involve, more than likely, the principle that each applicant has the right to be judged on the basis of all relevant considerations, that procedural safeguards are imperfect means of ensuring this right, and that when procedures have failed in this respect, they may be overridden, at least within limits. The important point is that talk about a friend's being wronged in this sort of situation need not involve talk about irresolvable moral conflict between special commitments and universal principles of fairness since the argument could be made that fairness, properly understood, allowed for the special initiative.

Variations on this case, admittedly, will be harder to resolve. For example, suppose that, having corrected the oversight regarding the friend, one then discovers that another candidate, to whom one has no special attachment, also possesses important qualifications gone undetected by the committee. Informing the committee accordingly would enhance the chances of this candidate, probably at the expense of the friend's own. Should one take the special initiative here also? In doing so, does one wrong the friend ("You didn't *have* to do that," she might say)? In failing to do so, does one wrong the other candidate ("What's sauce for the goose . . .")? Adjudication of these matters will naturally depend on assessing the deep conception of justice described above. Given the procedural failures depicted, does this conception *require* the special corrective measures or does it merely *allow* for such measures, which are rendered obligatory only by other conditions (e.g., when the person involved is a friend)? There are no simple answers to these questions. Yet to acknowledge perplexity about this sort of case is not to admit that *whatever* is done is a moral wrong. Needless to say, taking what is ultimately the right course of action may generate all kinds of unfortunate consequences, including the loss of one's friend, and these consequences may stimulate in turn appropriate forms of agent regret (indeed, one *ought* to regret the alienation of a friend's affections). Still, as we learned from earlier discussion, the fact of such regret or the fact of its appropriateness need not be taken as the sign of genuine moral dilemma; thus, the same phenomenon need not be regarded by the theological scheme under consideration as an expression of paradox in the divine will.

The immediately preceding reflections have been limited, of course, to one particular type of encounter between special-relations love and universal love, the encounter between friendship and vocational responsibility. Nonetheless, I am confident that analyses of other types would show that dilemmatic readings are unnecessary. At any rate, Meilaender's own commitment to divine paradox remains undetermined by the evidence he advances and is especially troublesome in light of the extraordinary theological difficulties that, as we have seen, such a commitment generates. Whether there are additional arguments he might employ in defense of his position is a matter we must leave open. Indeed, at one point Meilaender hints that his remarks about the coherence of God's purposes rest essentially not on normative considerations but rather on an unspecified premise derived from a distinctive theological conception of the relation between nature and grace.[10] If this is so, both the premise and the conception call for further discussion. Whatever course such a discussion might take, we can say with reasonable assurance that normative assessments abstracted from larger theological accounts will lack the conclusiveness necessary to sustain any unqualified affirmation of moral dilemmas spawned by irremediable tension between the two loves.

Love and Coercion

A second normative issue that has given rise to theological assertions of irresolvable moral conflict is the question whether the use of coercive means in the service of justice may be reconciled with commitment to the way of Christ, particularly as it is embodied in the Sermon on the Mount and in the picture of nonresistant, suffering love drawn by the narrative of the Cross. As is well known, a persistent, if not dominant, element in the Christian tradition has held that no reconciliation is possible and that witness to one's faith in Christ demands an unequivocal rejection of coercive means in theory and in practice. As is also well known, however, the more typical assessment of the tradition has been that, given the realities of a sinful world, the use of coercive means in the cause of justice is sometimes a permissible, if regrettable, option for the Christian believer. Interestingly enough for our purposes, this second assessment now and then is advanced with an important proviso: Though coercive means are frequently warranted in practice, their employment is morally ambiguous at best. On the one hand, it is said, responsibility for the world's preservation will often require the use of force, for example, when such force is necessary to protect the innocent against unjust aggression. On the other hand, it is also insisted, coercive means always stand morally convicted by the command of love, whose content is captured by the prescriptions of the Sermon on the Mount and by the general account of Christ's own suffering, nonresistant history. The consequence, presumably, is that, while coercion may be *morally required* of the Christian believer, its employment always involves some *moral guilt*. In recent times, of course, this line of thinking has been characteristic of the "Christian realism" articulated by Reinhold Niebuhr, and it is on his ethical analysis of coercion that I shall focus here.

The general contours of Niebuhr's view are familiar, so only a brief review will be necessary.[11] According to Niebuhr, Christian love is to be understood essentially in terms of the radical altruism or "perfect disinterestedness" at the core of the divine love itself, which is revealed historically in the life and ethic of Jesus. In Jesus' existence love is disclosed as unadulterated self-sacrifice, an attribute given supreme expression in the utterly self-denying gesture symbolized by the Cross.[12] Correspondingly, the ethical teaching of Jesus is distinguished by the relentless consistency with which it identifies and criticizes the various tendencies toward self-assertion that naturally manifest themselves in human life. Among these tendencies, of course, is the natural inclination to defend the self against the unjust onslaught of the enemy. From the perspective of the love that Jesus enjoins, forgiveness, not resistance, is the appropriate response to such onslaught. The justification for this response, moreover, cannot be the prudential, and thus egocentric, concern to heighten the enemy's conscience in the hope that his behavior will be transformed, nor, for that matter, can it be any other consequentialist concern. Rather, the warrant is simply in the fact that the prescribed reaction mirrors the operation of the divine love itself.

> The justification for these demands is put in purely religious and not in socio-moral terms. We are to forgive because God forgives; we are to love our enemies because God is impartial in his love. The points of reference are vertical and not horizontal. Neither natural impulses nor social consequences are taken into consideration. It is always possible, of course, that absolute ethical attitudes have desirable social consequences. To do good to an enemy may prompt him to overcome his enmity; and forgiveness of evil may be a method of redemption which commends itself to the most prudent.

It must be observed, however, that no appeal to social consequences could ever fully justify these demands of Jesus. Nonresistance may shame an aggressor into goodness, but it may also prompt him to further aggression.[13]

Thus, the absolute prohibition of resistance is impossible to justify on purely consequentialist grounds. In any case, consequentialist considerations are irrelevant, as Niebuhr sees it, to assessing the prohibition's obligatory force, which remains intact no matter what effects obedience has on the world.

Of course, as Niebuhr admits, this ethic of love is not one that speaks in any direct fashion to the exigencies of social life, including "the problem of arranging some kind of armistice between various factions and forces."[14] Given the character of the world, where individuals and especially groups unceasingly press claims of self-interest against each other and where the claims are typically backed by various forms of coercion, society requires institutions that will adjudicate disputes in accordance with certain principles of equal justice and that will enforce just decisions with sanctions compelling recalcitrant losers to abide by the outcomes. Moreover, in instances where just systems are threatened by unjust forces or where the systems themselves fall short of justice, resistance, even *violent* resistance, may be necessary to set matters aright. All in all, refusing, in the name of selfless love, to press one's own interests against the interests of others is likely to be suicidal in a world where advantage is characteristically taken at every opportunity; and categorically rejecting, in the name of nonresistant love, the use of coercive strategies, whether they be violent or not, is *morally irresponsible* in a world where the unjust prey upon the just.[15] The conclusion to be drawn is that the ethic of Jesus, while *morally* binding on human agents, is inadequate to meet either the practical or the *moral* demands of social life in a sinful world. To reach this conclusion is not, as Niebuhr sees it, to disavow altogether any connection between love and social justice since "equality is always the regulative principle of justice; and in the ideal of equality there is an echo of the law of love, 'Thou shalt love thy neighbor AS THYSELF.'"[16] Nonetheless, to the extent that coercion is employed as a way of promoting equality, there is also a departure from the full meaning of the command to love. Under the conditions of historical existence, moreover, such a departure is a moral necessity.

For Niebuhr, then, there can be no unambiguous politics of love in a fallen world, and thus any claims to the contrary are misconceived. One instance of such misconception is the position of the Christian pacifist who argues that strategies of nonviolent resistance (e.g., civil disobedience) properly reflect in the political order the love Jesus espouses. Niebuhr's response is simply that this sort of position misunderstands the nature of that love. "If Christians are to live by the 'way of the Cross' they ought to practice non-resistance. They will find nothing in the Gospels which justifies non-violent resistance as an instrument of love perfectionism."[17] Indeed, a compromise of that perfectionism is already forged once one has accepted the necessity of engaging in any resistance at all. At that point, the question of whether to employ violent or nonviolent strategy is merely a matter of tactics, though one may concede that nonviolent methods most often ought to be preferred for pragmatic reasons. The point is that, short of an entire withdrawal from the social and political realms, perfect fidelity to nonassertive love is impossible. Furthermore, such a withdrawal is itself morally tainted inasmuch as it profits parasitically from the sinful work of others.[18] What we are left with, then, is a state of affairs in which irresolvable moral conflict is inescapable: "Justification by faith in the realm of justice means that we will not regard the pressures and counter pressures, the tensions, the overt and the covert conflicts by which justice is achieved and maintained, as normative in the absolute sense; but neither will we ease our conscience by seeking to escape from involvement in them. We will know that we cannot purge ourselves of the sin and guilt in which we are involved by the moral ambiguities of politics without also disavowing responsibility for the creative possibilities of justice."[19] Accepting that responsibility is a moral requirement. Yet such acceptance stands morally convicted by the "impossible possibility" represented in the law of love.

Thus, according to Niebuhr, the collision between love in its fullest meaning and social justice as it can be maintained in the world is a collision that creates moral dilemma. And though he does not say so explicitly, what he does say implies that the ultimate source of the problem is a tension in the divine will as it is reflected in the requirements of the love command. For while Niebuhr is unbending in his insistence that the command calls for unqualified commitment to nonresistance, he also suggests, as I have intimated already, that the moral requirement to seek justice is itself a function of that command. Once again, if equality is the regulative principle of justice, it is also an "echo" of the law of love. Niebuhr sometimes brings this tension to the surface by remarking that the relation between love and justice is *dialectical.* While love condemns the coercion necessary to achieve and sustain justice, it also seems to enjoin in no uncertain terms the pursuit of "brotherhood," an end-state approximated, though not fully captured, in social systems governed by principles of justice.[20] God's command to love, then, appears both to prohibit and to require coercive policies when their outcome is justice and when such justice can be achieved in no other fashion. In defense of Niebuhr it might be argued that God does not command such coercive policies but rather that he simply prescribes the goal of brotherhood. Yet if this argument is intended to suggest that God wills the goal *only* as it is realizable through noncoercive means, then it is difficult to see what sense could be made of Niebuhr's claims that the use of coercion to achieve justice is a moral obligation binding all who bear a responsible relationship to the social order. What is the obligation's source if it is not the divine will? Niebuhr speaks of no source independent of that will, and the links he forges between love and justice via the mediating concept of *brotherhood* points to a grounding of the obligation in God's love command. Given this grounding, the conclusion seems inescapable that the moral ambiguities Niebuhr describes must be attributed, on his own terms, to conflict within the divine will itself.

Such a conclusion calls for a reexamination of the overall position, and in this spirit it is fruitful to consider whether the problematic normative judgments Niebuhr advances follow necessarily from the premises that structure his argument. For instance, does Niebuhr's general characterization of agape in combination with his realistic assessments of the world necessarily yield the conclusions he draws about moral dilemmas? Let us assume for the purpose of discussion that he is correct in his interpretation of love as perfect disinterestedness and that in this world such disinterestedness manifests itself as a disposition to sacrifice one's own interests for the sake of the neighbor's. In this rendering, the command to love would prohibit asserting one's interests at the expense of the neighbor's, including the enemy's. Thus, coercion of others would be ruled out as long as it were employed to protect or advance the self's own welfare, and the scope of the prohibition would appear to extend to resistance of the enemy's unjust attacks on one's own person. Yet a prohibition of coercion for the sake of self-interest does not entail a prohibition of coercion *simpliciter.* Indeed, it is perfectly reasonable to propose that when the interests of an innocent third party are unjustly threatened and when defense of those interests against the aggressor may be offered only at considerable expense to the self, love as *self-sacrifice* requires such defense even if it necessitates the use of coercive means. After all, sacrificing one's own interests does not imply sacrificing the interests of the innocent neighbor. Neither does it imply a lack of discrimination about whom to sacrifice for when there is conflict between interests other than the self's. In cases of such conflict a moral judgment will naturally be required to determine which neighbor is rightly served. Interestingly enough, Niebuhr himself seems to recognize this necessity, and he suggests, moreover, that the moral judgment in question will be a function of love itself: "A relation between the self and one other may be partly ecstatic; and in any case the calculation of relative interests may be reduced to a minimum. But as soon as a third person is introduced into the relation even the most perfect love requires a rational estimate of conflicting needs and interests."[21] What he does not go on to say is that once the estimate is made "the most perfect love" may then demand coercive defense of the innocent against the unjust.[22] Yet there is nothing in his general account of agape as self-sacrifice that rules out such a conclusion.

If this judgment is accurate, then the Niebuhrian construction of Christian love generates no theoretical need to posit moral dilemmas even when one considers the bearing of that love on the exigencies of a sinful world. Any use of coercive means motivated by self-interest will be morally wrong from the perspective of selfless love, but such use will always be avoidable. Under certain conditions, of course, refusing to employ coercion in one's own behalf will require self-restraint of heroic proportions; yet to concede that the way of agape is difficult is not to say that it is impossible. On the other hand, coercion employed in defense of another against aggression will involve no moral guilt as long as the action is governed by a prior determination that the aggression is unjust. Naturally, in certain circumstances this determination may be hard to make with any reasonable degree of certainty, and proper judgments can be obscured by hidden motivations of self-interest. Still, even assuming that self-sacrifice and the pursuit of justice are both absolute moral requirements, we need not conclude that whatever one does in such a situation is morally wrong. That conclusion would follow only if there were a logical connection between the notions of self-sacrifice and nonresistance; yet there is clearly no such connection.

Now it might be argued in response that, while Niebuhr is mistaken in his movement from love as self-sacrifice to love as nonresistance, he is correct, nonetheless, in specifying nonresistance as an essential feature of agape and thus is also correct to speak of genuine moral dilemmas generated by a conflict between agape and justice. According to this view, the connection between Christian love and nonresistance is established not via the mediating notion of disinterestedness but rather via independent reflection on agape's meaning as it is disclosed generally in the biblical account of Jesus' history. For in that account, it could be argued, Jesus reveals, through his rejection of ordinary political solutions to human problems and through his acceptance of execution by the political authorities, that the way of love is not the way of the world, which understands both events and persons as forces to be manipulated by counterforces in an ongoing struggle to direct the course of human history. What Jesus shows, more particularly, is that the way of love reflects the character of the providential power, which genuinely directs history on its ultimate course, and that this providential power in the final analysis is paradoxically no power at all but rather powerlessness, submission, suffering—*passion*, in the radical sense of the term. Agape, then, as it properly signifies the operation of providence, rejects the coercive strategies of the world and embraces without qualification a policy of nonresistance.

The question, of course, is whether this conception of agape can be marshaled in defense of Niebuhr's claims about the moral ambiguities inherent in social life. The argument would be, presumably, that the requirements of love as powerlessness conflict irremediably with the requirements of justice, which cannot be approximated, much less fully realized, without a willingness to employ coercive means. Thus dilemmas are unavoidable. Now there is certainly no incoherence in such an argument per se. Yet it is essential to note also that there are alternative normative assessments, even given the rendering of agape under consideration. For it might be argued, and indeed has been argued, that full appreciation of the character of God's love as powerlessness and a faithful witness to that love's strength as the informing principle of history's movement, will be reflected precisely in a politics of a wholly different kind, one that seeks justice in the world without employing the coercive policies that mark the standard way of the world (i.e., through protest, conscientious objection, and other forms of nonresistant witness).[23] According to this account, Christians are faced with no moral dilemmas, at least as far as the use of coercion is concerned; with respect to this matter the divine command is clear, albeit extraordinarily difficult at times to obey.

Undoubtedly, the Niebuhrian will respond to this account by arguing (a) that such a "politics of Jesus" ignores the painful realities of a sinful world; (b) that the recommended strategy, if universally employed by those in the right, would mean the surrendering of history to those in the wrong; (c) that morality consequently requires the willingness of some to seek justice by way of coercion; and (d) that, were Christians to refuse participation in realistic efforts to secure justice, they would be abandoning their moral responsibility to share in the sinful work of preservation. But the counterresponse to this Niebuhrian line will be simply (a) that it is unduly pessimistic about the possibilities of nonresistant activity as an instrument for advancing the cause of justice in the world and (b) that, more important, it reflects a profound absence of faith in the power of God's love to ensure victory of the right in the *final* scheme of things. Genuine faith in providence, as this view would have it, includes the belief "that the cross and not the sword, suffering and not brute power determines the meaning of history," and this belief should manifest itself practically as a commitment to nonresistance.[24] There need be no denial in such a view that under certain conditions the innocent will suffer as a consequence of acting on this belief, and this outcome will always be an occasion for heartfelt regret and deep sorrow. Indeed, tragedy of this sort may also be an occasion for moral guilt, if, for example, the disaster is partially the result of a slothful imprudence in conceiving or executing a particular nonresistant strategy. Yet, for this politics of Jesus, an industrious, intelligent, faithful witness to the suffering love that guides the universe can never, in itself, be regarded as morally irresponsible, even when it issues in tragedy as far as one can see. Thus, according to this position, a choice between the use and rejection of force is no moral dilemma since only by embracing the second alternative can one express genuine belief in the efficacy of God's providential love.

My point is not to suggest that this defense of nonresistance is without its own problems. Final assessment of the theory would depend on resolving a host of extremely difficult questions regarding the precise relation between taking an active responsibility for the direction of history and remaining faithful to certain convictions about the scope and power of God's providential economy. I cannot pursue these questions here. But enough has been said to demonstrate that Niebuhr's normative proposals about the nature of Christian love and its bearing on the necessities of social life are simply insufficient in themselves to establish the existence of moral dilemmas. If agape is essentially selfless, there need be no irresolvable conflict between its requirements and the use of force in the cause of justice. If love is essentially nonresistant, then its requirements do prohibit coercion, but the prohibition may be taken as absolutely binding both in theory and in practice. And whatever might be said about these alternative normative positions, they avoid one theological problem that Niebuhr's theory cannot escape, the problem of attributing paradox or incoherence to the divine will itself.

Conscience and Consequences

Niebuhrian realism has focused on another normative issue that has generated assertions of irreparable moral conflict. That issue is the problem of coordinating the requirements of an individual conscience, which often seems to reject as a matter of principle the use of certain means to achieve morally worthy ends, with the requirements of social responsibility, which is goal-oriented in nature and perhaps open *de jure* to the employment of means that individual conscience condemns. Of course, in our previous discussion of the moral status of coercion, we attended to one sort of means/ends problem. And, indeed, Niebuhr himself seems at times to reduce the means/ends question to the question of the morality of coercion. Nonetheless, the issues are separate. For one may admit that coercion is sometimes warranted morally by the ends that it secures and still argue that there are certain coercive means (e.g., torture) or certain means not obviously coercive in character (e.g., deceiving, bribing, stealing) that no ends may justify to an upright conscience. Thus, the more general question merits examination in its own right.

We have already touched on that question, at least indirectly, in our earlier descriptions and analyses of politicians who must contemplate doing morally questionable things in order to achieve politically desirable ends, the realization of which in some cases may appear to be mandated by the moral requirements of political office. This sort of phenomenon, needless to say, is not limited to governmental officials. Indeed, union leaders, business executives, representatives of public interest groups, and others all may be faced with similar quandaries, where the social responsibilities

174 THEOLOGICAL ETHICS AND MORAL CONFLICT

attached to an official position demand the securing of certain ends but where the means necessary to achieve those ends are ones that would be judged unethical, at least under ordinary circumstances. For the morally sensitive individual such situations may be perceived as dilemmas involving conflict between the judgments of conscience and the duties of office. If the individual conscientiously refuses to perform the morally questionable act, she may see herself as guilty of abandoning her social responsibilities. If she realizes the desired ends by performing the act, then she may see herself as having violated the dictates of her conscience.

As is well known, Niebuhr claims that these situations are indeed dilemmas, and he attributes the difficulty to an apparently ineradicable dualism in the moral consciousness: "A realistic analysis of the problem of human society reveals a constant and seemingly irreconcilable conflict between the needs of society and the imperatives of a sensitive conscience. This conflict, which could be most briefly defined as the conflict between ethics and politics, is made inevitable by the double focus of the moral life."[25] On the one hand, for Niebuhr, there is an *individual* morality, which judges all human behavior from an *internal* perspective. Given this view, actions are right or wrong to the extent that they reflect a "good will" or an upright intention, that is, to the degree that they are in accord with the inner voice of an individual's conscience. On the other hand, there is a *social* morality, which evaluates all human behavior from an *external* perspective. Given this view, actions are judged right or wrong based on the consequences they generate in the outer world. If a particular act promotes the "greatest good for the greatest number" when compared with its alternatives, then the act is justified from the vantage point of social morality. As Niebuhr sees it, this consequentialism is unmitigated. Social morality, in other words, embraces without qualification the dictum that the ends justify the means, and thus no types of action are prohibited in principle as far as this morality is concerned. Of course, it is this unabashed consequentialism which explains in large measure the tension between the competing moral points of view. For the introspective conscience prized by individual morality often judges that certain kinds of actions are unethical even when, all things considered, they happen to promote favorable social consequences.[26]

Niebuhr does acknowledge that the "two moral perspectives are not mutually exclusive" and thus that "the contradiction between them is not absolute."[27] If the pursuit of worthy ends with questionable means is not checked intermittently by the power of individual conscience, then society will eventually lose sight of the ends themselves. At the same time, a preoccupation with upright intentions to the exclusion of consequentialist considerations borders on moral absurdity. Still, while there is some overlap between the two moralities, they simply cannot, according to Niebuhr, be reconciled without remainder. Certain tactics warranted by the utilitarian canons of social morality will elicit condemnation by the individual conscience. Alternatively, from the perspective of social morality, the fastidiousness of conscience will seem both practically foolish and morally disastrous in a world where the forces of injustice are less than scrupulous about the means employed to secure immoral ends. The result for Niebuhr is an unbridgeable normative dichotomy in the experience of persons who assume positions of social responsibility. With respect to the political arena, for instance, he speaks of "a moral breach in the inner life of statesmen, who find themselves torn between the necessities of statecraft and the sometimes sensitive promptings of an individual conscience."[28] Such a breach is often papered over with hypocritical or self-deceptive rationalizations, but the rift cannot be repaired, according to Niebuhr, in a way that completely resolves the moral conflict.

It is important to note that Niebuhr typically associates the collision between individual and social morality with the opposition between love and justice discussed in the previous section. The logic behind the connection is as follows: From the internal perspective assumed by individual morality, moral acts are those motivated by disinterestedness or unselfishness, a disposition that, as we have observed, forms the normative core of agape in the Niebuhrian scheme. From the external vantage point of social morality, however, the supreme value is equal justice and the preferred actions are those that promote consequences favorable to the cause of such justice. What this means in a real world marked by the "assertion of interest against interest" is that social morality will require *self-assertion* on the part of the just in order to counteract "the self-assertion of those who infringe on the rights of others."[29] According to Niebuhr, then, there is an egocentricity built into the dicta of social morality, an egocentricity that comes into conflict with the disinterested or selfless character of individual conscience. He often illustrates the point by describing the situation of a person in an official position of responsibility for the welfare of some group. In such a position, it is the individual's moral duty to defend the concerns of that group. This person may not act disinterestedly with the interests of others:

> A high type of unselfishness, even if it brings ultimate rewards, demands immediate sacrifices. An individual may sacrifice his own interests, either without hope of reward or in the hope of an ultimate compensation. But how is an individual, who is responsible for the interests of his group, to justify the sacrifice of interests other than his own? "It follows," declares Hugh Cecil, "that all that department of morality which requires an individual to sacrifice his interests to others, everything which falls under the heading of unselfishness, is inappropriate to the action of the state. No one has a right to be unselfish with other people's interests."[30]

At least, this is the verdict of social morality. Yet for Niebuhr pressing even the just claims of a group for which one is accountable always involves some moral compromise of the selfless ideal. Given this state of affairs, responsible social advocacy stands under the negative judgment of individual conscience.

Clearly, something is missing in the argument here. Even if one grants Niebuhr's general point that social morality requires things that are unacceptable to conscience, it is not at all obvious that the conflict can be explained by appealing to a collision between egocentricity and selfless motivation. For the fundamental intention behind a representative's defense of her group's interests (even with morally dubious means) may be entirely self-sacrificial in character; after all, she may give up her life for the sake of the group's just cause. Admittedly, apart from such radical altruism, an individual may profit personally from the gains she secures for the collectivity she represents. But this fact in itself hardly demonstrates a conflict between individual and social morality since such personal profit is surely incidental to what social morality requires, namely, the promotion of consequences favorable to *justice*. Indeed, it scarcely needs saying that under certain conditions the goals of social justice can *collide* with the self-interested concerns of groups and their representatives. Niebuhr himself admits as much: "A wise statesman is hardly justified in insisting on the interests of his group when they are obviously in unjust relation to the total interests of the community of mankind."[31] Yet if such a collision between justice and self-interest is possible and if self-sacrifice might be expressed in the pursuit of justice, then it is difficult to see how any tension between conscience and social morality could be explained by appealing to the opposition between disinterestedness and selfishness. Of course, as we observed earlier, Niebuhr's remarks about justice's egocentricity often appear to rest on a conceptual link between self-assertiveness and the use of coercion. Given this link, he frequently seems to be saying that social morality effectively condones self-assertion by justifying coercive means and that in this respect it conflicts with the self-sacrificial ideal of individual conscience. The problem with this argument, once again, is that the logical connection between self-assertion and coercion is simply untenable because we can easily conceive of instances in which coercion is employed for entirely altruistic purposes (e.g., defending, at great risk to oneself, an innocent person against unjust aggression). Thus, the argument fails to explain the sort of conflict we have been considering. More generally, even if Niebuhr is correct in his assumption that the claims of conscience are irreconcilable with the claims of social morality, it seems that he will not be able to locate the source of the problem in a deeper tension between self-sacrifice and self-assertion.

But is the initial assumption correct? In order to answer this query we need to get a clearer picture of what Niebuhr means by conscience, a task made none too easy by the sketchiness of his general account. Nonetheless, while he needs to say more about conscience than he actually does, his undeveloped remarks on the subject suggest that he comes very close to adopting an interpretation according to which conscience is the faculty that determines the worth of an action on the basis of whether it is right or wrong, that is, on the basis of whether it conforms or fails to conform to duty impartially conceived, not on the grounds of whether it serves personal interest or contingently promotes any number of social goods. Moreover, to act conscientiously, according to this view, is to act on conscience's determination to perform or refuse to perform actions simply because they are right or wrong and not because they are expedient or inexpedient. It is such an understanding, I believe, that Niebuhr wishes to convey when he claims that individual morality "makes good motives the criterion of good conduct."[32] This morality, in other words, calls for acting on the dictates of conscience, even if so doing turns out to be unhappy in its effects either on the self or on the society at large.

At this point two questions naturally arise: (1) *What* particular judgments does conscience issue? (2) *How* does it arrive at these judgments? Niebuhr's treatment of both these questions is vague at best, and it is doubtful that all of his explicit pronouncements could be brought together into one coherent whole; yet his overall discussion permits us to draw some tentative conclusions about his views on the determinations and procedures of conscientious reflection. In the first place, such reflection, for Niebuhr, seems to issue in a number of prescriptions prohibiting and commending acts that fall under certain descriptions (e.g., 'Refrain from violence'; 'Do not steal'; 'Tell the truth'; 'Keep promises'.). These prescriptions admit of no qualification as far as their moral bindingness is concerned; that is, an agent's violation of them always involves at least some moral guilt. Practically speaking, however, they cannot be taken as absolutes since there will be conflict among them (a fact suggesting conflict internal to conscience itself) and since they will often collide with the pragmatic requirements of social existence.[33] Niebuhr sometimes expresses this point about the practical necessity of compromise by stating, rather misleadingly, that no actions are intrinsically immoral and that, to the contrary, the status of any act depends solely on the social consequences it generates.[34] As should be obvious, such a position amounts to an unadulterated utilitarianism, which renders senseless his claims about conflict between the requirements of conscience and the utilitarian canons of social morality. What Niebuhr means to say, I think, is that *from the perspective of social morality* actions have only instrumental value. One can make this claim and still hold, as any dualist such as Niebuhr must, that individual conscience condemns as *intrinsically immoral* a range of actions that social morality justifies on *instrumental* grounds.

So much for the content of conscience. What about its procedures? How does conscience arrive at its determinations? Here Niebuhr is especially vague. Yet his characterization of individual morality as entirely introspective, delivering its judgments without regard to consequentialist considerations, suggests a view of conscience as a faculty that simply intuits in some unmediated fashion the intrinsic rightness or wrongness of various actions. Such intuition, when it escapes distortion by external circumstances, presumably reflects the claims of human nature in its "original righteousness."[35] Of course, Niebuhr always remains sensitive to the ways in which social and historical conditions or even sin can refract the intuitions of conscience and thus warp moral judgments. Indeed, such refraction is said to account for much of the moral diversity one finds across space and time. Still, with persistent regularity the true voice of conscience breaks through the contingencies of human existence and expresses the "requirements of action dictated by man's essential nature."[36] And in a world where social exigencies frequently demand the doing of things that violate that nature, the voice will often be heard to speak the word of self-incrimination and moral guilt.

This understanding of conscience as an inner tribunal of moral intuition immediately discerning the intrinsic value of acts irrespective of consequences is an understanding that naturally makes possible Niebuhr's talk about irresolvable conflict between the respective claims of individual and social morality. Yet at this juncture one is compelled to ask just why Niebuhr separates consequentialist considerations from the operations of conscience in the way he does. Unfortunately, he provides no clear-cut answer to this question, but I think, if pressed, he would repair to phenomenological arguments claiming that departures from certain moral principles on consequentialist grounds always result in an uneasy conscience, the experience of moral guilt, and that such an experience attests to the violation of a binding moral requirement. As should be clear by now, however, this sort of phenomenological maneuver is simply inconclusive. Even if we grant that the sense of self-conviction is often an experiential datum of decision making in these contexts, we need not admit that the datum signifies the violation of a genuine moral requirement since the experience may be pathological, albeit understandable. Most important for present purposes, in an alternative view of *conscience,* there may be reason for saying that such an experience *is* pathological even when it is the result of employing ordinarily questionable means that have been justified on consequentialist grounds.

According to this alternative view, conscientious reflection is to be generally conceived not as a source of moral conflict, in the manner Niebuhr suggests, but rather as a process set in motion by such conflict, a process whose goal is the *adjudication* of moral perplexity. The operations of conscience understood in this sense are marked by a number of distinctive procedural features.[37] For an agent to reflect conscientiously on a moral problem, that is, she must take into full account the circumstances surrounding her decision, including prior explicit or implicit commitments, personal ideals, special bonds to persons or institutions, the more general network of human relations, and the nature of the contemplated means as well as the consequences of performing or refusing to perform the considered action. In assessing the circumstances, she must be self-critical, open to the possibility of any prejudice that might skew her perceptions of the factual or moral state of affairs. Having surveyed the entire range of circumstances, at least to the extent her power permits, she must then decide which course is morally preferred all things considered, and she must regard this moral judgment as both the necessary and the sufficient condition of her own performance or nonperformance. In this account, any action that is the outcome of such a deliberate process may fairly be taken as an action of conscience.

If this view of conscientious reflection and action is correct, then Niebuhr is much too quick in assuming that the judgments of conscience are wholly *internal* affairs and thus in conflict with the *external* requirements of genuine social responsibility. For one thing, in the alternative view, any moral assessment that refuses to *consider* all the consequences of a contemplated act cannot be regarded as a conscientious assessment in the full sense of the term. Moreover, it will not be difficult to imagine conditions under which *conscience*, understood in this alternative way, judges that consequentialist considerations are weighty enough to override scruples about the means employed. All other things being equal, for example, politicians should not abuse their patronage powers. But matters are cast in a somewhat different light when we learn that Abraham Lincoln's possible bribery of lame-duck congressmen with federal jobs was motivated by a concern to secure the necessary votes for the antislavery amendment, passage of which, he believed, would hasten the ending of a bloody civil war.[38] It is certainly not unintelligible to suggest that Lincoln's judgments and actions in this matter were a function of his personal conscience, duly informed by careful consideration of the moral requirements of his office. Needless to say, and as Niebuhr is wont to remind us, the potential for self-deception in such contexts always exists; a clear conscience, when all is said and done, may simply be a mistaken one. Indeed, one might argue that Lincoln badly misjudged the moral demands of his station. Yet it is one thing to admit the possibility of an erroneous conscience in its assessment of social responsibility and quite another thing to claim, as Niebuhr's dualism does, that the *correct* judgments of conscience conflict irreparably with the *correct* determinations of social responsibility. As far as I can tell, there is nothing in Niebuhr's explicit position that compels this dilemmatic rendering.

To reach this conclusion is not to deny that there may be deeper theological reasons for Niebuhr's dualism, reasons he occasionally hints at but fails to explore fully. We have already seen that his descriptions of moral ambiguity are sometimes connected in an ad hoc way to the doctrine of justification by faith; and his remarks about the "uneasy conscience" are delivered in the midst of discussing the moral law's power to convict humans of their sinfulness. Yet in Niebuhr's case, the precise nature of the links between these overarching theological commitments and the moral dilemmas thesis remains unclear. In view of this unclarity and the enormous theoretical difficulties that dilemmas pose for any Christian theological ethic, it seems reasonable to conclude that Niebuhr's affirmation of an irresolvable moral dualism is simply premature.

Borderline Situations

Up to now the discussion of this chapter has focused on pro-dilemmas arguments grounded in normative analyses of specific moral problems. If my assessments have been accurate, these analyses are inconclusive and consequently fail to prove beyond reasonable doubt that agents are ever faced with genuine moral dilemmas. At best such normative assessments drive us to deeper reflection on possible connections between a theoretical commitment to dilemmas and certain fundamental theological beliefs. In the remainder of this chapter I want to consider Helmut Thielicke's elaborate attempt to forge these sorts of connections. In Thielicke's view, dilemmatic interpretations of moral perplexity are required not simply by normative analyses taken in isolation but rather by basic theological doctrines, which constitute the Christian view of the world and which impose theoretical constraints on Christian ethical assessments of specific moral problems. As I have already suggested, Thielicke's position arguably provides the most comprehensive theological defense of the moral dilemmas thesis in the history of Christian ethics. For this reason his general account warrants extended treatment here.

According to Thielicke, the fundamental task of theological ethics is not essentially one of applied normative ethics or casuistry; that is, it does not primarily involve the resolution of moral problems through appeals to principles grounded in theological doctrine. Rather, that task is one of *theological diagnosis* or the theological interpretation and explanation of moral phenomena

selected in accordance with certain theological canons of significance. Thielicke detects in this procedure a kind of circularity but
regards such as the inevitable condition of any systematic inquiry.
More particularly, he claims in a Weberian manner that the presupposition of any theoretical investigation is a principle of phenomena selection that has its roots in some idiosyncratic way of
viewing the world (TE 1:462).[39] Theological ethics constitutes no
exception to this rule of inquiry. On the contrary, the moral phenomena to be explained by ethical theory are chosen with an eye
to their potential for illuminating fundamental theological truths.
As a result, certain features of moral experience will be emphasized at the expense of others in any theological explanatory
account.

It is this methodological understanding that informs Thielicke's
strategy of selecting instances of moral perplexity for theological
interpretation. The specific justification for the selection is that
such instances present the clearest examples of disruption in the
moral life, and as Thielicke sees it, only in such disruption is the
authentic structure of the world disclosed, namely, its extreme
disorder, its fallenness. Preoccupation with the normal cases of
moral experience, that is, those in which our general principles
provide unambiguous guidance, tends to obscure this fact about
the world. Only when our principles fail to serve us in this manner do we come to experience in our moral lives what the Bible
and Reformation theology teach—that the world is entirely
broken by sin. More specifically, the point of departure for Christian theological ethics must be the examination of cases of conflict between our moral principles. In such cases we are forced to
compromise one or more of our moral values, and this fact of
moral compromise makes manifest the condition of the world in
which we live. For this reason Thielicke states that moral conflict
or, as he often categorizes such conflict, the "borderline situation" serves as "an instructive example in terms of which to study
the fact of the fallen world and to put the problem of ethics in its
sharpest form" (TE 1:582).

Exactly how moral conflict highlights the fact of the world's
fallenness is an intricate matter that occupies a substantial portion of Thielicke's attention. At this point, however, it is essential
to emphasize that for him the theological significance of the
borderline situation is inextricably bound up with its genuinely
dilemmatic structure. Borderline situations present us with conflicts that in principle are beyond unequivocal moral resolution,

and it is in virtue of this specific feature that they are important from the perspective of theological ethics. For this reason Thielicke refuses to construe moral perplexity in simple epistemic terms, a refusal brought out unambiguously in his critical analysis of the Thomistic theory of natural law. He rightly identifies the tendency of that theory to attribute the cause of moral perplexity to limitations in our cognitive apprehension of moral truth. As we saw in earlier discussion, these limitations manifest themselves primarily in the application of the general principles of natural law to particular cases. Because subsumption of particular cases to general principles is always difficult, the practical conclusions deduced from the basic norms are often, according to the Thomistic theory, less than certain. What Thielicke objects to in this account is the operative presumption that moral perplexity is purely and simply an epistemological problem. Such a presumption reflects, according to him, a fundamental misunderstanding of the significance of moral conflict, which is said to depict essentially a defect in the moral order itself rather than a defect in our perception of that order. In other words, moral perplexity is first and foremost for Thielicke an ontological rather than an epistemological problem: "It would thus be a mistake to ascribe wholly to the subjective imperfection of our cognitive acts, as they take place within that zone where deduction and empiricism intersect, all the uncertainty involved in making concrete applications of the natural law. No, we must see that this uncertainty is grounded rather in the very structure of the world itself, an objective structure which is so permeated by guilt that there are in fact no 'pure' cases at all, such as those which the Thomistic view of order and nature is compelled to assume" (*TE* 1:415). Thus, Thielicke resists any purely epistemological interpretation of moral conflict. When faced with such conflict, he maintains, "We cannot even conceive of that which ought unequivocally and unreservedly to be" (*TE* 1:417).

What prompts Thielicke's refusal to cast conflict situations as problems of moral knowledge is presumably the concern to sustain a certain fit between the normative descriptions of such situations and the doctrine of justification *sola fide*. If moral conflict is merely a problem of epistemology, if there is in principle a resolution to such conflict in every case despite our occasional failures to discern the conditions of such resolution, then the way is open for the agent to escape morally unscathed provided that she hits on the correct answer either by extended ethical reflection or by sheer luck. Yet for Thielicke admitting this posibility of a way out betrays a failure to take seriously the fact that this world is one in which the autonomous achievement of objective righteousness is impossible. Given a full appreciation of this fact, conflict situations will come to be seen for what they actually are—genuine moral dilemmas in which the commission of a moral wrong is an inevitability, in which the agent ineluctably incurs moral guilt and thereby stands in need of divine forgiveness. Thus, Thielicke can say that belief in the adjudicability of moral conflict even as a matter of principle "is only a variation of that righteousness by the Law which feeds on the illusion that man is capable of satisfying the claim of God." It is for this reason also that he postulates the unity of the subject matter of dogmatics and ethics in "the doctrine of justification" (*TE* 1 : xviii).

Interestingly enough, while he is relentless in asserting that borderline situations present us with genuine moral dilemmas, Thielicke is reluctant to conclude that there are no optimal courses of action in these situations. Dilemmas can never be resolved without moral guilt, but the alternatives do admit of comparative assessment, and it is part of the agent's responsibility to engage in such assessment. Thielicke often puts the point in terms of a distinction between *qualitative* and *quantitative* adjudication, a distinction that he never clearly defines but one that is crucial, nonetheless, to certain of his normative analyses (*TE* 3 : 226–47). A particular instance is his assessment of abortion cases in which one is confronted with a choice between killing the fetus and allowing the mother to die. In discussing such cases Thielicke postulates the full humanity of the fetus's existence and subsequently concludes that from the "qualitative point of view" no resolution of the conflict is possible (*TE* 3 : 245). Both the decision to abort and the decision not to abort incur moral guilt. At the same time, this qualitative judgment is said to leave open the possibility of certain quantitative discriminations grounded in "empirical observations" (*TE* 3 : 244). Thus, while the fetus's status is qualitatively equivalent to the mother's, we may still speak in quantitative terms of the mother's having a "higher sacrosanctity" (*TE* 3 : 245). We are presumably led to such an assessment by observing, for instance, that in general a mother's willingness to sacrifice her life for her fetus is not as strong as when a comparable sacrifice is required to save the life of a child already born. This quantitative discrimination is similarly buttressed, according to Thielicke, by the appearance of certain distinctions in the criminal law between the comparative values of the fetus at different stages of development. He never tells us why such empirical indicators of social attitude are morally relevant, and this, of course, is a serious omission. However that issue might be resolved, the important point for present purposes is that Thielicke regards such considerations as establishing a quantitative presumption in favor of abortion for cases such as the one described.

In his treatment of abortion, Thielicke is careful to maintain a boundary between this sort of quantitative analysis and an unabashed utilitarian calculation, which he rejects explicitly (*TE* 3:229–32). Thus, state abortion policies could never be justified on the basis of eugenic or economic considerations, even in this secondary, quantitative sense. The rejection of an unqualified utilitarianism seems to have its roots in two concerns. First, as indicated by such policies, utilitarianism allows for the balancing of the value of human life against other sorts of social values (population quality, social wealth, and so forth). According to Thielicke, this balancing, at least in the case of abortion, is ruled out. Abortion admits of quantitative justification only when another's life (the mother's) is at stake (*TE* 3:247). Second, a purely utilitarian calculation reduces the worth of human existence to its instrumental value. Yet human life, according to Thielicke, is not so reducible; it retains, on the contrary, an intrinsic value or "alien dignity," which by definition is not cashable in terms of its functional utility or "value for producing 'good works'" (*TE* 3:231). This irreducible, intrinsic value makes itself felt in the qualitative indictment of *any* abortion justified on quantitative grounds. Utilitarianism cannot explain this indictment since it does not allow for a residual moral wrong consequent on performing the most favorable action, all things considered. In the final analysis, then, for Thielicke the problem with utilitarianism is that its unqualifiedly reductionistic program denies the ineradicable ambiguity of moral conflict. While there may be better and worse courses of action in conflict cases, taking even the best course involves the agent in moral guilt.

This second criticism of utilitarianism is part of a larger attack by Thielicke on any normative ethical theory that seeks refuge from moral guilt in the quantitative calculation of consequences: "The weighing of quantitative distinctions is certainly demanded. Bearing in mind the fallen form of the world, however, makes it impossible to assume that whatever action is determined on that basis to be the best possible automatically establishes of itself an

ontic righteousness" (*TE* 1:501). According to Thielicke, any refusal to accept this impossibility is symptomatic of a deep-seated
wish to achieve *securitas* in moral righteousness, a *securitas* beyond attainment in this world (*TE* 1:491–93). That such consola-
tion is beyond human grasp, he sometimes suggests, is attested to
by the fact that conscience convicts even those decisions justified
on consequentialist grounds (*TE* 1:492). At other times he claims
that the futility of the search for *securitas* in the context of moral
conflict is a function of the sheer incommensurability of the competing values (*TE* 1:491–92). It should be noted that Thielicke
never says explicitly just how much weight such phenomenological and conceptual considerations are supposed to carry in his
overall argument against consequentialism. What is clear is that
the load they can bear is limited. The constraint of internal consistency would seem to prohibit his appeal to incommensurability as
an *exhaustive* account of the impossibility of *securitas* since,
as we have seen, he does admit instances in which quantitative
assessments (implying commensurability of some sort) are both
possible and obligatory. Even if one allowed for some cases where
the competing values were genuinely incommensurable, however,
problems would remain. As I have already argued, neither the putative facts of an uneasy conscience nor assessments of incommensurability are sufficient to establish the radical insolubility of
moral conflict. Consequently, neither can be cited by Thielicke as
conclusive evidence that such conflict inevitably generates moral
guilt and that therefore the search for *securitas* is ill-conceived.
Yet, most likely, these are not decisive objections to Thielicke's
position. For he probably regards such phenomenological and conceptual considerations as ancillary to his fundamental argument,
which is *theological* in nature. *Securitas* is deemed impossible
mainly because, in Thielicke's view, it is inconsistent with the
doctrine of justification by faith.

In any event, Thielicke's general assessment of an unadulterated
consequentialism is clear. The theory's inadequacy resides in its
incapacity to do justice to the ambiguity of moral conflict. He
often makes the point in terms of the language of means and ends.
Because it restricts normative analysis to a determination and assessment of the ends of human action, a purely consequentialist
ethic ignores the moral significance of means. It assumes, in other
words, that ends justify means in every case and without equivocation. For Thielicke this assumption is unquestionably mistaken since there do occur instances in which the means em-

ployed are morally wrong despite the fact that they are justified in terms of the ends to be achieved. The abortion problem discussed earlier is a case in point. Abortion involves the direct killing of a human being, and as such it constitutes, from Thielicke's perspective, a morally corrupt means even when employed as part of the most favored course of action from the moral point of view. No matter how weighty, consequentialist considerations cannot erase this fact. For Thielicke the point is generalizable: "This implies quite simply that even in the name of an end which seems to be commanded I cannot disregard the means; I cannot scorn the commands which restrain or the safeguards which impede me, as though the situation of conflict could that easily be resolved" (*TE* 1:612).

While consequentialism is in error inasmuch as it emphasizes the moral relevance of ends to the exclusion of means, there is, according to Thielicke, another interpretation of the means/ends relation that is just as problematic. The position under consideration is one he sometimes refers to as "legalistic moralism" (*TE* 1:613), which has come to be discussed in philosophical circles under the heading of *ethical absolutism*. By this account, the moral life is seen primarily in terms of an absolute obedience to moral principles prohibiting the performance of acts falling under certain descriptions. The content of the prohibitions will vary depending on which version of absolutism is being considered. Thus, conservative versions of the theory will prohibit the direct killing of innocent human life while more radical versions (e.g., absolute pacifism) will prohibit all forms of violent resistance. Whatever the content of the principles, however, consequentialist considerations, according to the absolutist, are never sufficient to override these prohibitions, and, therefore, the actions denoted by the prohibitive rules may never be engaged in as means to achieving one's end, no matter how important that end may be.

Now Thielicke sees in such an absolutism the same concern for *securitas* in moral righteousness that was detected in consequentialism (*TE* 1:613). The difference, of course, is that the absolutists believe moral guilt to be avoidable through rigid adherence to a set of moral rules rather than through promotion of the most favorable consequences, all things considered. But for Thielicke this absolutist belief is a delusion since there are certain situations in which the consequences of adhering to a prohibitory rule would be so grave that it is a matter of ethical responsibility to consider setting the rule aside. He suggests that this condition may

188 THEOLOGICAL ETHICS AND MORAL CONFLICT

have obtained in the case of the Nazi concentration camps where prisoners were instructed to select from among themselves those who were "unfit" and thus ready for execution (*TE* 1 : 589–91). Refusal to cooperate would result, as past experience had proven, in the execution of an even greater number. According to Thielicke, the most favored course of action in such a case cannot be decided in advance. But whatever the solution to that problem, he maintains, *any* decision in this sort of situation "stands under an ineluctable burden of guilt which apart from forgiveness would be quite unbearable" (*TE* 1:591). And this includes a decision to refuse cooperation out of respect for the principle that prohibits participation in the murder of innocents. Absolutism, therefore, provides no unambiguous escape from such conflict, which for Thielicke cannot be resolved without moral remainder.

Thielicke's criticism of absolutism is not qualified, however, for he does allow that certain types of acts may not be performed under any circumstances. The rules prohibiting such acts provide what he calls "a casuistical minimum" specifying "certain limits which cannot be transgressed."

> That we have to reckon with such limits is grounded in the fact that at certain points in life there are confrontations with transcendence in which it is impossible for us to regard that which is encountered as on the same level with various other possibilities of decision. Now it is of the very essence of conflict that two possibilities which are relatively co-ordinated and of relatively equal validity stand over against one another. If, however, one of these possibilities is transcendence itself, it loses its character as one "possibility" among others. It then becomes an "impossibility" to think that the choice before us is still wide open and that we have the possibility of decision. In such a case the situation is precisely not one of conflict. It is these limits which are imposed upon the very existence of the conflict situation—and the consequent need for and possibility of decision—to which we make reference when we employ the phrase "casuistical minimum" as a technical term. (*TE* 1:643–44)

For Thielicke an act is prohibited absolutely if it falls roughly under one of two descriptions—*blasphemy* (e.g., denying Christ) or *violation of personhood* (*TE* 1:644–47). Paradigm cases of the latter include the use of torture or truth drugs for the purpose of compelling confessions or releasing vital information. Such methods are said to dehumanize inasmuch as they rob human beings of the capacity for decision in freedom, a capacity Thielicke implies is essential to authentic personhood. In any event, conflict situations in which one of the colliding principles is either that forbidding blasphemy or that prohibiting violation of personhood are for Thielicke never genuinely dilemmatic. Notwithstanding the gravity of the consequences, the refusal to commit blasphemy or engage in depersonalizing activities is absolutely required, and such refusal presumably can be issued under any condition in good conscience, that is, without the sense that moral guilt is incurred. The upshot is that for Thielicke *certain* conflict situations may be resolved unequivocally by the absolute adherence to principle. What he apparently wishes to deny is the absolutist's claim that *all* conflict situations may be so resolved. Now one may question whether Thielicke is allowed even this partial concession to absolutism. For, after all, his most explicit argument against an unqualified absolutism is that in any given case it seeks *securitas* in moral righteousness, a *securitas* that is beyond attainment in this world. Yet might not the same criticism be lodged against Thielicke's own minimalist version of absolutism? Indeed, his position implies that an agent who rejects blasphemy or depersonalization can always rest assured that the right thing was done even when the consequences of such a rejection are disastrous (e.g., when innocent lives are lost as a result). If this assurance is to be distinguished from the *securitas* that has been dismissed, then some explanation of the distinction is in order. Thielicke, however, provides no such explanation.

Whatever the status of Thielicke's partial concession to absolutism, his rejection of an unqualified absolutism is clear. Again, like consequentialism in its pure form, an unrestricted absolutism is false because it assumes that every situation of moral conflict admits of unambiguous resolution. Of course, Thielicke believes this assumption must be rejected since, as he sees it, there do exist genuinely dilemmatic circumstances in which moral guilt is incurred no matter what course of action is taken.

While consequentialism and absolutism attempt to eradicate the guilt of moral conflict by suggesting unequivocally *moral* resolutions, there is, according to Thielicke, another type of theory that aims to dissolve such guilt by maintaining that certain realms of human activity are not bound by moral principles at all. The area of practical life most frequently accorded this autonomous status is the realm of politics. It is sometimes claimed that political activity is governed normatively not by morality but rather by laws of political necessity which are bereft of moral content. Thus, politicians, in order to secure some political goal, will often lie, cheat, bribe, blackmail, and so forth. Yet according to the position under consideration, they do not incur moral guilt thereby, since the norms of morality prohibiting such action are not applicable to political life. Furthermore, while the political goals in question often have a utilitarian character (e.g., the preservation of the common good), they need not be of this type. Political necessity is often interpreted simply as the need to conserve or achieve political power irrespective of the particular use to which such power might be put. At any rate, it is important to distinguish this sort of political amoralism from an ethical consequentialism that claims politicians are often *morally* justified in setting aside moral principles that are binding ordinarily. Even when the political goals are of a utilitarian nature, the amoralist construes them in nonmoral terms. Such goals provide distinctively political rather than moral justifications of the activities described. The question of *moral* assessment simply cannot arise in a political context. It is for this reason, according to the amoralist, that we must reject any talk of a politician's acquiring moral guilt in the way of doing what is politically required. The so-called paradox of dirty hands is, in this view, simply meaningless.

Now, while he cannot countenance an unrestrained *Realpolitik*, which justifies setting morality aside for the sake of preserving political power *simpliciter*, Thielicke does admit that political necessity—interpreted in terms denoting the common good—often requires the abandonment of some moral principle or other. He differs from the amoralist even on this matter, however, in his reluctance to dismiss the relevance of the principle left behind. Although politicians, in discharging the duties attached to their office, are frequently obliged to engage in ethically dubious activities, they dirty their hands, morally speaking, in so doing. In Thielicke's view, the politician's recognition of this fact serves as a safeguard against excessive moral compromise:

> Whoever retains an awareness that in certain fields and situations some crookedness is inevitable is still under a restraint which no longer applies to the man who no longer makes any distinction whatever between crooked and straight, evil and good. "Having to sin" is basically quite a different idea from that of eliminating the concept of sin altogether. Luther's "sin boldly and believe even more

boldly" still grasps the horns of the altar, whereas in Machiavelli there is an unending level plain where once the temple stood, and with the temple there has disappeared also the sign, the reminder [*Anamnesis*] that the world as it is ought not to be, and that we can thus live in it only under forgiveness. (*TE* 1 : 539)

Theological ethics, then, must reject the tenets of political amoralism and thus must realize "that there can be no complete separation between the sphere of a political realism which is supposed to be morally neutral and the personal sphere of ethical obligation" (*TE* 1 : 543). The politician simply occupies a space on which conflicting moral requirements converge.

All in all, for Thielicke any normative theory that attempts to explain away the moral guilt native to borderline situations finally must be dismissed. As I have already noted, the fundamental reason for the dismissal, in his view, is intimately related to the doctrine of justification *sola fide*. Now on its face this is a surprising position. The argument appears to be that the doctrine of justification inexorably forces a dilemmatic reading of moral perplexity. Stated so simply, the correlation is certainly questionable. It is one thing to say, as the doctrine implies in its standard form, that under the conditions of fallen existence persons inevitably fail to achieve what morality requires and therefore stand in need of forgiveness as well as the alien righteousness imparted by God's grace. It is quite another thing to say that the inevitability of human failing is sometimes of the sort that would be generated by a moral dilemma. Indeed, one could argue quite plausibly that the moral guilt which would be associated with a genuine dilemma is categorically distinct from the moral guilt conceptually related to the doctrine of justification. After all, it is reasonable to propose that the sin standing in need of divine grace, according to the doctrine, involves a moral violation willfully embraced and prompted by wayward inclination. In this view, the condition of sin is simply that persistent, *internal* impediment preventing agents from doing what they know they ought to do. But the "sin" that would be generated by a moral dilemma appears to be not like that at all. In such a case it seems possible to say that the agent's psychological integrity is maintained, that her intentions are good, that she is perfectly prepared to do what she ought to do even if it conflicts with her inclinations, but that she is prevented from so doing because of *external* constraints imposed by the world. The general point is that, given the distinction elaborated here, one could intelligibly assent to the doctrine of justification by faith and its correlative notion of sin as *internal* impediment to moral righteousness without admitting the existence of situations where "sin" is generated by *external* factors. And if such a position can be sustained, then there would appear to be no necessary connection between the doctrine and the moral dilemmas thesis.

Thielicke objects to this line of reasoning simply because he believes that the distinction between internal and external is untenable. The reason it is untenable, presumably, is that it rests on a mistaken understanding of the relation between individual sin and the sin of the world. The latter, which supposedly manifests itself in the borderline situation, is not something imposed on the individual agent entirely from without. Rather, this sinful world is a state of affairs for which every individual moral agent is in some sense responsible. Thus, it is wrong to suggest that the guilt of a moral dilemma is unrelated to the agent's own internal sin, for the world that produces the dilemma is in some way the creation of a human subjectivity in which all individual agents participate:

> The process involved here points essentially to a theological circumstance which will repeatedly occupy our attention, namely, that wherever there is a borderline situation we must speak not only of a fate which comes upon us but also of a guilt in which we are implicated. This guilt consists in the fact that our origin and point of departure is always to be found in a complex of wrong decisions, those made by ourselves and by others.
>
> The fact that conflict situations and conflicts of values exist at all in this world is not due to the "structure" of the world itself. More accurately, it is not due to the character imparted to the world by creation, as though "from the beginning" (Matt. 19:8) this included tragic features. It is due rather to the complex of wrong decisions which lie behind us, which have their ultimate root in that primal decision recorded in the story of the fall.
>
> It is not that "the world" is so perverse that it constantly thrusts us into borderline situations. It is rather that man has perverted his world, and no man is exempt from sharing responsibility for this human character of his world, this demonic humanizing of the world. No man is merely the object of a conflict situation. We are all part of the human subject that has helped to bring it about. (*TE* 1:596–97)

Against the background of such reflections, Thielicke often appears to draw a systematic connection between the dilemmas thesis and the construct of a sinful world. The logic of the connection is as follows: Borderline situations, through the moral guilt they display, illustrate microcosmically the fallen character of the world. To deny that such situations, because they are externally imposed, inevitably involve the agent in some moral wrong is to deny the agent's participation in the sin of the world, a participation that includes a shared responsibility for the conditions generating the conflict. Yet this second denial is inconsistent with the position, internal to the Christian (i.e., Reformation) view of reality, that all humans bear some guilt for the world's sinful structure. Thus, if it is to remain faithful to its fundamental anthropological tenets, Christian ethics must acknowledge that human agents are morally guilty no matter what course of action they take in conflict situations (cf. *TE* 1 : xx–xxi, 499–500).

There are two major difficulties with this argument. First, on the surface it seems implausible to suggest that in every case of moral conflict the agent bears some responsibility for the conditions that create the problem. True enough, we can point to instances where such an analysis does apply. If I promise to lie for my friend, for example, I am clearly responsible for the ensuing conflict between the values of promise keeping and veracity. Moreover, there might be cases where the responsibility is less obvious. Thus, a politician may be forced either to bribe a corrupt operative or to lose an important piece of social legislation, but she may also be indirectly accountable for the difficulty through her failure to work for reform of the system in which such deals are routinely made. Still, while it is necessary to recognize that agents are often responsible for the conflicts they find themselves in, it is also necessary to admit that for certain conflict situations such agent responsibility cannot reasonably be assigned. If the politician just described has spent her entire career battling political corruption and striving for social justice but is still faced with the conflict noted, it would seem unreasonable to claim that she was responsible, nonetheless, for the fix she was in. The only way to sustain such a judgment would be to argue for some notion of collective responsibility whereby each individual is accountable for every moral wrong in the world even though in certain cases no specific connections can be drawn between one agent's actions and another's moral transgressions. Not surprisingly, Thielicke does employ such a notion in his characterization of the guilt endemic to borderline situations. "Compromise does not mean that we have an excuse. It means that we participate in the supra-personal guilt of this aeon" (*TE* 1 : 500). Yet one can only wonder about the intelligibility of such a claim. Indeed, it seems reasonable to propose that the idea of an individual's incurring moral guilt merely by virtue of membership in a collectivity remains a mystification unless the guilt can be tied in one way or another to a specific dereliction of duty on that individual's part. At any rate, while they appear to be necessary to sustain his position, Thielicke's appeals to collective responsibility require more substantial explanation and defense than he provides.

The second difficulty with the argument under consideration is that it undoubtedly rests on an equivocation. Even if one grants that some agents are morally responsible for the conflicts they face, one need not grant the *further* point that such conflicts are genuine moral dilemmas. It is one thing to claim that an agent has incurred moral guilt for generating a borderline situation. It is another thing to argue that she incurs guilt for whatever she does in the situation itself. Thus, one might agree with Thielicke that the borderline situation is a sign of the world's fallenness (in which the agent participates) without agreeing that the situation is beyond unambiguous moral resolution. This distinction is subtle but important. For the first claim raises no obvious problems with regard to the coherence of God's commands, while the second claim does. On the one hand, to say that an agent is morally guilty for creating conditions that lead to moral conflict is to suggest that she has violated some moral obligation forbidding such behavior, and on Thielicke's terms (he is clearly a theological voluntarist) the existence of this obligation attests to a divine command prohibiting the conduct. Yet to acknowledge such a command is to acknowledge nothing ambiguous about the content of God's will. On the other hand, as we have seen, the theological voluntarist's admission of dilemmas does imply an admission of incoherence in God's purposes. The general point is that there is considerable reason for Thielicke to avoid a commitment to dilemmas; he can avoid this commitment apparently without abandoning his claims about the sin of human agents who create the conditions of conflict as well as the suffering almost invariably associated with such conflict. The notion of a sinful world, in this sense at least, does not entail the existence of moral dilemmas.

Thielicke's remarks about dilemmas, however, often seem to

follow from a somewhat different understanding of the sinful world. According to this view, borderline situations are the result of conflicts arising out of the normative orders of creation. Under pre-lapsarian conditions these orders would yield unambiguous moral guidance in every instance, but the effects of the fall are such that the specific dictates of those orders clash. This conflict between the orders of creation is illustrated among other places in his aforementioned analysis of situations where aborting the fetus is the only alternative to permitting the mother's death (TE 3: 226–47). His argument appears to take the following form: The normative order inherent in creation requires that God's creative work be sustained in various ways. Among the principles generated by this requirement are those demanding the preservation of human life—more specifically, a principle of nonmaleficence (that human beings not be harmed) and a principle of beneficence (that the lives of human beings be actively promoted). Under pre-lapsarian conditions the specific duties arising from these principles can be discharged without difficulty. But given the circumstances of the fallen world in which there is "conflict between life and life" such as that manifested in the abortion case, the dictates of the principles inevitably collide. Abortion to save a mother's life conforms to the requirement of beneficence but at the same time violates the requirement of nonmaleficence with respect to the fetus. As a result, "the order of creation cannot provide a direct solution of the conflict" (TE 3:236). Nonetheless, that order retains its binding force; consequently, in such cases "we know that whatever we do we incur moral guilt" and "that we can decide only subject to forgiveness" (TE 3:242).

Now Thielicke suggests that the theological beliefs sustaining such an analysis are given particularly in the Reformation conception of the fall as a radical break with the created order, a conception that, he claims, differs significantly from the Catholic conception of sin. It is this difference, presumably, that accounts for the competing normative assessments generated by the respective traditions. According to Thielicke, the Catholic determination that there are unambiguous moral resolutions to conflict cases (a determination expressed in the judgment that only indirect abortion to save the mother's life is permissible) depends on the assumption that the normative created order is unequivocally applicable to human beings in their fallen condition. And this assumption in turn presumes that a measure of continuity obtains between the pre- and post-lapsarian states:

We can show how in the borderline situation there appears that distortion of perspective which demonstrates all too clearly the derangement of the order of creation and the conflict of values which has intruded into it. All this we can state at the level of theological argument. But we cannot proceed with the same style of argumentation and "solve" that conflict. For in order for us to be able to proceed in this way the order of creation would have to be an immediately applicable standard. But this it is not.

The order of creation would be this kind of standard only if we did not view the incursion of sin as radically as did the Reformers; in other words, if we did not interpret it as a break in the continuity between the original state and the fallen world. If, however, one accepts this almost unbroken continuity and introduces the doctrine of original sin accordingly, then both members of the continuity remain commensurable and the order of creation can be taken as a critical rule and standard and applied directly to the realities of our world. This experiment took form in the Catholic doctrine of natural law! (TE 3:240)

The details of the argument leading to these conclusions are not easily discerned, but the following would appear to be a reasonable extrapolation (TE 1:147–221). For the Catholic tradition the moral principles constitutive of the created order are part of a natural law that is grounded in human nature as it was created, that is, in the *imago dei*. What this means is that the normative bindingness of those principles on human behavior is inextricably tied to the fact that humans have an essential nature and that the natural law is peculiarly suited to that nature. To suggest, then, that the norms of the created order are directly and unambiguously applicable to human beings in their present sinful state is to imply that human nature has not been altered radically by the fall. It is this implication that, Thielicke maintains, the Reformation tradition rejects. According to that tradition, the effect of the fall on human nature is total. Since the *imago dei* is not a property constitutive of the human essence per se but is rather an attribute of relationship with God, human retention of the *imago* depends on the maintenance of that relationship. Yet sin, interpreted fundamentally as disobedience, involves the complete disruption of the relation between God and humanity. By this account, then, sin can only mean the obliteration of the *imago*. Thus, any talk of a direct and unequivocal application of the created normative order to humanity must be dismissed by the Reformation tradition.

Whatever one makes of Thielicke's readings of the respective traditions, the major problem with the foregoing is that it is not made entirely clear just how such theological considerations connect with the moral dilemmas thesis. What we need to hear is a specific argument supporting the claims (a) that the changes in human nature effected by the fall manifest themselves, among other ways, in the conflicts between goods that characterize historical existence and (b) that under such conditions the created orders cannot provide unambiguous guidance since the content of the principles constituting those orders contain no provisions for conflicting circumstances. While establishment of the first claim may be unproblematic, it is difficult to see how any appeal even to the most radical conception of the fall could aid in establishing the second. Presumably, what lies behind such a conception is the concern to preserve the integrity of the doctrine of justification *sola fide* by maintaining that human beings in their fallen state lack the inherent capacity either to know what morality requires or to fulfill its demands. None of this is to say, however, that the specific moral requirements generated by the created order conflict irresolvably under sinful conditions. On the contrary, all that follows from the radical conception is that, if the created order affords solutions to moral perplexity, then fallen persons either cannot know the content of those solutions or, knowing the content, cannot, because of sinful inclinations, live their lives in accordance with those solutions. The point is that adoption of the radical conception of the fall *simpliciter* seems not to require embracing the further claim that the orders of creation produce genuine moral dilemmas in the context of historical existence.

It would appear, then, that the issue here between Thielicke and the Catholics (as he reads them) has to do more with divergent understandings of the *completeness* or *extensiveness* of the moral system constitutive of the created order than with competing doctrines of human fallenness. The Catholic position would seem to hold that the moral system applicable to the pre-lapsarian state (the natural law) is rich enough in the content of its principles to make possible the adjudication of moral conflict even under post-lapsarian conditions. In other words, those principles are viewed as containing provisions for the peculiar circumstances that prevail in the sinful world, circumstances characterized by conflicts between goods. Once again, this is not to say that such provisions are regarded as unproblematically knowable by human beings in their present state. As Thielicke himself recognizes and as we saw earlier, the tenets of Thomistic natural law leave considerable room for moral perplexity as a serious epistemic problem. The important point is that the natural law is said to afford in principle resolutions to such perplexity even though the resolutions may be difficult to discern in any given case. It is precisely this last claim that Thielicke rejects. According to his account, the moral system informing the created normative order is comparatively impoverished in its content. Its principles provide unambiguous prescriptions for pre-lapsarian situations but are neither ordered nor qualified in a way that is sufficient for their rendering unequivocal solutions to conflicts they generate in post-lapsarian circumstances.

The intriguing thing about Thielicke's position as just outlined is that it seems to make moral dilemmas partially a function of God's unwillingness to adjust entirely to history. If irresolvable conflict is the product of a system of moral principles whose content is designed only for a pre-lapsarian world and if these principles reflect God's commands, then dilemmas are partly the product of God's failure to modify these commands for the conditions of historical existence. The reason this feature of the position is interesting is that in other places Thielicke does allow, up to a point, for God's adjusting his commands to meet the exigencies of the fallen world (*TE* 1 : 359–82, 567–77). Thus, violence between life and life symbolizes a disruption of the created order. But such violence is justifiable in history where the innocent must be protected against unjust aggression, and this justification signifies a concession to human sin on God's part (*TE* 1 : 357). It is such a concession, presumably, that is reflected in the quantitative justification of abortion mentioned earlier. In the created order killing the fetus is prohibited, yet such killing is allowable under historical conditions. At the same time, for Thielicke these divine concessions never completely resolve the moral conflict. On the one hand, they do establish new moral directives that are genuinely obligatory. Violence in defense of the innocent, for example, is not simply permissible; it is required. To deny this fact is fanatical. On the other hand, the new directives cannot extinguish the binding force of the created order left behind; rather, they call for a "compromise" of that order, a compromise that "stands in need of forgiveness" (*TE* 1 : 567). The upshot is that, while God adjusts his mandates for the fallen world, the accommodations are partial at best.

What does the partiality of God's adjustments tell us about the coherence of his purposes? Interestingly enough, Thielicke denies explicitly that the moral ambiguities of historical existence actually reflect genuine tension in the divine will: "For the borderline situation, being a case of extreme conflict, is characterized by the fact that . . . it implies an extreme concentration of the forces of revolt which are at work in this aeon. To this degree it involves a conflict with God, not a conflict within God" (*TE* 1:666). Yet it is difficult to see how this assessment can be sustained. If the compromises of the created order are authentic moral requirements, then presumably God wills such compromises. If the moral bindingness of the created order is preserved in spite of the compromises, then God also wills that creation's dictates be fulfilled. Of course, Thielicke is undoubtedly correct to suggest that this state of affairs also signifies in some sense a collision between the fallen world and God's primitive commands. The sin of the world, after all, remains in tension with God's original purposes as constituted in the created order. But to the extent that he *requires sinful actions* for the sake of the world's preservation, God also commands things that are simply inconsistent with other things he commands. This conclusion follows inevitably from Thielicke's characterization of the moral ambiguities native to historical existence.

The irony here is that such a characterization seems unnecessary to preserve what Thielicke regards as essential to Christian faith, that is, the doctrine of justification *sola fide* and its corresponding notion of a sinful world. As I have noted already, we may grant, at least in some cases, that humans are morally responsible for the historical conditions generating moral conflict and for the suffering such conflict typically involves.[40] We may grant also that this state of affairs requires divine forgiveness, that humans, in light of their responsibility for the sinful world, are made righteous only by their faith in God's gracious dispensation. Yet having conceded all of this, we need not admit that borderline situations are beyond unequivocal moral resolution. Of course, to claim that such situations are adjudicable in principle is not to deny the reality of honest disagreement about proper courses of action. With respect to violence in defense of the innocent, for instance, the pacifist will argue that such means are to be eschewed, that God does not compromise his demands in the face of sin. On the other hand, there will be those who contend that such violence is permissible, if not required, that God, in his providential concern for the welfare of his creation, unequivocally adjusts his requirements to meet the conditions of sin, and that humans may act accordingly with a clear conscience. Needless to say, there are numerous disagreements of this sort, and the questions they pose are not easily decided. But to acknowledge the poverty of our moral perceptions in these matters is not to conclude that the problems are functions of divine equivocations. And, indeed, if Christians have a stake in preserving the coherence of God's purposes, they will have every reason to resist such a conclusion.

In his explicit denial of ultimate tension in the divine will, Thielicke himself seems to appreciate the importance of this theoretical concern. Indeed, there are times when his considerations of God's unity appear to force him into a reinterpretation of conflict situations as purely epistemological problems. According to this reading, resolutions are not readily perceived, but judgments are made in the hope that the right course is taken and in the belief that apparent contradictions are merely apparent (*TE* 1:663–67). The trouble is that this sort of characterization hardly seems reconcilable with the rudiments of his moral theory. Perhaps it is not unfair to say that in the rare moments when he speaks this way Thielicke unwittingly illustrates the fundamental strain between the moral dilemmas thesis and an ethic that grounds moral requirement in the purposes of a reasonable God. At any rate, as should be clear by now, the strain is there. And what this means in more positive terms is that faith in such a God can only promote the conviction that moral perplexity is less an occasion for despair over inevitable moral guilt than a call for further ethical reflection to determine precisely what this reasonable God requires. There always remains the danger, of course, that the motivation behind such a conviction will be tainted. Thielicke is at his best when he reminds us that sometimes the search for solutions to our moral problems may be nothing more than a hubristic quest for self-justification. But he overstates his case in claiming that *any* belief in the adjudicability of moral conflict is finally reducible without remainder to such self-righteous concern. On the contrary, if I am correct, then that belief is simply a corollary of the view that moral requirement is a sign of divine guidance rather than an emblem of divine confusion. And it is difficult to see how one might sustain any Christian ethic that calls this view into question.

Conclusion

In this chapter I have focused on a number of theological considerations which have been or might be taken to demonstrate the existence of irresolvable moral conflict. I have tried to show that, whatever plausibility such considerations have in their own right, they are simply insufficient to establish the moral dilemmas thesis. Commonly proposed normative arguments frequently do underline real tensions in the moral life, but there is nothing in such arguments that excludes the possibility that such tensions are resolvable in principle. More often than not, pronouncements to the contrary rest on concealed theological premises that ought to be brought to light, or they rest on ad hoc appeals to theological constructs that call for further clarification. In Thielicke's case, where an elaborate attempt is made to link dilemmatic normative assessments systematically to points of fundamental theological doctrine, the arguments offered are finally inconclusive. Despite his claims suggesting otherwise, there appears to be no theoretical connection between the moral dilemmas thesis and the doctrine of justification *sola fide* or between that thesis and the idea of a world in sinful rebellion against the will of God. Consequently, it seems that everything of theological importance that Thielicke wishes to preserve can be preserved while acknowledging that moral perplexity admits of adjudication in principle.

Of course, there may be other theological constructs that can be tied systematically to the moral dilemmas thesis. Nothing I have said rules out this possibility, though I am unaware of theological programs that affirm dilemmas and proceed along lines substantially different from those discussed in this chapter.[41] In any event, my arguments have shown, I think, that the specific positions considered here cannot bear the theoretical burden of proof established earlier. If Christian ethics makes moral requirement a function either of divine providential guidance or of divine command, then it also has a stake in claiming that no moral conflict situations are beyond the possibility of unambiguous resolution. According to this view, moral perplexity, even in the most extreme cases, will have to be taken essentially as an epistemological problem. Given that supposition, our experience of such perplexity can only serve as an incentive for sustained involvement in the practice of normative inquiry.

POSTSCRIPT

THE general purpose of this essay has been to suggest that from the view of Christian ethics moral perplexity ought to be assessed essentially as a problem of moral knowledge. That is to say, situations in which it appears as though whatever we do is morally wrong should not be seen as authentic moral dilemmas, as functions of *real* conflict in the structure of moral reality itself, but instead as consequences of limitations on our capacities for discerning what that reality actually requires. This conclusion cannot be reached via pure philosophical reflection of the sort that draws exclusively on logical, phenomenological, or normative evidence. Indeed, as I have tried to show, such evidence is finally indeterminate regarding the question of moral perplexity's proper construal. Rather, the conclusion presented here is derived wholly from theological considerations of the relation between God and the moral life. Whether moral requirement is interpreted as an expression of providential guidance or as a representation of divine command, there are serious reasons for dismissing the possibility of genuinely irresolvable moral conflict. Standard theological arguments that suggest otherwise cannot, in the final analysis, bear the burden of proof such reasons impose. For the Christian believer, then, the experience of moral perplexity will always appropriately elicit the response of increased ethical reflection, whose point is to discover precisely what it is that morality demands.

This overall position undoubtedly will prompt the following question: "If it is true that situations of moral conflict are always resolvable in principle, that God is never absent in such instances, that his providential guidance is unequivocal, his commands, coherent, then what sense could possibly be made of the indisputably *tragic* character of these situations?" The question will be raised by those who have argued in recent years that the category of moral tragedy is an essential component of any adequate ethical theory. Among Christian ethicists, the most prominent defender of this view has been Stanley Hauerwas. According to Hauerwas, ethical theory in the twentieth century too often has been dominated by a model that depicts moral reasoning as a decision procedure yielding *solutions* to our moral problems. Such a model, as he sees it, cannot capture the most outstanding feature of our moral decision making in problem contexts, namely, that in such contexts there is often no unequivocal solution to be found. To assume otherwise is presumably to engage in self-deception, which typically manifests itself in distorted normative descriptions of our activities:

> For our difficulty with such matters is that morally we lack the
> skills to describe what happens in such dilemmas—especially
> since the dilemmas result from our own power of intervention. Be
> cause we lack a sense of the tragic we are tempted to try to justify
> what we do in such circumstances by using the language of the
> good—"It is a good thing that we let the child die." But what we
> must learn to see is that this is to misdescribe the situation by giv
> ing in to our need for moral justification. We must simply learn
> that often in such situations there is no right or wrong thing to
> do—whatever we do will involve both. Such situations are tragic
> and we only pervert ourselves . . . if we try to describe them in
> terms that deny they are anything else.[1]

Given this state of affairs, the primary task of ethical theory, particularly Christian ethical theory, is not to generate procedures for making moral decisions but rather to articulate "a truthful narrative," which "gives us the means to accept the tragic without succumbing to self-deceiving explanations."[2]

There is a good deal in Hauerwas's general account that cannot be considered here. But for our purposes the important issues are why he regards the concept of tragedy as essential to our moral descriptions and why he understands this notion as one compelling the dilemmatic interpretations of moral conflict. After all, it has frequently been suggested that the idea of tragedy is finally inimical to the Christian construction of reality, a construction whose "narrative," among other things, counterbalances the tragic subplot of Jesus' crucifixion with the *comic* denouement of his resurrection.[3] And even if one grants that there is room in the Christian world view for certain tragic *elements* (e.g., frustrated expectations, missed opportunities, broken friendships, physical and psychological harms), it still seems intelligible to claim that such elements never conspire to take the form of genuine moral dilemmas. Indeed, I have argued throughout this essay that there is every reason for Christian theology to exclude the possibility of tragedy in this more extreme sense. Why, then, does Hauerwas insist both that tragic characterizations are appropriate and that these categorizations must affirm the irresolvable character of moral conflict?

The answer to this question, I believe, is to be found not in any distinctively *theological* position he assumes but rather in a particular *sociological* theory that informs his reading of moral phenomena.[4] According to that theory, our moral quandaries are nothing more than symptoms of fragmentation in the moral discourse employed by the contemporary world. This fragmentation is a reflection of the fact that the various axiological and deontic concepts constituting our moral language are actually vestiges of diverse moral traditions, which arose in different historical contexts marked by idiosyncratic discursive practices. To propose that such quandaries are adjudicable is to assume that the diverse traditions are commensurable or orderable, but this assumption is sociologically naive. A historically informed ethical theory will recognize that such conflicts cannot be resolved and that this state of affairs makes for the moral tragedy endemic to modern life.

As far as I can tell, Hauerwas accepts this explanation virtually without qualification. Consequently, an issue he fails to address is whether the metaethical presuppositions of the sociological account just proposed can be reconciled with an ethic that ties moral concepts in various ways to the metaphysical beliefs of Christian theism. It may be true that the ethical discourse of the present is a collection of bits and pieces from conceptual schemes of different historical epochs and that this state of affairs explains the fact of moral conflict in the modern world. To infer from all of this, however, that moral conflict cannot be resolved is almost certainly to assume the truth of a kind of positivism, which holds that moral practices are no more than conventional systems created by human beings for the purpose of meeting the problems of community. Moral quandaries, in this view, are simply the product of a system's assimilating incompatible conventions derived from practices of an earlier time. Such quandaries are irresolvable in the modern world because the present system, *as a matter of brute fact*, does not contain further conventions ordering the competing conventions borrowed from the past.

Now it is difficult to see how this explanation could be entirely acceptable to Christian ethics. For in the Christian view, systems of moral discourse are not simply reducible without remainder to the brute factual conventions of a given society. Quite the contrary, the Christian will at least have to say that some of these moral systems represent more or less accurate attempts to capture the contents of an independent moral reality transcending in varying degrees the conventions themselves. This moral reality might be interpreted in terms of either providential directives or divine commands, but the crucial point is that, given such a reality, however interpreted, a conflict between the explicit normative canons of a system cannot in itself be regarded as evidence that the conflict is irresolvable in principle. It may simply be the case that a resolution is available (in moral reality) but has not been captured by the canons of the system in question. Indeed, if my previous assessments were correct, then Christian ethics must assume the availability of such a resolution. But whatever the score on that matter, the argument here is merely that, in explaining the "fact" of dilemmas and the necessity of tragic interpretations, Hauerwas cannot appeal to the sociological theory described without also denying implicitly what Christian ethics must affirm, namely, the existence of a moral reality that transcends any given moral system.

Having made this point, however, I think it necessary to concede that, despite the foundational difficulties with his program, Hauerwas still leads us in the right direction by bringing our attention to the tragic character of conflict cases. For whatever we want to say about the solubility of such cases, it would be hard to disavow the tragic interpretations given by morally scrupulous agents embroiled in these situations. Once again, in making even the most conscientious choices, such agents must often face the prospects, nonetheless, of generating bruised sensibilities, ruptured relations, broken commitments, and other harms of various sorts. Most important, even when the deleterious consequences are minimal, it still seems appropriate to speak of a *moral loss* inevitably incurred. Thus, deceiving a corrupt legislator to secure

a crucial piece of social legislation may be morally justifiable, all
things considered, but such an action will be and should be morally regretted by the conscientious agent. In these senses, then,
the tragedy of moral conflict would appear to be undeniable. And
any adequate moral theory, Christian or otherwise, will need to
provide an account of this element in the moral life. On that
matter, at any rate, Hauerwas seems substantially correct.

Yet he is mistaken in suggesting that a suitable explanation of
the tragedy signified by moral regret demands the admission of
genuine moral dilemmas.[5] On the contrary, as I noted earlier, acknowledging the appropriateness of moral regret in conflict situations does not require acknowledging further that the agent has
violated some binding moral obligation. Of course, when moral
regret is appropriate, this fact always attests to the sacrifice of
some moral value. But the loss of a moral value or a moral good
does not imply the doing of a moral wrong. To assume otherwise
is to confuse the categories of the moral good and the moral right.
Given this distinction, it is possible, after all, to explain the phenomenon of morally tragic conflict without referring to conflicting rights and wrongs. In the alternative account, such tragic conflict will be interpreted as a sign of the world's having fallen away
from the moral ideal and not as a sign of moral transgression. The
real issue before us is how this alternative account might be given
expression in the terms of an ethical theory grounded in Christian
theism.

Needless to say, much hangs on the type of theistic ethic being
considered. Take first the case of theological voluntarism. It might
be argued that according to this theory genuine moral tragedy will
be impossible to explain simply because, as Brunner noted, it is
hard to see how there could be tragedy in obeying a divine command. If God is the source of all moral value and if his unambiguous command is actually present in every situation of conflict, then what room could there be for talk of an agent's moral
regret in such situations?

This is a difficult question to answer, but I do believe a plausible response is available. The response turns on a conception of
the morally ideal world as a function of God's *desires* rather than
as an object of his *will*. Whatever the actual condition of the
world, for instance, God desires that lies not be told, that promises be kept, that bribes not be offered, and so forth; he desires
these things in the sense that, all other things being equal, he prefers the *possible* world in which such states of affairs are pre-

served. To make this claim, however, is not to deny that in the *actual* world God may will the telling of lies, the breaking of promises, the offering of bribes, and other such actions, when competing moral values are at stake. Indeed, God may will any of these things, but in so doing he always overrides one or more of his desires. It is important to emphasize that there is no suggestion here of God's willing incompatible courses of action in the real world; such a suggestion would naturally raise questions about God's coherence. Yet there is no incoherence in a being's willing something that has undesirable features as long as that something is also desirable in other respects. And given the rationality of willing under these circumstances, moral tragedy can be explicated without attributing irrationality to the divine volition. For now the appropriateness of an agent's moral regret in conflict cases will be explained by the fact that the morally required course of action, the course *willed* by God, is one that would not be taken in the morally ideal world, that is, the world constituted by God's desires. On the interpretation offered here, one might say, moral tragedy is always a sign of *divine* regret over the actual state of affairs.

How might such tragedy be accounted for in terms of Thomistic natural law? One is unlikely to find an explicit answer to this question in the theory's classical expression. Thus, there is some truth to the claim, advanced by certain commentators, that the notion of tragic conflict is foreign to Aquinas's ethics.[6] At the same time, I do think it is possible to reconstruct an analysis of moral tragedy from the elements of Thomistic theory without violating its spirit. In brief, moral tragedy, given this reconstructed view, will be seen as a function of conflict among the various goods of human existence, and moral regret will be interpreted as an indispensable feature of the virtuous agent's response to instances of such conflict.

It will be remembered that for Aquinas doing what is morally right contributes substantially to the agent's self-realization, while doing what is morally wrong impedes such self-realization. Both these points are related to the Thomistic presupposition that the principles of moral requirement, the precepts of the natural law, are expressions of the eternal law through which God providentially directs his creatures to their specific ends. Given this relation, moral dilemmas would be theoretically problematic inasmuch as their existence would signify disorder in the providential scheme. More particularly, a dilemma would have to be taken as an instance in which an agent paradoxically frustrated her progress toward self-realization by performing the very action demanded by that self-realization. Yet to claim that for this reason dilemmas must be excluded theoretically is not to deny that there can be conflict among the various goods of human life. On the contrary, the exclusion of dilemmas requires only the affirmation that such conflict is resolvable, that for the agent there is always available some course of action affording an unambiguous path to self-realization. Needless to say, the resolutions will always involve the sacrifice of some human good, and a reasonable agent will respond to the loss with a measure of regret. Under certain conditions, moreover, the loss in question will be characterized most appropriately as a *moral* one.

This last conclusion derives support from Aquinas's understanding of moral activity as behavior that promotes in one way or another the bonding of human communities.[7] In this view, the moral worth of actions such as promise keeping and truth telling at least partially depends on their capacities for creating and sustaining relations among persons. In an ideal world these relations would flourish without qualification, but in the real world breakdowns frequently occur. Sometimes the breakdowns are the consequences of out-and-out violations of moral right. This individual fails to keep a promise merely because keeping it would be inconvenient. That individual tells a lie simply to gain undue advantage. Yet at other times the damaging or severing of human relations may be the result of doing precisely what is morally required. Breaking a promise may lead to alienation, but the action may also be morally justified by the fact that the alternatives would have even graver effects on the community. Telling a lie may, on its discovery, generate an irreparable rift between persons, but the falsehood may be necessary to protect the fundamental well-being of others. Of course, where such actions are indeed morally required, it is essential for Aquinas to say that their performance cannot impede the agent's progress toward self-realization. To claim otherwise, once again, would be to admit disorder in providential design or operation. Yet having conceded as much, it is still possible, on Aquinas's own terms, to speak of a moral loss in these cases, a loss constituted by the ruptures in human community. Given such a loss, the proper attitude of the virtuous agent will be one of moral regret.

If I am correct, then, nothing in the positions of theological voluntarism and Thomistic natural law makes it impossible for them to account for genuine tragedy in the moral life. Just as important, the necessary explanations can be provided without admitting the existence of moral dilemmas. While we may insist that an unequivocally right course of action is always available in situations of conflict, we may still speak intelligibly of a real moral cost in such situations, a cost that will elicit from the morally sensitive agent a response of heartfelt regret. The crucial point is that theological considerations prevent our interpreting such regret as evidence of an unavoidable moral transgression. If God's commands are coherent or if his providential directives are ordered, then we must assume that moral requirement in cases of conflict is always unambiguous as a matter of principle.

Of course, as I have stressed throughout this essay, to presume that in principle moral requirement is unambiguous is not to deny that its precise dictates will be hard to discern in certain instances. Indeed, such a denial would be foolish in the face of our moral experience, which shows that under the most extreme conditions agents may be thoroughly perplexed about what they ought to do. In light of that experience I have suggested that the most difficult conflict situations provide an incentive for engaging in serious and sustained ethical inquiry. Yet this suggestion may provoke the response that such inquiry is never productive, that ethical reflection can at best identify competing values and principles but can never yield solutions to our moral conflicts. The problem, according to the objection, is that the canons of our moral thinking simply do not include ruled procedures for adjudication. In the absence of such procedures, all we can do is choose, and practical necessity will compel our choosing in problem cases. The idea that our decisions ever reflect some truth of the matter discovered through considered reflection is an idea without foundation, however. That there are no ruled procedures shows that there is no truth of the matter; that there is no truth of the matter makes normative inquiry a waste of time.

This is a powerful objection, but two considerations diminish its force in the present context. First, the nihilism expressed (at least with respect to conflict cases) would be difficult to reconcile with certain fundamental beliefs about God's relation to the moral life. For if no moral truth remains to be discovered in situations of perplexity, then the implication for theological ethics would appear to be that God is absent from these situations, that neither divine commands nor providential directive is available to the agent. Second, such nihilism seems unduly pessimistic about the

possibilities afforded by normative reflection. Admittedly, it is
hard to see at times how many of our moral conflicts might be
adjudicated satisfactorily. We struggle to imagine, for instance,
what normative principles could possibly render an unequivocal
solution to the abortion problem. At the same time, it is also hard
to know in advance how much of our perplexity is the function of
social circumstances that distort our moral perceptions and blind
us to principles that could resolve our difficulties. History is instructive in this matter. As poignantly illustrated in Mark Twain's
characterization of Huck Finn, there was a time when individuals
were unsure about their moral responsibilities related to fugitive
slaves. On the one hand, Huck could not bring himself to inform
on his friend Jim, the runaway slave. On the other hand, the young
boy also concluded that as a slave Jim was the private property of
Miss Watson, a conclusion which prompted self-conviction:

> Well, I can tell you it made me all over trembly and feverish, too, to
> hear him, because I begun to get it through my head that he *was*
> most free—and who was to blame for it? Why, *me*. I couldn't get
> that out of my conscience, no how nor no way. It got to troubling
> me so I couldn't rest; I couldn't stay still in one place. It hadn't ever
> come home to me before, what this thing was that I was doing. But
> now it did; and it stayed with me, and scorched me more and more. I
> tried to make out to myself that *I* warn't to blame, because *I* didn't
> run Jim off from his rightful owner; but it warn't no use, conscience
> up and says, every time, "But you knowed he was running for
> his freedom, and you could 'a' paddled ashore and told somebody."
> That was so—I couldn't get around that no way. That was where it
> pinched. Conscience says to me, "What had poor Miss Watson done
> to you that you could see her nigger go off right under your eyes and
> never say one single word? What did that poor old woman do to you
> that you could treat her so mean? Why, she tried to learn you your
> book, she tried to learn you your manners, she tried to be good to
> you every way she knowed how. *That's* what she done."[8]

On this side of the nineteenth century we know, of course, that
Huck's perplexity was the result of a partial moral blindness,
which in turn was the product of mistaken social beliefs about
the nature of persons and property; we know now that his was a
blindness to principles and procedures that could have resolved
his difficulty. From our privileged historical perspective we realize
that the moral "truth of the matter" was there to be seen but that

for perfectly understandable reasons Huck was not able to see. The point is that what for Huck may have appeared to be an insoluble moral quandary no longer appears as such for us. The normative inquiry that might have appeared futile to him we know in retrospect to have been both morally necessary and ultimately productive.

Once again, we are unable to say in advance just how our conflicts in the present might be tied to moral visions distorted by social circumstances. Part of the difficulty is that, until we have gained the normative insight to see through our perplexities, we cannot discover which elements in our social surroundings have impeded our moral progress. Interestingly enough, sociological understanding in these matters is a reflexive understanding; it can only *follow* upon moral discovery. Yet to admit that such understanding characteristically must be deferred to a later time and that our normative insights often require favorable social conditions is not to admit that there are no normative insights to be achieved. Most important, if my assessments are correct, then the Christian believer, at any rate, will need to assume that a moral truth is always available for the resolutions of moral conflicts, no matter how intractable those conflicts may appear to be.

NOTES
BIBLIOGRAPHY
INDEX

NOTES

Introduction

1. The example is a modified version of Michael Walzer's. See his "Political Action: The Problem of Dirty Hands," in *War and Moral Responsibility*, ed. Marshall Cohen et al. (Princeton, N.J.: Princeton University Press, 1974), pp. 62–82.
2. Among those who have maintained such a position are the following: E. J. Lemmon, "Moral Dilemmas," *Philosophical Review* 71 (1962): 135–58; idem, "Deontic Logic and the Logic of Imperatives," *Logique et Analyse* 8 (1965): 39–71; Bernard Williams, *Problems of the Self* (Cambridge: Cambridge University Press, 1973), pp. 166–206; R. F. Atkinson, *Conduct: An Introduction to Moral Philosophy* (London: Macmillan, 1969), pp. 17–29; D. Z. Phillips and H. O. Mounce, *Moral Practices* (London: Routledge and Kegan Paul, 1969), pp. 79–103; R. W. Beardsmore, *Moral Reasoning* (New York: Schocken Books, 1969), pp. 104–19; Roger Trigg, "Moral Conflict," *Mind* 80 (1971): 41–55; Michael Walzer, "Political Action: The Problem of Dirty Hands," pp. 62–82; idem, *Just and Unjust Wars* (New York: Basic Books, 1977), pp. 225–83; Thomas Nagel, *Mortal Questions* (Cambridge: Cambridge University Press, 1979), pp. 53–74, 128–41; P. H. Nowell-Smith, "Some Reflections on Utilitarianism," *Canadian Journal of Philosophy* 2 (1972–73): 417–31; Bas C. van Fraassen, "Values and the Heart's Command," *Journal of Philosophy* 70 (1973): 5–19; Mark Platts, *Ways of Meaning: An Introduction to a Philosophy of Language* (London: Routledge and Kegan Paul, 1979), pp. 243–63; Ruth Marcus, "Moral Dilemmas and Consistency," *Journal of Philosophy* 77 (1980): 121–36; Samuel Guttenplan, "Moral Realism and Moral Dilemmas," *Proceedings of the Aristotelian Society*, n.s. 80 (1979–80): 61–80; Philippa Foot, "Moral Realism and Moral Dilemma," *Journal of Philosophy* 80 (1983): 379–98; Stuart Hampshire, *Morality and Conflict* (Cambridge: Harvard University Press, 1983).
3. For those who trade on this confrontation see Nagel, *Mortal Questions*, pp. 53–74, 128–41; Nowell-Smith, "Some Reflections on Utilitarianism," pp. 417–31; Walzer, "Political Action," pp. 62–82; and idem, *Just and Unjust Wars*, pp. 243–63.
4. For instance, see Phillips and Mounce, *Moral Practices*, pp. 79–103.

5. Of course, an interesting question in its own right is that asking which particular normative ethical theories are compatible with the moral dilemmas
thesis. Consider, for instance, act utilitarianism, the theory stating, roughly,
that whether one ought or ought not to perform a particular act depends on
the comparative utilities of performing and refraining from performing that
act. Suppose that with respect to some act z the utility of performance is
equal to the utility of refraining. In one possible reading of the theory this
situation is dilemmatic. The agent both ought and ought not to perform z.
According to another possible reading (and, I would argue, the more plausible one), however, the moral options are maximized. Whatever the agent
does in this case is morally correct. The phrase "moral dilemmas thesis" is
from Terrance McConnell, "Moral Dilemmas and Consistency in Ethics,"
Canadian Journal of Philosophy 7 (1978): 221.
6. See Immanuel Kant, *Lectures on Ethics*, trans. Louis Infield (New York: Harper
and Row, 1963), p. 20; idem, *The Metaphysical Elements of Justice*, trans.
John Ladd (Indianapolis and New York: Bobbs-Merrill, 1965), p. 25; John
Stuart Mill, *Utilitarianism*, ed. Osker Priest (Indianapolis and New York:
Bobbs-Merrill, 1957), pp. 32–33; W. D. Ross, *The Right and the Good*
(Oxford: Clarendon Press, 1930), pp. 16–47; and idem, *Foundations of Ethics*
(Oxford: Clarendon Press, 1939), pp. 60–86. For more recent adherents of
this position see David Lyons, *Forms and Limits of Utilitarianism* (Oxford:
Clarendon Press, 1965), p. 21; John Rawls, *A Theory of Justice* (Cambridge:
Harvard University Press, 1971), pp. 133–34; Alan Gewirth, *Reason and
Morality* (Chicago and London: University of Chicago Press, 1978), pp. 338–
54; and Earl Conee, "Against Moral Dilemmas," *Philosophical Review* 91
(1982): 87–97. Arguing that morally innocent persons can never be faced
with genuine moral dilemmas, while allowing that such dilemmas might be
consequent on some wrongdoing, are: Georg Henrik von Wright, *An Essay
on Deontic Logic and the General Theory of Action* (Amsterdam: North
Holland Publishing, 1968), pp. 79–81; Alan Donagan, *The Theory of Morality* (Chicago and London: University of Chicago Press, 1977), pp. 144–45;
McConnell, "Moral Dilemmas and Consistency in Ethics," 269–87. I am
indebted to McConnell's account of the moral dilemmas debate.
7. Thus, Kant writes: "A conflict of duties (*collisio officiorum s. obligationem*)
would be that relationship between duties by virtue of which one would
(wholly or partially) cancel the other. Because, however, duty and obligation
are in general concepts that express the objective practical necessity of
certain actions and because two mutually opposing rules cannot be necessary at the same time, then, if it is a duty to act according to one of them, it is
not only not a duty but contrary to duty to act according to the other. It
follows, therefore, that a conflict of duties and obligations is inconceivable
(*obligationes non colinduntur*)." *The Metaphysical Elements of Justice*, p.
25. It should be noted that what Kant means by a conflict of duties is what I
mean by a moral dilemma. Ross writes in a similar vein: "But while we
might agree that the same act may be in some respects right and in others
wrong, we do not suppose that the same act can be in fact right on the whole
and wrong on the whole. To think this would be to put an end to all ethical
judgment." *Foundations of Ethics*, p. 60.

1. Moral Perplexity and Consistency

1. A *general moral principle*, as I am using the term, states that an act of a general
type ought to be performed or ought not to be performed by a certain class of
agent(s). A *singular moral judgment*, on the other hand, states that a par-

ticular act ought to be performed or ought not to be performed by some particular agent(s). On this understanding, 'Persons ought to keep their promises' qualifies as a general moral principle while 'Jane ought to perform *that*
act in keeping with her promise to John' counts as a singular moral judgment. Although general moral principles often will include no expressions
denoting particulars (e.g., proper names, uniquely referring expressions, in-
dexical terms), I shall not stipulate that they will always be devoid of such
expressions. Thus, the sentence 'Persons ought to perform acts commanded
by God', though containing a proper name (or, at least, a covert, uniquely
referring description), counts as a general moral principle inasmuch as it enjoins the performance of a general type of act by a determinate class of
agents. Of course, singular moral judgments qua singular will always contain some uniquely referring expressions. Ordinarily, general moral principles will serve as major premises in moral syllogisms, and singular moral
judgments will serve as conclusions to moral syllogisms, though this will
not always be the case. In any event, the distinction between general principles and singular judgments expounded here is not intended to carry enormous theoretical weight. Its articulation is provided merely to facilitate discussion. Accordingly, whenever I mention moral principles I shall mean
general moral principles, and whenever I mention moral judgments I shall
mean *singular* moral judgments. I shall often use the term *rule* as a syn-
onym for *principle*.

2. This argument for moral revision has often been attributed, mistakenly I think,
to R. M. Hare. See, for example, Trigg's "Moral Conflict," pp. 41–55. While
Hare does hold a strong theory of prescriptivity, he does not in my judgment
ground his claims about revision in that theory. See *The Language of Morals*
(Oxford: Clarendon Press, 1952), pp. 56–78.

3. Hare agrees that in cases of moral weakness the 'ought' in question is "down-
graded" in such a way that it "no longer carries prescriptive force in the particular case, though it may continue to do so with regard to actions in similar circumstances." *Freedom and Reason* (Oxford: Clarendon Press, 1963),
p. 80. Yet such cases, he maintains, do not constitute counterexamples to
the theory, which states simply that an assent to a self-addressed imperative
entails the performance of the appropriate action *given the requisite psychological ability* and that cases of moral weakness are to be analyzed in
terms of *psychological inability*. The problem with Hare's defense is that it
renders the theory immune to counterexample by definition. This trivi-
alization can be avoided only by providing independent criteria for determining cases of psychological inability. As far as I can tell, Hare specifies no
such criteria.

4. This is the course that Hare seems to take in justifying the sort of revision I
have been discussing. Cf. *The Language of Morals*, pp. 56–78.

5. This account of universalizability is indebted to Alan Gewirth's discussion in
Reason and Morality, p. 105.

6. Marcus, "Moral Dilemmas and Consistency," p. 121; Lemmon, "Moral Dilemmas," pp. 151–52; Trigg, "Moral Conflict," pp. 50–55; Williams, *Problems
of the Self*, pp. 184–86.

7. Trigg, "Moral Conflict," pp. 50–51. The following example is a modified version of Trigg's.

8. See p. 11.

9. Trigg does remark that the analogy "is not intended to be particularly close,"
but he never spells out what he means by this qualification. "Moral Conflict," p. 50.

10. Williams, *Problems of the Self*, pp. 184–86.

11. Needless to say, we are speaking of 'moral' as a term of classification rather
than as a term of approval or appraisal. In the first case the term's contradic-

tory is 'nonmoral'. In the second instance the contradictory is 'immoral'. For a survey of the positions taken on the meaning of the term in its classi- ficatory sense see G. Wallace and A. D. M. Walker, eds., *The Definition of Morality* (London: Methuen, 1970), pp. 1–20.

12. Lemmon, "Moral Dilemmas," p. 152. Incidentally, I find Lemmon's parenthetical remark especially unconvincing. If it were correct, we would be forced to admit that the language of supererogation, a language comprising terms like 'good', 'better', and 'best', is a nonmoral language, and this conclusion strikes me as counterintuitive.

13. Phillips and Mounce, *Moral Practices*, pp. 86–87.

14. Lyons, *Forms and Limits of Utilitarianism*, p. 21.

15. Marcus, "Moral Dilemmas and Consistency," pp. 128–29.

16. See p. 3.

17. Alvin Goldman, *A Theory of Human Action* (Princeton, N.J.: Princeton University Press, 1970), pp. 1–19. My argument of the previous two pages is largely indebted to Goldman, pp. 6–7.

18. Ibid., p. 2.

19. Lemmon, "Moral Dilemmas," pp. 149–50.

20. See McConnell, "Moral Dilemmas and Consistency in Ethics," pp. 272–73; also Conee, "Against Moral Dilemmas," pp. 87–97.

21. Cf. Williams, *Problems of the Self*, pp. 204–5. My general account is indebted to Williams and to Ross Harrison, "Ethical Consistency," in *Rational Action: Studies in Philosophy and Social Science*, ed. Ross Harrison (Cambridge: Cambridge University Press, 1979), pp. 30–31.

22. Cf. van Fraasen, "Values and the Heart's Command," pp. 11–12.

23. See Harrison, "Ethical Consistency," pp. 32–35.

24. What follows is a modified version of an argument presented and rejected by Bernard Williams in *Problems of the Self*, p. 180. For a formalized rendition of the argument see McConnell, "Moral Dilemmas and Consistency in Ethics," p. 271.

25. This is one strategy adopted by McConnell. Cf. "Moral Dilemmas and Consistency in Ethics," pp. 273–87.

26. This argument from analogy is suggested by Williams in *Problems of the Self*, pp. 181–82. As for question-begging maneuvers, it has been argued that moral dilemmas do exist and that therefore the factoring principle must be rejected. See, for example, Marcus, "Moral Dilemmas and Consistency," p. 134. At one point Williams appears also to adopt this line. *Problems of the Self*, p. 182.

27. Representative of the literature on the subject are the following: Doreen Bretherton, "'Ought' Implies 'Can Say'," *Proceedings of the Aristotelian Society* 63 (1962–63): 145–66; F. E. Brouwer, "A Difficulty with 'Ought' Implies 'Can'," *Southern Journal of Philosophy* 7 (1969): 45–50; James Brown, "Moral Theory and the Ought-Can Principle," *Mind* 86 (1977): 206–23; D. G. Collingridge, "'Ought-Implies-Can' and Hume's Rule," *Philosophy* 52 (1977): 348–51; Norman O. Dahl, "'Ought' Implies 'Can' and Deontic Logic," *Philosophia* (Israel) 4 (1974): 485–511; William Frankena, "Obligation and Ability," in *Philosophical Analysis*, ed. Max Black (Englewood Cliffs, N.J.: Prentice Hall, 1950), pp. 148–65; Nicolas Haines, "Ought and Can," *Philosophy* 47 (1972): 263; Lawrence Heintz, "Excuses and 'Ought' Implies 'Can'," *Canadian Journal of Philosophy* 2 (1975): 449–62; Jaakko Hintikka, *Models for Modalities* (Dordrecht: D. Reidel, 1969), pp. 184–214; Joseph Margolis, "One Last Time—Ought Implies Can," *Personalist* 48 (1967): 33–41; idem, "'Ought' Implies 'Can'," *Philosophical Forum* (Boston) 2 (1971): 479–88; H. Ofstad, "Frankena on Ought and Can," *Mind* 68 (1959): 73–79; Richard Robinson, "Ought and Ought Not," *Philosophy* 46 (1971): 193–202; P. D. Shaw, "Ought and Can," *Analysis* 25 (1965):

196–97; Michael Stocker, "'Ought' and 'Can'," *Australasian Journal of Philosophy* 49 (1971): 303–17; K. E. Tranøy, "'Ought' Implies 'Can': A Bridge from Fact to Norm," *Ratio* 14 (1972): 116–30; idem, "'Ought' Implies 'Can': A Bridge from Fact to Norm (Part II)," *Ratio* 17 (1975): 147–75; George Henrik von Wright, *Norm and Action: A Logical Enquiry* (London: Routledge and Kegan Paul, 1963), pp. 108–16, 122–25; Alan White, *Modal Thinking* (Ithaca, N.Y.: Cornell University Press, 1975), pp. 147–57; Morton White, "Oughts and Cans," in *The Idea of Freedom: Essays in Honour of Isaiah Berlin,* ed. Alan Ryan (Oxford: Oxford University Press, 1979), pp. 211–19.

28. Hare, *Freedom and Reason*, pp. 51–66. I say "seems" to provide a defense because of an ambiguity in Hare's presentation. At times he appears not to be giving a *justification* of the principle at all but rather an *explanation* of how it can be true.
29. See P. F. Strawson, "On Referring," *Mind* 59 (1950): 320–44.
30. Hare, *Freedom and Reason*, p. 51.
31. Hare does acknowledge two exceptions to the principle's application. According to him, 'ought' does not imply 'can' in cases where the 'ought' denotes a sociological fact or moral convention (analysis: There is a moral convention which requires that x ought to be performed) or in instances of moral weakness. See *Freedom and Reason*, pp. 52–53. Neither of these exceptions, however, affects the antidilemmas argument under consideration.
32. Cf. Stocker, "'Ought' and 'Can'," p. 312.
33. See Brown, "Moral Theory and the Ought-Can Principle," pp. 216–19.
34. I leave aside questions about the reliability of the intuitions themselves. Cases of culpable inability might prove to be counterinstances to the weaker principle that 'blame' implies 'can'. Thus, we might blame an agent for failing to do x when he *could not*, on the grounds that negligence generated the inability. This sort of case is difficult to analyze since in almost every instance we are talking about a situation that *could have been* avoided. Does this fact save the claim that 'blame' implies 'can'?
35. See Brown, "Moral Theory and the Ought-Can Principle," pp. 213–23.
36. On the distinction between excuse and justification see J. L. Austin, "A Plea for Excuses," in *Philosophical Papers*, ed. J. O. Urmson and G. J. Warnock (Oxford: Oxford University Press, 1970), pp. 175–204. On the distinction's relation to the 'ought'/'can' question see Heintz, "Excuses and 'Ought' Implies 'Can'," pp. 449–62.

2. *Perplexity as Dilemma*

1. Marcus, "Moral Dilemmas and Consistency," pp. 129–33.
2. Ibid., p. 133. Cf. Rawls, *A Theory of Justice*, p. 483.
3. Marcus, "Moral Dilemmas and Consistency," p. 121.
4. Amelie Oksenberg Rorty, "Agent Regret," in *Explaining Emotions*, ed. Amelie Oksenberg Rorty (Berkeley and Los Angeles: University of California Press, 1980), p. 501.
5. Marcus, "Moral Dilemmas and Consistency," p. 133.
6. Ross's doctrine of *prima facie* duties has been the subject of considerable philosophical discussion. The following is a representative sampling: P. Jones, "Doubts About Prima Facie Duties," *Philosophy* 45 (1970): 39–54; Maurice Mandelbaum, *The Phenomenology of Moral Experience* (Baltimore: Johns Hopkins Press, 1955), pp. 73–80; John Searle, "*Prima Facie* Obligations," in *Practical Reasoning*, ed. Joseph Raz (Oxford: Oxford University Press, 1978), pp. 81–90; Robert K. Shope, "Prima Facie Duty," *Journal of Philosophy* 62 (1965): 279–87; Frank Snare, "The Definition of *Prima Facie* Du-

ties," *Philosophical Quarterly* 24 (1974): 235–44; P. F. Strawson, "Ethical Intuitionism," *Philosophy* 24 (1949): 23–33.

7. I shall focus on Ross's exposition of the distinction in *The Right and the Good*, pp. 16–47.

8. Ross provides the following classification (which he admits is incomplete) of *prima facie* duties: duties of fidelity, duties of reparation, duties of gratitude, duties of justice, duties of beneficence, duties of self-improvement, and duties of non-maleficence. Cf. *The Right and the Good*, pp. 20–21.

9. Ibid., p. 42.

10. See p. 216, note 7. Ross does say that drawing the distinction between *prima facie* and actual duties or obligations solves the apparent problem of conflict between duties, indeed, "show[s] it to be non-existent." *Foundations of Ethics*, p. 86. Yet as McConnell has pointed out, drawing the distinction hardly solves the problem of moral conflict; it rather presupposes that the problem has been solved. See McConnell, "Moral Dilemmas and Consistency in Ethics," p. 270.

11. Ross, *The Right and the Good*, p. 28.

12. Searle, *"Prima Facie* Obligations," p. 83.

13. Ibid., pp. 85–86; also Williams, *Problems of the Self*, pp. 175–76. Williams puts the point as follows: "Ross—whom unfairly I shall mention without discussing in detail—makes a valiant attempt to get nearer to the facts than this, with his doctrine that the *prima facie* obligations are not just *seeming* obligations, but more in the nature of a claim, which can generate residual obligations if not fulfilled. But it remains obscure how all this is supposed to be so within the general structure of his theory; a claim, on these views, must surely be a claim for consideration as the only thing that matters, a duty, and if a course of action has failed to make this claim in a situation of conflict, how can it maintain in that situation some residual influence on my moral thought?" *Problems of the Self*, p. 176.

14. Cf. Williams, *Problems of the Self*, pp. 172–79; also Trigg, "Moral Conflict," pp. 47–52.

15. Ross, *The Right and the Good*, p. 30.

16. McConnell, "Moral Dilemmas and Consistency in Ethics," pp. 280–82.

17. Mandelbaum, *The Phenomenology of Moral Experience*, pp. 79–80.

18. Williams, *Problems of the Self*, p. 175.

19. Rorty, "Agent Regret," p. 499.

20. See David A. J. Richards, *A Theory of Reasons for Action* (Oxford: Oxford University Press, 1971), pp. 251–53. See McConnell, "Moral Dilemmas," p. 278, for a version of the general argument stated here.

21. Trigg, "Moral Conflict," pp. 46–47; see also note 13.

22. See pp. 52–53.

23. Thus, Williams writes: "I may rather learn that I ought not to get into situations of this kind—and this lesson seems to imply very much the opposite of the previous one, since my reason for avoiding such situations in the future is that I have learned that in them both *ought's do* apply." *Problems of the Self*, pp. 176–77.

24. Bernard Williams, "Politics and Moral Character," in *Public and Private Morality*, ed. Stuart Hampshire (Cambridge: Cambridge University Press, 1978), pp. 55–73.

25. Ibid., p. 62.

26. Ibid., p. 65.

27. What has been presented, of course, is a positivistic account of legal decision making. Of late this account has come under attack by Ronald Dworkin, who argues roughly that there may be a "right answer" to a legal problem of the sort we are discussing even though no resolution is anticipated explicitly in a statute. See especially his "No Right Answer?" in *Law, Mo-*

rality, and Society: Essays in Honour of H. L. A. Hart, ed. P.M.S. Hacker and J. Raz (Oxford: Clarendon Press, 1977), pp. 58–84. For a criticism of Dworkin's view see A. D. Woozley, "No Right Answer," *Philosophical Quarterly* 29 (1979): 25–34. Though I think the legal positivist position is the correct one on this particular issue, I shall not attempt a defense here. Suffice it to say at this juncture that one may take a positivist view of legal decision making without abandoning realism in the realm of morals.

28. J. L. Mackie, *Ethics: Inventing Right and Wrong* (Middlesex and New York: Penguin, 1977), p. 36.
29. Ibid., p. 37.
30. For example, the cross-cultural collision between the belief of the Ik that it is permissible to let youngsters fend for themselves and the belief of, say, westerners that such a practice is abhorrent from the moral point of view may be attributed to the mistaken nature of the former belief, an error due to conditions of resource scarcity. See Colin M. Turnbull, *The Mountain People* (New York: Simon and Schuster, 1972), pp. 109–54.
31. Mackie, *Ethics: Inventing Right and Wrong*, p. 41.
32. Ibid., pp. 21–22. See also R. M. Hare, *Applications of Moral Philosophy* (Berkeley and Los Angeles: University of California Press, 1972), pp. 32–47.
33. Platts, *Ways of Meaning*, pp. 243–63.
34. Ibid., p. 247.
35. Ibid., p. 243.
36. Ibid., p. 244.
37. Ibid., p. 246.
38. Ibid., pp. 247–55.
39. Ibid., p. 252.
40. Nagel, *Mortal Questions*, pp. 128–41.
41. Ibid., p. 129.
42. Ibid., pp. 141–42.
43. In another section of the book Nagel remarks that to admit irreducibility is to "deny that there is a single world." *Mortal Questions*, p. 212.
44. Ibid., pp. 134–35.
45. Ibid., p. 131.
46. Bernard Williams, "Conflicts of Values," in *The Idea of Freedom: Essays in Honour of Isaiah Berlin*, ed. Alan Ryan (Oxford: Oxford University Press, 1979), p. 225.

3. Thomistic Natural Law and the Order of Value

1. See Frederick A. Olafson, *Principles and Persons: An Ethical Interpretation of Existentialism* (Baltimore: Johns Hopkins Press, 1967), pp. 19–33. For Olafson theological voluntarism is to be regarded as a species of *ethical voluntarism*, which "may be said to amount to a demand that moral phenomena be comprehensively redescribed in a vocabulary that explicitly recognizes the decisional and logically autonomous character of moral judgment." Ibid., p. 15. On *theism* see Van Harvey, *A Handbook of Theological Terms* (New York: Macmillan, 1964), p. 235.
2. Olafson, pp. 3–17.
3. For a representative expression of this position as well as a summary account of similar views see Nicholas Crotty, "Conscience and Conflict," *Theological Studies* 32 (1971): 208–32.
4. "In discussion of natural law, should the concept of the 'conflict of rights' be used as if the norms deriving from different 'objects' were at variance with one another, it would seem in this case also that theonomy had been abandoned; God can demand only one thing at a time. The nature law theorist,

even before giving a definite solution, will certainly remark that all orders deriving from different 'objects' are connected with one another in a harmonious cosmos of orders, and that therefore a true 'conflict of rights' is already excluded. He will tend to hold this without even looking for God's demanding will." Joseph Fuchs, *Natural Law: A Theological Investigation,* trans. Helmut Reckter and John A. Dowling (New York: Sheed and Ward, 1965), p. 69. For a more recent statement of Fuchs's position, articulated in response to the revisionists, see "The 'Sin of the World' and Normative Morality," *Gregorianum* 61 (1981): 51–76. See also Richard McCormick, "A Commentary on the Commentaries," in *Doing Evil to Achieve Good,* ed. Richard McCormick and Paul Ramsey (Chicago: Loyola University Press, 1978), p. 222.

5. Aquinas, *Summa Theologiae* 1a 2ae, 91.2. For the most part I rely on the English translation given in *The 'Summa Theologica' of St. Thomas Aquinas,* trans. the Fathers of the English Dominican Province (London: Burns Oates and Washbourne, 1920). Departures from this translation will be noted. In all cases translations have been checked against the Latin text as provided in *Summa Theologiae: Latin Text and English Translation, Introductions, Notes, Appendices and Glossaries,* ed. Thomas Gilby and T. C. O'Brien (London: Blackfriars, Eyre and Spottiswoode; New York: McGraw-Hill, 1964–).

6. Aquinas, *Summa Theologiae* 1a 2ae, 94.2. What follows is an interpretation of Aquinas's discussion in this article. My analysis is indebted to Germain Grisez, "The First Principle of Practical Reason: *A Commentary on the* Summa theologiae, *1–2, Question 94, Article 2,"* in *Aquinas: A Collection of Essays,* ed. Anthony Kenny (Notre Dame, Ind.: University of Notre Dame Press, 1976), pp. 340–82.

7. The translation of *ratio* as "sense" or "meaning" is my own and departs from the Dominican Fathers' translation, which has it as "notion." Grisez translates it as "intelligibility." Yet Grisez's extended discussion of the concept of *intelligibility* suggests that "sense" or "meaning" is an appropriate rendering: "An intelligibility (*ratio*) is all that would be included in the meaning of a word that is used correctly if the things referred to in that use were fully known in all ways relevant to the aspect then signified by the word in question. Thus the intelligibility includes the meaning with which a word is used, but it also includes whatever increment of meaning the same word would have in a similar use if what is denoted by the word were more perfectly known." Grisez, "First Principle of Practical Reason," p. 349.

8. Here I follow Grisez's translation of *appetunt* as "tend toward." Ibid., p. 345. The Dominican Fathers' translation has it as "desire."

9. Apparently, Aquinas does not intend this list to be taken as exhaustive. In other places he makes additions. See *Summa Theologiae* 1a 2ae, 94.4, where he speaks of rational activity as a good in itself.

10. Grisez, "First Principle of Practical Reason," p. 346. Aquinas's remark occurs at *Summa Theologiae* 1a 2ae, 94.2, *ad* 1.

11. It should be noted that, apart from Aquinas's cryptic remark in *Summa Theologiae* 1a 2ae, 94.2, *ad* 1, there is, as far as I can tell, no textual support for Grisez's interpretation.

12. John Finnis, *Natural Law and Natural Rights* (Oxford: Clarendon Press, 1980), pp. 92–95. It should be remarked that Finnis presents and advocates a *reconstructed* version of Aquinas's theory. For instance, his delineation of the basic goods of human existence (which he identifies as knowledge, life, play, aesthetic experience, sociability or friendship, practical reasonableness, and religion) differs from that of Aquinas. Despite the differences in content, however, the structural parallels are sufficient for present purposes.

13. Ibid., p. 92.

14. Ibid., pp. 92–93.
15. Ibid., p. 118. What is expressed here is actually just one condition of the doctrine of double effect as it is classically formulated. In brief, the doctrine states that an act which issues in two effects (the one good, the other evil) is morally permissible if and only if (1) the act in itself is not morally evil, (2) the evil effect (the damaging of some good) is not directly intended, (3) the evil effect does not serve as a means to bring about the good effect, and (4) the good effect is proportionate to the evil effect. Finnis's principle constitutes his reformulation of the second condition. The place where Aquinas is said to have articulated the doctrine of double effect is *Summa Theologiae* 2a 2ae, 64.7.
16. One of the most difficult problems involves articulating the criteria for determining just when a basic good is *directly* damaged and when it is only *indirectly* damaged. See Finnis, *Natural Law and Natural Rights*, pp. 122–25.
17. Aquinas, *Summa Theologiae* 1a 2ae, 93.4.
18. For Aquinas's discussion of the eternal law as exemplar or *ratio* see *Summa Theologiae* 1a 2ae, 93.1. For his discussion of God's essence as the primary object of his intellect see *Summa Theologiae* 1a, 14.4. See also *Summa Contra Gentiles*, bk. 1, ch. 45. I rely on the English translation of the *Summa Contra Gentiles* in *The Summa Contra Gentiles*, trans. the English Dominican Fathers (New York, Cincinnati, Chicago: Benziger Brothers, 1924).
19. Aquinas, *Summa Contra Gentiles*, bk. 1, ch. 74.
20. Ibid., bk. 1, ch. 73.
21. Aquinas, *Summa Theologiae* 1a 2ae, 93.4, *ad* 1.
22. Adherents of the standard interpretation include von Wright, *An Essay on Deontic Logic and the General Theory of Action*, p. 81; Donagan, *The Theory of Morality*, pp. 144–45; Alasdair MacIntyre, *After Virtue* (Notre Dame, Ind.: University of Notre Dame Press, 1981), p. 167. Von Wright credits Peter Geach with originating the interpretation.
23. Aquinas, *De Veritate*, 17.4, *obj.* and *ad* 8. For the most part I rely on the English translation given in *Truth*, trans. R. W. Mulligan et al., 3 vols. (Chicago: Henry Regnery, 1953). Departures from this translation will be noted. In all cases translations have been checked against the Latin text as given in *Quaestiones Disputatae de Veritate*, ed. R. M. Spiazzi (Turin, 1949).
24. Aquinas, *De Veritate*, 17.4, *ad* 8. Here I depart from the Mulligan edition's translation. The Latin text is: ". . . quod ille qui habet conscientiam faciendi fornicationem, non est *simpliciter* perplexus, quia potest aliquid facere quo facto non incidet in peccatum, scilicet conscientiam erroneam deponere; sed perplexus *secundum quid*, scilicet conscientia erronea manente. Et hoc non est inconveniens, ut aliquo supposito, homo peccatum vitare non possit; sicut supposita intentione inanis gloriae, ille qui tenetur eleemosynam dare, peccatum evitare non potest: si enim dat ex tali intentione, peccat; si vero non dat, transgressor est."
25. Aquinas, *Summa Theologiae* 1a 2ae, 19.6, *ad* 3; 2a 2ae, 62.2, *obj.* 2; 3a, 64.6, *ad* 3.
26. Donagan, *The Theory of Morality*, pp. 144–45.
27. Donagan's assumption that Aquinas's rejection of dilemmas is motivated by logical concerns appears to hinge on the former's translation of *inconveniens* in *De Veritate* 17.4, *ad* 8 as "inconsistent." Yet the term *inconveniens*, as Aquinas uses it, need not denote strict logical inconsistency. On the contrary, it often means, more generally, unbecoming, unsuitable, unfitting, or incongruous. See R. A. Armstrong, *Primary and Secondary Precepts in Thomistic Natural Law Teaching* (The Hague: Martinus Nijhoff, 1966), pp. 60–61.
28. See my discussion in Chapter 1.

224

NOTES

29. Aquinas, *Summa Theologiae* 1a 2ae, 20.6.
30. "Evil is more comprehensive than sin, so also is good than right. For every privation of good, in whatever subject, is an evil; but sin consists properly in an action done for a certain end, and lacking due order to that end." Ibid., 1a 2ae, 20.1.
31. Ibid., 1a 2ae, 94.4.
32. Aquinas, *De Veritate* 21.2. For an illuminating discussion of Aquinas's definition of 'good' in *De Veritate* see Ronald Duska, "Aquinas's Definition of Good: Ethical-Theoretical Notes on *De Veritate*, Q21," *The Monist* 58 (1974): 151–62.
33. Aquinas, *Summa Theologiae* 1a 2ae, 109.
34. For Aquinas's discussion of humanity's last end and the relation of its attainment to natural capacities see especially *Summa Theologiae* 1a 2ae, 1–5.
35. "For the words, 'God is good,' or 'wise,' signify not only that He is the cause of wisdom or goodness, but that these preexist in Him in a more excellent way. Hence as regards the thing which the name signifies, these names are applied primarily to God rather than to creatures, because these perfections flow from God to creatures." Ibid., 1a, 13.6.
36. Ibid., 1a, 12.
37. Aquinas, *Summa Contra Gentiles*, bk. 3, ch. 20.
38. Aquinas, *Summa Theologiae* 1a 2ae, 94.4. Here I follow Bigongiari in departing from the Dominican Fathers' translation. See *The Political Ideas of St. Thomas Aquinas: Representative Selections*, ed. Dino Bigongiari (New York: Hafner Publishing, 1953), pp. 49–50.
39. Aquinas, *Summa Theologiae* 1a 2ae, 94.6.
40. Ibid., 1a 2ae, 98.6.
41. Ibid., 1a 2ae, 91.3, *ad* 1.
42. It is interesting to note that with some important differences Aquinas in effect provides a *theological* foundation for one modern account of the semantic elusiveness of moral concepts. See Platts, *Ways of Meaning*, pp. 261–62.
43. Once again, it is useful to note the way Aquinas affords a *theological* rationale for subscribing to a modern ethical account, in this case, an account that regards the *good* as the epistemologically elusive source of unity in the moral life. See Iris Murdoch, *The Sovereignty of Good* (New York: Schocken Books, 1971), pp. 94–98.
44. Crotty, "Conscience and Conflict," pp. 218–19.
45. Alvin Plantinga, *Does God Have a Nature?* (Milwaukee: Marquette University Press, 1980), pp. 34–35.
46. Ibid., pp. 37–61.
47. Aquinas, *Summa Contra Gentiles*, bk. 1, ch. 18.
48. Robert Leet Patterson, *The Conception of God in the Philosophy of Aquinas* (London: George Allen and Unwin, 1933), p. 138.
49. McCormick, "A Commentary on the Commentaries," p. 222.

4. Divine Commands and Moral Dilemmas

1. As is well known, the adequacy of the theory has been challenged on a number of different grounds. See the discussion of Janine Idziak, "Divine Command Morality: A Guide to the Literature," in *Divine Command Morality: Historical and Contemporary Readings*, ed. Janine Idziak (New York and Toronto: Edwin Mellen Press, 1979), pp. 13–21. See in addition Paul Helm, ed., *Divine Commands and Morality* (New York: Oxford University Press, 1981), passim; also Gene Outka and John Reeder, eds., *Religion and Morality* (Garden City, N.Y.: Anchor Press/Doubleday, 1973), passim.
2. Philip Quinn, "Divine Command Morality: A Causal Theory," in *Divine Com-*

mand Morality: Historical and Contemporary Readings, ed. Janine Idziak (New York and Toronto: Edwin Mellen Press, 1979), pp. 305–25.

3. Ibid., p. 311.
4. Ibid., pp. 319–20.
5. Ibid., p. 320.
6. Ibid.
7. Joel Feinberg, *Doing and Deserving: Essays in the Theory of Responsibility* (Princeton, N.J.: Princeton University Press, 1970), pp. 8–9.
8. Quinn, "Divine Command Morality," p. 324. See van Fraassen, "Values and the Heart's Command," pp. 5–19.
9. See pp. 60–61.
10. Van Fraassen, "Values and the Heart's Command," pp. 11–12.
11. See pp. 64–66.
12. Quinn, "Divine Command Morality," pp. 320–21.
13. See Chapter 2.
14. See pp. 47–60.
15. Quinn, "Divine Command Morality," p. 320.
16. Interestingly enough, Quinn does seem to be aware of this possibility, a fact evidenced in his discussion of the Abraham and Isaac case: "So in the situation we are imagining Abraham is confronted with a conflict of obligations. Moreover, our theory offers Abraham no way out of the conflict, since it makes no provision for one obligation to override another. The point of the example is not to show that such conflicts do in fact occur; an omniscient God is undoubtedly smart enough never to command a proposition and also command its negation, if he so chooses." "Divine Command Morality," p. 319. The problem is that Quinn never makes clear (a) why the property of omniscience rules out the possibility of dilemmas and (b) how his claims about the existence of dilemmas is consistent with this claim about God's "never" issuing conflicting imperatives as a matter of fact.
17. Peter Geach, *God and the Soul* (London: Routledge and Kegan Paul, 1969), pp. 117–29.
18. Ibid., p. 122.
19. Ibid., p. 123. In fact, despite his claims, Geach never demonstrates that belief in God is a logically necessary condition of rational adherence to absolute moral principles. All he shows, if his arguments are sound, is that absolutes cannot be justified by appealing to agent wants.
20. Ibid., p. 124.
21. Ibid., pp. 126–29.
22. Kenneth E. Kirk, *Conscience and Its Problems: An Introduction to Casuistry* (London and New York: Longman's Green, 1927), p. 331. Quoted in Donagan, *The Theory of Morality*, p. 146. Much of the present discussion is indebted to Donagan, though my analysis departs from his at some points. Cf. *The Theory of Morality*, pp. 146–47.
23. Donagan, *The Theory of Morality*, p. 146.
24. Geach, *God and the Soul*, p. 128.
25. See Peter Geach, *The Virtues* (Cambridge: Cambridge University Press, 1977), pp. 1–19.
26. Ibid., p. 155.
27. Emil Brunner, *The Divine Imperative: A Study in Christian Ethics*, trans. Olive Wyon (London: Lutterworth Press, 1937).
28. The account of the next two paragraphs is based on ibid., pp. 111–39, 198–233.
29. Ibid., p. 224.
30. Ibid., p. 228.
31. Ibid., p. 229.
32. For an illuminating analysis of Brunner on conflicts among duties of the cre-

ated orders see Dale Burrington, "The Command and the Orders in Brunner's Ethic," *Scottish Journal of Theology* 20 (1967): 149–64.
33. Brunner, *The Divine Imperative*, p. 204.
34. Ibid., pp. 204–5.
35. Ibid., p. 225.
36. Ibid., p. 206.
37. Ibid., pp. 132–39.
38. See Hare, *The Language of Morals*, pp. 17–55; idem, *Practical Inferences*
    (Berkeley and Los Angeles: University of California Press, 1972), pp. 59–73.
39. Hare, *The Language of Morals*, pp. 22–23.
40. W. D. Hudson, *Modern Moral Philosophy* (Garden City, N.Y.: Doubleday,
    1970), pp. 231–32.
41. Hare, *Practical Inferences*, p. 70.
42. Roy Edgley, *Reason in Theory and Practice* (London: Hutchinson University
    Library, 1969), p. 84.
43. Von Wright, *Norm and Action*, pp. 107–67.
44. Ibid., pp. 118–19.
45. Ibid., p. 119.
46. Both the analysis and the examples are von Wright's. See ibid., pp. 149–52.
47. Ibid., p. 151.
48. Ibid., pp. 151–52.
49. Williams, *Problems of the Self*, pp. 187–206.
50. Williams, *Problems of the Self*, p. 191. Williams's definition of imperatival
    inconsistency does not distinguish between imperatives whose sources
    are single norm-authorities and those whose sources are divergent norm-
    authorities. As we shall see later on, he argues that this distinction is not all
    that important for understanding the rationality of commanding.
51. Ibid., p. 197.
52. Ibid., p. 198.
53. Ibid., pp. 200–201.
54. Augustine, *A Treatise Concerning Man's Perfection in Righteousness*, vol. 5
    of *A Select Library of the Nicene and Post-Nicene Fathers of the Christian
    Church*, ed. Philip Schaff (New York: Christian Literature, 1887), 161.
55. As we shall see later on, Helmut Thielicke comes very close to adopting this
    position. See pp. 181–200.
56. For a survey of the options see Idziak, "Divine Command Morality," pp. 9–10.
57. Karl Barth, *Church Dogmatics*, trans. G. W. Bromiley et al. (Edinburgh: T. and
    T. Clark, 1936–68), vol. 2, pt. 2, pp. 555–65.
58. Richard Swinburne, *The Coherence of Theism* (Oxford: Oxford University
    Press, 1977), p. 146.

5. Theological Ethics and Moral Conflict

1. Perhaps the best of recent discussions are Gene Outka, *Agape: An Ethical
   Analysis* (New Haven and London: Yale University Press, 1972), pp. 7–24,
   34–42, 207–14, 268–74; and Gilbert C. Meilaender, *Friendship: A Study in
   Theological Ethics* (Notre Dame, Ind., and London: University of Notre
   Dame Press, 1981), pp. 1–35, 86–103.
2. Outka, *Agape*, p. 24.
3. It should be noted that other contrasts are often drawn but are less significant
   for the present discussion. Gilbert Meilaender's remarks comparing the love
   of friendship with neighbor love nicely summarize some standard differ-
   entiations, though there will be disagreement on certain points: "Philia is
   clearly a preferential bond in which we are drawn by what is attractive or
   choiceworthy in the friend; agape is to be nonpreferential, like the love of

the Father in heaven who 'makes his sun rise on the evil and the good and sends rain on the just and the unjust (Matthew 5:45). Philia is in addition, a mutual bond, marked by the inner reciprocities of love; agape is to be shown even to the enemy, who, of course, cannot be expected to return such love. Philia is recognized to be subject to change; agape is to be characterized by the same fidelity which God shows to his covenant. Philia was the noblest thing in the world in an age when 'civic friendship' was a widely shared ideal; agape has dominated our understanding of love in a world in which the sphere of politics has been desacralized by the search of the restless heart for a suprahistorical resting place in God. Philia was the preeminent bond in a world for which work was of relatively little personal significance; agape helped shape a world in which vocation was seen as a supremely important form of service to the neighbor." Meilaender, *Friendship*, p. 3. See also Outka, *Agape*, pp. 9–21, 268–74.

4. Meilaender, *Friendship*, pp. 16–35, 86–103.
5. Ibid., p. 20.
6. Ibid., p. 33.
7. Ibid., p. 100.
8. Ibid., pp. 100–101.
9. Ibid., p. 102.
10. As evidenced in the following remarks: "In short, this is to some extent a case study in what used to be called the relation of nature and grace. And if the discerning reader perceives in my obvious unwillingness to transcend some tensions a certain residual Lutheranism, I hope that the matter of the discussion will also bear witness to a growing appreciation of Catholicism." Ibid., p. 4.
11. Cf. Reinhold Niebuhr, *An Interpretation of Christian Ethics* (New York: Seabury Press, 1979), pp. 22–38, 103–22; idem, *Moral Man and Immoral Society* (New York: Charles Scribner's Sons, 1932), pp. 169–99, 231–77; idem, *The Nature and Destiny of Man*, 2 vols. (New York: Charles Scribner's Sons, 1943), 2:68–97, 244–86. See also Outka, *Agape*, pp. 24–34.
12. Niebuhr, *Nature and Destiny of Man*, 2:72.
13. Niebuhr, *An Interpretation of Christian Ethics*, p. 28.
14. Ibid., p. 23.
15. "The very essence of politics is the achievement of justice through equilibrium of power. A balance of power is not conflict; but a tension between opposing forces underlies it. Where there is tension there is potential for conflict, and where there is conflict there is potential for violence. A responsible relationship to the political order, therefore, makes an unqualified disavowal of violence impossible. There may always be crises in which the course of justice will have to be defended against those who will attempt its violent destruction." Ibid., p. 116.
16. Ibid., p. 65.
17. Ibid., p. 114.
18. Ibid., p. 115.
19. Niebuhr, *Nature and Destiny of Man*, 2:284.
20. Ibid., p. 246.
21. Ibid., p. 248.
22. This conclusion was drawn by Paul Ramsey in defense of just war theory: "At the point of decision in a concrete case there takes place a convergence of judgments guided in these ways, a convergence in which sometimes love does more than justice requires but never less, and sometimes love acts in a quite different way from what justice alone can enable us to discern to be right. When one's own interests are alone at stake, the Christian governs himself by love and resists not one who is evil. When his neighbor's need and the just order of society are at stake, the Christian still governs himself

by love and suffers no injustice to be done nor the order necessary to earthly life to be injured. He governs himself by love and develops the theory of justified war as a reflection of the action which he judges is demanded of him." *War and the Christian Conscience* (Durham, N.C.: Duke University Press, 1961), p. 178. See also his *Basic Christian Ethics* (New York: Charles Scribner's Sons, 1950), pp. 166–84. For a discussion of the relation between agape and the defense of third-party interests see Outka, *Agape*, p. 23.

23. See, for instance, John Yoder, *The Politics of Jesus* (Grand Rapids, Mich.: William B. Eerdmans Publishing, 1972), pp. 11–26, 94–115, 135–62, 233–50.
24. Ibid., p. 238.
25. Niebuhr, *Moral Man and Immoral Society*, p. 257.
26. Ibid., pp. 257–77; also pp. 170–75.
27. Ibid., p. 257.
28. Ibid., p. 105.
29. Ibid., p. 259.
30. Ibid., p. 267.
31. Ibid.
32. Ibid., p. 259.
33. Ibid., p. 174.
34. Ibid., p. 173.
35. Niebuhr, *Nature and Destiny of Man*, 1 : 269–80.
36. Ibid., p. 275.
37. See C. D. Broad, "Conscience and Conscientious Action," in *Moral Concepts*, ed. Joel Feinberg (New York: Oxford University Press, 1970), p. 75; also David Little, "Duties of Station vs. Duties of Conscience: Are There Two Moralities?" in *Public and Private Ethics*, ed. Donald G. Jones (New York and Toronto: Edwin Mellen Press, 1978), pp. 140–42.
38. See J. G. Randall and Richard N. Current, *Lincoln the President: Last Full Measure* (New York: Dodd, Mead and Company, 1955), pp. 309–10.
39. References in the text to Helmut Thielicke's *Theological Ethics* (vols. 1–2, ed. William H. Lazareth, vol. 3 trans. John B. Doberstein, 2d ed. [Grand Rapids, Mich.: William B. Eerdmans Publishing, 1979]) are given using the abbreviation *TE* with volume and page numbers.
40. I say "in some cases" because it is difficult to see how certain instances of conflict can be explained in this way. For example, it is hard to see how humans could be held responsible for the conflict between life and life captured in the abortion case Thielicke describes.
41. As we shall see, however, there is one other theological program that affirms dilemmas and grounds the affirmation in a *sociological* theory. See pp. 202–5.

Postscript

1. Stanley Hauerwas, *Truthfulness and Tragedy: Further Investigations in Christian Ethics* (Notre Dame, Ind., and London: University of Notre Dame Press, 1977), p. 201.
2. Ibid., p. 12.
3. See D. D. Raphael, *The Paradox of Tragedy* (Bloomington, Ind.: Indiana University Press, 1960), pp. 37–68; also Reinhold Niebuhr, *Beyond Tragedy: Essays on the Christian Interpretation of History* (New York: Charles Scribner's Sons, 1937), pp. 3–24.
4. Cf. Stanley Hauerwas, *The Peaceable Kingdom: A Primer in Christian Ethics* (Notre Dame, Ind., and London: University of Notre Dame Press, 1983), pp. 1–6. Most will recognize the theory as that of Alasdair MacIntyre. See his *After Virtue*, passim.

5. At points Hauerwas appears to concede as much. See *The Peaceable Kingdom,* p. 172.
6. MacIntyre, *After Virtue,* pp. 166–67; also Stanley Hauerwas, *A Community of Character: Toward a Constructive Christian Social Ethic* (Notre Dame, Ind., and London: University of Notre Dame Press, 1981), pp. 141–43.
7. Cf. Aquinas, *Summa Theologiae* 1a, 96.4; 1a 2ae, 19.10, 62.1, 90.2–4, 96.2–4, 105.1; 2a 2ae, 63.3, 69.4, 109.3, 114.2.
8. Mark Twain, *Adventures of Huckleberry Finn* (Boston: Houghton Mifflin, 1962), p. 87. Reprinted here with the permission of Houghton Mifflin Co. Huck's plight is discussed from a somewhat different perspective by Alan Donagan. See *The Theory of Morality,* pp. 131–42.

Bibliography

Aquinas, Saint Thomas. *The Political Ideas of St. Thomas Aquinas: Representative Selections*. Edited by Dino Bigongiari. New York: Hafner Publishing, 1953.

———. *Quaestiones Disputatae de Veritate*. Edited by R. M. Spiazzi. Turin, 1949.

———. *The Summa Contra Gentiles*. Translated by the English Dominican Fathers. New York, Cincinnati, Chicago: Benziger Brothers, 1924.

———. *Summa Theologiae: Latin Text and English Translation, Introductions, Notes, Appendices and Glossaries*. Edited by Thomas Gilby and T. C. O'Brien. London: Blackfriars, Eyre and Spottiswoode; New York: McGraw-Hill, 1964–.

———. *The 'Summa Theologica' of St. Thomas Aquinas*. Translated by the Fathers of the English Dominican Province. London: Burns Oates and Washbourne, 1920.

———. *Truth*. Translated by R. W. Mulligan, J. V. McGlynn, and R. W. Schmidt. 3 vols. Chicago: Henry Regnery, 1953.

Armstrong, R. A. *Primary and Secondary Precepts in Thomistic Natural Law Teaching*. The Hague: Martinus Nijhoff, 1966.

Atkinson, R. F. *Conduct: An Introduction to Moral Philosophy*. London: Macmillan, 1969.

Augustine, Saint. *A Treatise Concerning Man's Perfection in Righteousness*. Vol. 5 of *A Select Library of the Nicene and Post-Nicene Fathers of the Christian Church*, edited by Philip Schaff. New York: Christian Literature, 1887.

Austin, J. L. "A Plea for Excuses." In *Philosophical Papers*, edited by J. O. Urmson and G. J. Warnock. Oxford: Oxford University Press, 1970.

Barth, Karl. *Church Dogmatics.* Translated by G. W. Bromiley et al. Edinburgh: T. and T. Clark, 1936–68.

Beardsmore, R. W. *Moral Reasoning.* New York: Schocken Books, 1969.

Bretherton, Doreen. "'Ought' Implies 'Can Say'." *Proceedings of the Aristotelian Society* 63 (1962–63): 145–66.

Broad, C. D. "Conscience and Conscientious Action." In *Moral Concepts,* edited by Joel Feinberg. New York: Oxford University Press, 1970.

Brouwer, F. E. "A Difficulty with 'Ought' Implies 'Can'." *Southern Journal of Philosophy* 7 (1969): 45–50.

Brown, James. "Moral Theory and the Ought-Can Principle." *Mind* 86 (1977): 206–23.

Brunner, Emil. *The Divine Imperative: A Study in Christian Ethics.* Translated by Olive Wyon. London: Lutterworth Press, 1937.

Burrington, Dale. "The Command and the Orders in Brunner's Ethic." *Scottish Journal of Theology* 20 (1967): 149–64.

Collingridge, D. G. "'Ought-Implies-Can' and Hume's Rule." *Philosophy* 52 (1977): 348–51.

Conee, Earl. "Against Moral Dilemmas." *Philosophical Review* 91 (1982): 87–97.

Crotty, Nicholas. "Conscience and Conflict." *Theological Studies* 32 (1971): 208–32.

Dahl, Norman O. "'Ought' Implies 'Can' and Deontic Logic." *Philosophia* (Israel) 4 (1974): 485–511.

Donagan, Alan. "Consistency in Rationalist Moral Systems." *Journal of Philosophy* 81 (1984): 291–309.

———. *The Theory of Morality.* Chicago and London: University of Chicago Press, 1977.

Duska, Ronald. "Aquinas's Definition of Good: Ethical-Theoretical Notes on *De Veritate,* Q21." *The Monist* 58 (1974): 151–62.

Dworkin, Ronald. "No Right Answer?" In *Law, Morality, and Society: Essays in Honour of H. L. A. Hart,* edited by P. M. S. Hacker and J. Raz. Oxford: Clarendon Press, 1977.

Edgley, Roy. *Reason in Theory and Practice.* London: Hutchinson University Library, 1969.

Feinberg, Joel. *Doing and Deserving: Essays in the Theory of Responsibility.* Princeton, N.J.: Princeton University Press, 1970.

Finnis, John. *Natural Law and Natural Rights.* Oxford: Clarendon Press, 1980.

Foot, Philippa. "Moral Realism and Moral Dilemma." *Journal of Philosophy* 80 (1983): 379–98.

Frankena, William. "Obligation and Ability." In *Philosophical Analysis,* edited by Max Black. Englewood Cliffs, N.J.: Prentice Hall, 1950.

Fuchs, Joseph. *Natural Law: A Theological Investigation.* Translated by Helmut Reckter and John A. Dowling. New York: Sheed and Ward, 1965.

————. "The 'Sin of the World' and Normative Morality." *Gregorianum* 61 (1981): 51–76.

Geach, Peter. *God and the Soul.* London: Routledge and Kegan Paul, 1969.

————. *The Virtues.* Cambridge: Cambridge University Press, 1977.

Gewirth, Alan. *Reason and Morality.* Chicago and London: University of Chicago Press, 1978.

Goldman, Alvin. *A Theory of Human Action.* Princeton, N.J.: Princeton University Press, 1970.

Grisez, Germain. "The First Principle of Practical Reason: A Commentary on the *Summa theologiae, 1–2, Question 94, Article 2.*" In *Aquinas: A Collection of Essays,* edited by Anthony Kenny. Notre Dame, Ind.: University of Notre Dame Press, 1976.

Guttenplan, Samuel. "Moral Realism and Moral Dilemmas." *Proceedings of the Aristotelian Society,* n.s. 80 (1979–80): 61–80.

Haines, Nicolas. "Ought and Can." *Philosophy* 47 (1972): 263.

Hampshire, Stuart. *Morality and Conflict.* Cambridge: Harvard University Press, 1983.

Hare, R. M. *Applications of Moral Philosophy.* Berkeley and Los Angeles: University of California Press, 1972.

————. *Freedom and Reason.* Oxford: Clarendon Press, 1963.

————. *The Language of Morals.* Oxford: Clarendon Press, 1952.

————. *Practical Inferences.* Berkeley and Los Angeles: University of California Press, 1972.

Harrison, Ross. "Ethical Consistency." In *Rational Action: Studies in Philosophy and Social Science,* edited by Ross Harrison. Cambridge: Cambridge University Press, 1979.

Hauerwas, Stanley. *A Community of Character: Toward a Constructive Christian Social Ethic.* Notre Dame, Ind., and London: University of Notre Dame Press, 1981.

————. *The Peaceable Kingdom: A Primer in Christian Ethics.* Notre Dame, Ind., and London: University of Notre Dame Press, 1983.

————. *Truthfulness and Tragedy: Further Investigations in Christian Ethics.* Notre Dame, Ind., and London: University of Notre Dame Press, 1977.

Heintz, Lawrence. "Excuses and 'Ought' Implies 'Can'." *Canadian Journal of Philosophy* 2 (1975): 449–62.

Helm, Paul, ed. *Divine Commands and Morality.* New York: Oxford University Press, 1981.

Henderson, G. P. "'Ought' Implies 'Can'." *Philosophy* 41 (1966): 101–12.

Hintikka, Jaakko. *Models for Modalities.* Dordrecht: D. Reidel, 1969.

Hudson, W. D. *Modern Moral Philosophy.* Garden City, N.Y.: Doubleday, 1970.

Humberstone, I. L. "Two Sorts of Oughts." *Analysis* 32 (1971): 8–10.

Idziak, Janine. "Divine Command Morality: A Guide to the Literature." In *Divine Command Morality: Historical and Contemporary Read-*

ings, edited by Janine Idziak. New York and Toronto: Edwin Mellen Press, 1979.

Jones, P. "Doubts about Prima Facie Duties." *Philosophy* 45 (1970): 39–54.

Kant, Immanuel. *Lectures on Ethics.* Translated by Louis Infield. New York: Harper and Row, 1963.

———. *The Metaphysical Elements of Justice.* Translated by John Ladd. Indianapolis and New York: Bobbs-Merrill, 1965.

Kirk, Kenneth. *Conscience and Its Problems: An Introduction to Casuistry.* London and New York: Longman's Green, 1927.

Lemmon, E. J. "Deontic Logic and the Logic of Imperatives." *Logique et Analyse* 8 (1965): 39–71.

———. "Moral Dilemmas." *Philosophical Review* 71 (1962): 135–58.

Little, David. "Duties of Station vs. Duties of Conscience: Are There Two Moralities?" In *Public and Private Ethics,* edited by Donald G. Jones. New York and Toronto: Edwin Mellen Press, 1978.

Lyons, David. *Forms and Limits of Utilitarianism.* Oxford: Clarendon Press, 1965.

McConnell, Terrance. "Moral Dilemmas and Consistency in Ethics." *Canadian Journal of Philosophy* 7 (1978): 269–87.

McCormick, Richard. "A Commentary on the Commentaries." In *Doing Evil to Achieve Good,* edited by Richard McCormick and Paul Ramsey. Chicago: Loyola University Press, 1978.

MacIntyre, Alasdair. *After Virtue.* Notre Dame, Ind.: University of Notre Dame Press, 1981.

Mackie, J. L. *Ethics: Inventing Right and Wrong.* Middlesex and New York: Penguin, 1977.

Mandelbaum, Maurice. *The Phenomenology of Moral Experience.* Baltimore: Johns Hopkins Press, 1955.

Marcus, Ruth. "Moral Dilemmas and Consistency." *Journal of Philosophy* 77 (1980): 121–36.

Margolis, Joseph. "One Last Time—Ought Implies Can." *Personalist* 48 (1967): 33–41.

———. "'Ought' Implies 'Can'." *Philosophical Forum* (Boston) 2 (1971): 479–88.

Meilaender, Gilbert C. *Friendship: A Study in Theological Ethics.* Notre Dame, Ind., and London: University of Notre Dame Press, 1981.

Mill, John Stuart. *Utilitarianism.* Edited by Osker Priest. Indianapolis and New York: Bobbs-Merrill, 1957.

Murdoch, Iris. *The Sovereignty of Good.* New York: Schocken Books, 1971.

Nagel, Thomas. *Mortal Questions.* Cambridge: Cambridge University Press, 1979.

Niebuhr, Reinhold. *Beyond Tragedy: Essays on the Christian Interpretation of History.* New York: Charles Scribner's Sons, 1937.

———. *An Interpretation of Christian Ethics.* New York: Seabury Press, 1979.

------. *Moral Man and Immoral Society.* New York: Charles Scribner's Sons, 1932.

------. *The Nature and Destiny of Man.* 2 vols. New York: Charles Scribner's Sons, 1943.

Nowell-Smith, P. H. "Some Reflections on Utilitarianism." *Canadian Journal of Philosophy* 2 (1972–73): 417–31.

Ofstad, H. "Frankena on Ought and Can." *Mind* 68 (1959): 73–79.

Olafson, Frederick A. *Principles and Persons: An Ethical Interpretation of Existentialism.* Baltimore: Johns Hopkins Press, 1967.

Outka, Gene. *Agape: An Ethical Analysis.* New Haven and London: Yale University Press, 1972.

Outka, Gene, and John Reeder, eds. *Religion and Morality.* Garden City, N.Y.: Anchor Press/Doubleday, 1973.

Patterson, Robert Leet. *The Conception of God in the Philosophy of Aquinas.* London: George Allen and Unwin, 1933.

Phillips, D. Z., and H. O. Mounce. *Moral Practices.* London: Routledge and Kegan Paul, 1969.

Plantinga, Alvin. *Does God Have a Nature?* Milwaukee: Marquette University Press, 1980.

Platts, Mark. *Ways of Meaning: An Introduction to a Philosophy of Language.* London: Routledge and Kegan Paul, 1979.

Quinn, Philip. "Divine Command Morality: A Causal Theory." In *Divine Command Morality: Historical and Contemporary Readings,* edited by Janine Idziak. New York and Toronto: Edwin Mellen Press, 1979.

Ramsey, Paul. *Basic Christian Ethics.* New York: Charles Scribner's Sons, 1950.

------. *War and the Christian Conscience.* Durham, N.C.: Duke University Press, 1961.

Randall, J. G., and Richard N. Current. *Lincoln the President: Last Full Measure.* New York: Dodd, Mead and Company, 1955.

Raphael, D. D. *The Paradox of Tragedy.* Bloomington: Indiana University Press, 1960.

Rawls, John. *A Theory of Justice.* Cambridge: Harvard University Press, 1971.

Richards, David A. J. *A Theory of Reasons for Action.* Oxford: Oxford University Press, 1971.

Robinson, Richard. "Ought and Ought Not." *Philosophy* 46 (1971): 193–202.

Rorty, Amelie Oksenberg. "Agent Regret." In *Explaining Emotions,* edited by Amelie Oksenberg Rorty. Berkeley and Los Angeles: University of California Press, 1980.

Ross, W. D. *Foundations of Ethics.* Oxford: Clarendon Press, 1939.

------. *The Right and the Good.* Oxford: Clarendon Press, 1930.

Searle, John. "*Prima Facie* Obligations." In *Practical Reasoning,* edited by Joseph Raz. Oxford: Oxford University Press, 1978.

Shaw, P. D. "Ought and Can." *Analysis* 25 (1965): 196–97.

Shope, Robert K. "Prima Facie Duty." *Journal of Philosophy* 62 (1965): 279–87.

Snare, Frank. "The Definition of *Prima Facie* Duties." *Philosophical Quarterly* 24 (1974): 235–44.

Stocker, Michael. "'Ought' and 'Can'." *Australasian Journal of Philosophy* 49 (1971): 303–17.

Strawson, P. F. "Ethical Intuitionism." *Philosophy* 24 (1949): 23–33.

———. "On Referring." *Mind* 59 (1950): 320–44.

Swinburne, Richard. *The Coherence of Theism.* Oxford: Oxford University Press, 1977.

Thielicke, Helmut. *Theological Ethics.* 2d ed. 3 vols. Vols. 1–2 edited by William H. Lazareth. Vol. 3 translated by John B. Doberstein. Grand Rapids, Mich.: William B. Eerdmans Publishing, 1979.

Tranøy, K. E. "'Ought' Implies 'Can': A Bridge from Fact to Norm." *Ratio* 14 (1972): 116–30.

———. "'Ought' Implies 'Can': A Bridge from Fact to Norm (Part II)." *Ratio* 17 (1975): 147–75.

Trigg, Roger. "Moral Conflict." *Mind* 80 (1971): 41–55.

Turnbull, Colin M. *The Mountain People.* New York: Simon and Schuster, 1972.

Twain, Mark. *Adventures of Huckleberry Finn.* Boston: Houghton Mifflin, 1962.

van Fraassen, Bas C. "Values and the Heart's Command." *Journal of Philosophy* 70 (1973): 5–19.

von Wright, Georg Henrik. *An Essay on Deontic Logic and the General Theory of Action.* Amsterdam: North Holland Publishing, 1968.

———. *Norm and Action: A Logical Enquiry.* London: Routledge and Kegan Paul, 1963.

Wallace, G., and A. D. M. Walker, eds. *The Definition of Morality.* London: Methuen, 1970.

Walzer, Michael. *Just and Unjust Wars.* New York: Basic Books, 1977.

———. "Political Action: The Problem of Dirty Hands." In *War and Moral Responsibility,* edited by Marshall Cohen, Thomas Nagel, and Thomas Scanlon. Princeton, N.J.: Princeton University Press, 1974.

White, Alan. *Modal Thinking.* Ithaca, N.Y.: Cornell University Press, 1975.

White, Morton. "Oughts and Cans." In *The Idea of Freedom: Essays in Honour of Isaiah Berlin,* edited by Alan Ryan. Oxford: Oxford University Press, 1979.

Williams, Bernard. "Conflicts of Values." In *The Idea of Freedom: Essays in Honour of Isaiah Berlin,* edited by Alan Ryan. Oxford: Oxford University Press, 1979.

———. "Politics and Moral Character." In *Public and Private Morality,* edited by Stuart Hampshire. Cambridge: Cambridge University Press, 1978.

———. *Problems of the Self.* Cambridge: Cambridge University Press, 1973.

Woozley, A. D. "No Right Answer." *Philosophical Quarterly* 29 (1979): 25–34.

Yoder, John. *The Politics of Jesus.* Grand Rapids, Mich.: William B. Eerdmans Publishing, 1972.

INDEX